THE BOOK OF JOB

William Blake Inv. & Sc.

"WHEN THE MORNING STARS SANG TOGETHER,
AND ALL THE SONS OF GOD SHOUTED FOR JOY."
—*Job*, 38, 7

The Book of Job

ITS ORIGIN, GROWTH AND INTERPRETATION

TOGETHER WITH
A NEW TRANSLATION
BASED ON A REVISED TEXT

BY

MORRIS JASTROW, JR., PH.D., LL.D.
PROFESSOR IN THE UNIVERSITY OF PENNSYLVANIA

"A noble book; all men's book"
CARLYLE

Wipf & Stock
PUBLISHERS
Eugene, Oregon

Wipf and Stock Publishers
199 W 8th Ave, Suite 3
Eugene, OR 97401

The Book of Job
It's Origin, Growth and Interpretation
By Jastrow, Morris, Jr.
ISBN 13: 978-1-55635-617-9
ISBN 10: 1-55635-617-X
Publication date 9/7/2007
Previously published by J.B. Lippincott Company, 1920

TO
EDGAR FAHS SMITH
SCIENTIST AND ADMINISTRATOR

A TRIBUTE
OF ESTEEM AND APPRECIATION

"Let him not boast who puts his armor on,
As he who puts it off, the battle done."
                                    LONGFELLOW.

FOREWORD

A WITTY Frenchman once remarked of the Bible that as a collection it was *plus célèbre que connu*. It is in the hope of making a contribution towards having the most celebrated of the books of the Bible better known—and by that I mean a deeper penetration into its real meaning and significance—that I offer a new translation which, based on an entirely revised Hebrew text, will be found to differ materially from the current translations. Preceding the translation and forming the first part of the work, I have given the results of a study of the origin, growth and interpretation of the Book of Job, which represents the outcome of many years of devotion to this remarkable production of antiquity, dealing with problems that are as vital and as puzzling to-day as they were two milleniums ago when the book, after an extended process of amplification, reached its final form.

The Book of Job may be said to have suffered from its celebrity. Regarded by universal consent as the literary masterpiece of the Old Testament and, indeed, as one of the masterpieces in world literature, the average person feels himself dispensed by virtue of this admission from reading it, much as Milton's Paradise Lost is universally admired but compara-

FOREWORD

tively little read, except as a task frequently assigned to those whose immaturity prevents them from appreciating it. The attitude of the average person towards Job seems to be, why read in order to confirm an opinion which one is ready to take on faith?

It is perhaps not surprising that Job should be little read, for the English translations of the book—taking their cue from the King James Version of 1611—make it a most uninviting and, one is tempted to add, an unprofitable task. As an English classic the King James Version will, as a matter of course, always retain the distinguished position that it holds, but as a translation it is in need of a much more thorough revision than has been given to it either in the Revised Version of 1885 or in the many other English translations that have since been published. The translation of the whole Bible issued by the American Baptist Publication Society in 1913 goes further than others in adopting corrections where the text is manifestly corrupt, and while this is gratifying it leaves, in the case of the Book of Job, a large number of passages untouched in which the text cannot possibly be correct for the sufficient reason that it gives no sense. Another recent translation of the Old Testament is that published by the American Jewish Publication Society in 1916. It was prepared by a body of competent scholars whose authority is unquestioned. In their rendering these translators have endeavored, so far as possible, to preserve the wording of the Authorized Version, but in many instances they have deviated where, as a result of more recent investigations, a better interpretation of the text as it stands

FOREWORD

could be secured; but the translators have stopped short at this point. As they themselves are at pains to tell us, their aim has been to translate the received text as it stands; that is to say, in the form given to it by the Massoretes, as the Jewish scholars, who attached the vowels to the consonantal text are called.[1] Only in the very rarest instances have the translators ventured to deviate even by a hair's-breadth from the received text, though no doubt all of the learned translators would be willing to admit that the text is corrupt in a great many instances. As a translation of the *received* text, the one issued by the American Jewish Publication Society is, therefore, satisfactory; but it is also hopelessly defective, since it deliberately ignores the results of modern critical study.

Confining ourselves to the Book of Job, it is no exaggeration to say that barring the two introductory chapters, which tell the story of Job in prose form, and the prose epilogue at the end of the book,[2] there are not ten consecutive verses in the Symposium between Job and his friends or in the speeches of Elihu or in the magnificent closing chapters placed as speeches in the mouth of Yahweh, the text of which can be regarded as correct. The text of a poetic composition is more liable to corruption than that of a prose narrative. In the case of the Book of Job we have as an additional factor favorable to corruption the manipulation to which the book was subjected, in the course of the long period elapsing between the

---
[1] In Hebrew, as in Arabic, Syriac and Phœnician, only the consonants are written in inscriptions or manuscripts. When vowels are added, they are indicated by diacritical marks placed above or below the consonants.
[2] 42, 7-17.

FOREWORD

first draft and the final form, with a view of making the book more palatable to Jewish orthodoxy. In many instances the textual changes required in order to produce a satisfactory meaning are slight and as obvious as they are slight; but frequently a more radical process is required in order to restore the text to its correct form. Often we can only approximate the correct form, but sufficiently so as to obtain at least a satisfactory view; and occasionally the critical student finds himself baffled and must content himself either with a more or less plausible guess, or admit his inability to solve the puzzling problem as to the precise meaning and original form of a line, phrase or word, or an entire verse. The means at our disposal for correcting the text, and the method to be followed in doing so, are set forth in my study of the book and in the notes attached to the translation. All instances of a deviation from the received text are noted; and while I have avoided technical discussions, because both the study of the book and the translation are intended primarily for the general reader, I have given sufficient indications in the brief notes to enable scholars, who feel so inclined, to test the justification of the revision to which the text has been subjected.

There is another sense in which the celebrity which the Book of Job acquired has proved to be a real obstacle to a proper understanding of it. A tradition gradually grew up around the book, as around most of the books of the Old Testament collection, resulting in a totally unhistorical view of its origin and purpose. The growth of this traditional view

FOREWORD

of Job was in part due to the general lack of a critical spirit in the approach towards Biblical productions until comparatively recent days, and in part to circumstances of a more special character. With the slow evolution of the idea of individual authorship, which proceeded under the influence of the contact with Greek culture after the middle of the fourth century before this era, the tendency arose to regard the Biblical books as literary units, composed by some individual at some specific time. As a matter of fact, however, with the possible single exception of the Book of Esther, which is a propagandist romance that may not be earlier than 100 B. C., there is not a book of the Old Testament that can be assigned to any individual author, as none represents in its present form a genuine literary unity. Literary unity is not to be found even in so late a book as that of Daniel, written circa 160 B. C., when individual authorship among the Hebrews had already come to the fore, for even in this book it is recognized by scholars that the last chapters are not by the same writer as the one to whom we owe the earlier ones.

The composition of Job, dating in its earliest form from the period before the contact with Greek culture, was produced under the time-honored method, prevalent throughout the ancient East, of anonymous and composite authorship. The book as we have it is a gradual growth, and in view of this, the traditional attitude towards the book, which regards it as a unit, effectively blocks the way to a genuine understanding and appreciation. On the assumption of literary unity the book is full of most glaring contradictions,

FOREWORD

the most obvious of which is the irreconcilability of the Job of the folktale—a model of piety and of silent resignation to the Divine will—with Job as he is pictured in the Symposium, voluble in his denunciation of the Divine injustice under which he languishes. Furthermore, the traditional view that grew up around the book and which assumed that *all* sections of it were written in the spirit of Jewish orthodoxy is responsible for the many misunderstandings still current about the Book of Job and which, as long as they persist, will render the reading of it in the ordinary translations a bewildering mental exercise to anyone who approaches it in the spirit in which we take up, let us say, a literary work of our own days. In the current translations we are baffled at every point. We have to ask ourselves certainly at every tenth verse, if not oftener, what does the writer mean? We come across fine and impressive passages, but if we are the least bit critical, we are also thwarted at frequent intervals by the hopeless endeavor to obtain an intelligible view of the sequence of the thought. It is only because we have been so frequently told that the Book of Job is a literary masterpiece that we can read passage after passage which upon analysis can be shown to give no sense. Tradition has a way of warping our critical instinct, and permits us to close our eyes to the inherent difficulties with which the book, on the assumption of its being a unit composition and that the text is correct, teems.

In making the results of the modern study of the book, in which many scholars in many lands have participated, accessible to the general public, it is my

FOREWORD

main purpose to present Job, as I have tried to present "The Words of Koheleth"—"A Gentle Cynic," as I ventured to call the unknown writer who hid his personality behind a *nom de plume*,[3]—as a human document. By illuminating the conditions under which the composite production gradually received its present form, its literary excellence will be all the more clearly revealed, as well as the reason for the profound influence that it has exerted in the domain of religious thought.

No modern translator that I know of makes the attempt to distinguish between the original portion of the book and the amplification to which Job, as every literary production in the ancient Orient, was subject. Without such distinction it is entirely hopeless to obtain a correct view of the great masterpiece—hopeless indeed to recognize it *as* a masterpiece. The starting point, therefore, in my study of the origin, growth and interpretation of Job, is a recognition of the separation of the story of Job from the poetical composition in which the two problems suggested by the story, the reason for innocent suffering in the world and for the frequent escape of the wicked from merited punishment, are discussed. The story of Job is like the text of a sermon, or like a parable on which a preacher enlarges. The story is the peg upon which is hung the discussion of two vital problems from which we cannot escape, if we look at things in this world as they are. Equally fundamental is the recognition that the poetical composition consists of three distinct strata in which the two problems involved are viewed from

---
[3] See *A Gentle Cynic*, p. 62-71.

FOREWORD

totally different angles. The first stratum is the Symposium between Job and his three friends (chapters 3–27), and constitutes the original book. The trend of this stratum is distinctly skeptical. It emanated from a circle of bold and independent thinkers who questioned conventional beliefs. Because of this and because the Symposium ended in an unsatisfactory manner, orthodox circles among the Jews as vitally interested in the problems as unorthodox Jews, took up the book and proceeded to amplify it. As the result of an extended process we have comments and reflections by pious commentators and other additions, as well as a rearrangement of some chapters, and above all, two additional strata represented by the speeches of Elihu (chapters 32-37) and the closing chapters of the book (chapters 38-41) which represent the endeavor of Jewish orthodoxy to *counteract* the influence of the original book, and to furnish more satisfactory answers to the questions raised in the Symposium.

It is to the elucidation of the various aspects of these three strata and their relationship to one another that the first part of this work is devoted; and I trust that after a consideration of what has been set forth, the reader will agree with me in the view that in the magnificent nature poems with which the book closes and which from the literary point of view are the finest in the composite production, there is suggested as a definite and final answer to the two main problems of Job that simple faith in a mysterious power, whose manifestations are to be seen in the world of inanimate and animate nature, constitutes a resting point for man in the ceaseless search to which he is irresistibly led

FOREWORD

by his own nature to penetrate the mystery surrounding his life. I am aware that to many, as I suggest at various points in my study, it will seem startling as well as painful, to be asked to lay aside views which have the force of time-honored tradition and to look at the great masterpiece from a new and unaccustomed angle. But I am also in hopes that after carefully considering the justification brought forward for the interpretation and for the new translation, my readers will reach the conclusion that the new Job is a greater masterpiece than the traditional one, because relieved of contradictions and freed from inherent difficulties that persist under the traditional view of the book. Let me not be understood as setting up the extravagant claim of having solved all the difficulties in the book. That were presumptuous indeed. An author unless carried away by vanity is always his severest critic. I feel, however, that without exceeding the bounds of proper modesty I may lay claim to having advanced the interpretation of the book to which I have given years of patient study and to which I have become ever more closely attached as I have penetrated deeper into its spirit. That at all events is my hope which, I trust, will not turn out to be a delusion.

In closing this foreword I wish to make special acknowledgment to a modern student of the Old Testament who in my judgment has been more successful than almost any other scholar of the present or past generation, in freeing the Old Testament of textual errors and in illuminating hundreds of passages in all of the books. Alas that the acknowledgment must take the form of a tribute to his memory. Arnold

FOREWORD

B. Ehrlich, whose name is little known beyond the small circle of special workers, passed away a few months ago after a lifetime devoted to research. He left behind him as his monument a comprehensive work in seven volumes which he modestly called "Marginal Notes (Randglossen) to the Hebrew Bible," in which as he passes from book to book he makes his comments and textual suggestions in brief but always striking form, with an unfailing instinct as the fruit of profound learning. Though he spent most of his life in New York, he wrote this comprehensive commentary in German, because it was only in Germany that he could find a publisher for a work of this character appealing naturally to a restricted circle. To all students of the Old Testament, however, these Marginal Notes are an indispensible handbook which every one engaged in the study must have constantly at his side. If I were to have made full acknowledgment to Ehrlich in the notes to my translation, his name would have appeared on every page.

I also wish to make special acknowledgment to my colleague Professor Clarence G. Child, of the English Department of the University of Pennsylvania, who was kind enough to go over my rendering very carefully and to make quite a number of valuable suggestions, which I was glad to accept. For the very reason that my rendering deviates so widely from that of the classic Authorized Version, I was the more anxious to have the benefit of Professor Child's expert knowledge and excellent judgment.

To Mr. E. S. Holloway, of the J. B. Lippincott Co., I am likewise indebted for various helpful sugges-

FOREWORD

tions, and more particularly for the very attractive cover design which is his work. As in the case of all my writings I am overwhelmed, on the completion of this particularly difficult task, with gratitude to my wife for her large share in bringing the work nearer to a high standard by her careful supervision and unerring judgment, as well as by her ever sympathetic encouragement of my labors.

Lastly, I regard it as a privilege to be permitted to dedicate the book to a distinguished scientist and administrator whose life, devoted to the highest ideals, furnishes a rare example of unselfishness and of untiring industry.

MORRIS JASTROW Jr.

University of Pennsylvania
June, 1920

CONTENTS

PART I

THE ORIGIN, GROWTH AND INTERPRETATION OF THE BOOK OF JOB

CHAPTER	PAGE
FOREWORD	7
I THE FOLKTALE OF JOB AND THE BOOK OF JOB	
I The Skeptical Spirit in the Original Book of Job	25
II The Origin of the Literary Symposium	30
III The Date of the Symposium	33
IV The Two Jobs	39
V The Friends in the Folktale and in the Symposium	41
VI The Two Conceptions of God	43
VII The Non-Hebraic Origin of the Story of Job	46
VIII Oral Transmission *Versus* Literary Production	49
IX The Modifications in the Folktale. The Figure of Satan	52
X "The Sons of God"	56
XI The Four Epilogues to the Book of Job	59
II THE THREE STRATA IN THE BOOK OF JOB	
I Collective and Anonymous Authorship	64
II The Original Book of Job and the Supplements to it	67
III The Third Series of Speeches of Job and His Friends	70
IV The Two Appendices to the Original Book of Job	74
V The Composite Character of the Speeches of Elihu	77

CONTENTS

  VI A Collection of Nature Poems as the Third Stratum.............................. 82
  VII The Message of the Nature Poems........... 86
III CHANGES AND ADDITIONS WITHIN THE ORIGINAL BOOK OF JOB
  I Jewish Orthodoxy *Versus* Skepticism......... 88
  II Varying Versions of the Hebrew Text........ 92
  III Additions to the Original Book of Job of a Purely Explanatory Character........... 97
  IV Superfluous Lines....................... 103
IV HOW A SKEPTICAL BOOK WAS TRANSFORMED INTO A BULWARK OF ORTHODOXY
  I Changes in the Original Book of Job Made in the Interests of Jewish Orthodoxy........ 109
  II Additions by Pious Commentators.......... 112
  III The Transformation of Crucial Passages..... 120
  IV Orthodox Sentiments Placed in the Mouth of Job................................ 130
  V The "Search for Wisdom"................. 135
  VI The Virtues of Job...................... 137
  VII The Two Appendices as the Coping to the Structure of Jewish Orthodoxy........... 140
V THE BOOK OF JOB AS PHILOSOPHY AND LITERATURE
  I The Insoluble Problem.................... 148
  II The Religious Strain in the Original Book of Job................................. 153
  III Individualism in Religion................. 156
  IV The Defects in Job's Philosophy........... 159
  V The Attitude Towards the Problem of Evil in the Speeches of Elihu.................... 162
  VI The Solution of the Problem in the Nature Poems............................... 167
  VII The New Doctrine of Retribution in a Future World................................ 170

CONTENTS

VIII The Literary Form of Job. A Symposium not a Drama.............................. 174
IX Zoroastrianism and the Book of Job......... 181
X Job and Prometheus....................... 185
XI The Message of Job to the Present Age...... 188

PART II

A NEW TRANSLATION OF THE BOOK OF JOB

I THE STORY OF JOB (CHAPTERS 1 AND 2)......... 197
II THE SYMPOSIUM BETWEEN JOB AND HIS FRIENDS (CHAPTERS 3 TO 21)........................ 206
III A THIRD SERIES OF SPEECHES (CHAPTERS 22 TO 27)..................................... 275
IV TWO SUPPLEMENTARY SPEECHES OF JOB. (CHAPTERS 29 TO 31)............................... 298
V THE SEARCH FOR WISDOM (CHAPTER 28).......... 310
VI FIRST APPENDIX TO BOOK OF JOB—THE FOUR SPEECHES OF ELIHU WITH THREE INSERTED POEMS (CHAPTERS 32 TO 37)........................ 314
VII SECOND APPENDIX TO THE BOOK OF JOB—A COLLECTION OF EIGHT NATURE POEMS (CHAPTERS 38 TO 41) 343
VIII THE FOUR EPILOGUES TO THE BOOK OF JOB....... 361
  (a) Chapter 40, 1–5 (Poetical Epilogue, added to the first Speech put in the Mouth of Yahweh)
  (b) Chapter 40, 6–14 with 42, 1–6 (Poetical Epilogue, combined with an Introduction, and added to the Description of the Hippopotamus and the Crocodile, as the Second Speech put in the Mouth of Yahweh)
  (c) 42, 7ᵇ–9 (The Prose Epilogue to the Symposium)
  (d) 42, 10–17 (The Original Close of the Folktale)

PART I
THE ORIGIN, GROWTH AND INTERPRETATION OF THE BOOK OF JOB

The Book of Job

CHAPTER I

THE FOLKTALE OF JOB AND THE BOOK OF JOB

I

THE SKEPTICAL SPIRIT IN THE ORIGINAL BOOK OF JOB

THE ambition of the student of Biblical Literature to try his hand at an interpretation of the Book of Job[1] appears to be as irresistible as the longing of every actor—even though he begins his career with low comedy—to end as Hamlet. The difficulties with which the book bristles form its challenge, as the intensely human problem with which it deals explains the fascination which it has ever exercised on every one who can sympathize—and who can not?—with the pathetic effort of the human soul to pierce the encompassing darkness and mystery of human life. Carlyle calls it "A noble book; all men's book."[2] It makes, in

---

[1] The list of interpretators of Job extends from Theodore of Mopsuestia who in the fifth century of our era endeavored to show that Job is a tragedy after the pattern of the Greek drama, to the year 1918 in which Dr. H. M. Kallen made the same futile attempt. The interpreters include the greater lights and smaller satellites among Biblical scholars from the Jewish commentators of the Middle Ages: Ibn Ezra, Kimchi and Rashi, to Ewald, Renan, Dillman, Duhm, Budde, Graetz, Cheyne, Szold, Genung, Delitzsch, Siegfried, Peake, Cox, Barton, Strahan, Blake, Ehrlich, Driver, Gray and Buttenwieser in the nineteenth and twentieth centuries.

[2] The Hero as Prophet (Heroes and Hero Worshippers, II).

truth, a universal appeal, and this is the more remarkable because there is no other book in the Biblical collection which is so puzzling the moment one endeavors to penetrate beneath the surface, as there is none in regard to which so many misunderstandings are still current. It may be said without exaggeration that every thing about the book is puzzling. The language is difficult and in many cases almost hopelessly obscure, the text has come down to us in a very corrupt form, in part due to the obscurity of the language, the arrangement is most complicated, the setting is as strange as it is non-Jewish, and what adds to these difficulties, the entire book has been manipulated in the interest of conventional orthodoxy, so that its original import can only be discovered by a most exacting study.

We must at the outset recognize that the Book of Job in its original form was a skeptical composition—skeptical in the sense of putting a question mark after the fundamental axiom in the teachings of the Hebrew prophets of the ninth and succeeding centuries, that the government of the universe rests on justice. We will see that there is no single author in the modern sense to any part of the book. The group that produced the original book, while not denying the existence of a watchful Creator, is not satisfied with the mere repetition of a pious phrase,

> "God's in His heaven,
> All's right with the world!"

They wish to test the phrase. Anatole France tells us in that charming narrative of his childhood—

THE BOOK OF JOB

Le Petit Pierre—in which one suspects that he has used the Goethean device of combining "Wahrheit und Dichtung"—that he declined to follow his mother's suggestion to put an interrogation mark after the title of his earliest composition "What is God," because, as he insisted, he purposed to answer the question. Since then, he tells us, he has changed his mind and is inclined to put a question mark after everything that he writes, thinks or does. The unknown thinker to whom we owe the first draft of the Book of Job is one of the great questioners of antiquity, and those who followed in his wake in enlarging the book often add two interrogation marks to statements that were accepted as a matter of course by the age in which they lived.

The personage of Job is merely an illustration of a man who endured in patience. The folktale is a peg on which to hang the discussion of the problem involved in Job's sufferings. This problem is resolved into the question—Why should the just man suffer? Job is "Everyman," and what happened to him represents merely on a large scale what on a smaller one may be taken as typical of the common human experience. For who has not at some time in his life suffered innocently and felt convinced of his martyrdom? Even the most fortunate experience disappointments which seem to involve injustice towards them. We are all at some time buffeted by the waves of fortune, and when we look about us we behold on all sides the sea strewn with the wrecks of human careers, as a result of the merciless fury of the elements aroused to anger through no cause that can be reconciled with the

THE BOOK OF JOB

conception of a moral and just Neptune. In the larger field of human history—the fate of nations and countries—cunning, deceit, brute power, oppression of the masses seem to be the forces in control.

> "Right forever on the scaffold,
> Wrong forever on the throne."

A "gentle cynic" like Koheleth can deal lightly with a topsy-turvy world in which he sees "a righteous man who perishes by his righteousness, and there a wicked man rounding out his life in his wickedness."[3] The one who is willing to take things as they come can reach the conclusion that there is "nothing better for a man than to be happy and enjoy himself in his life."[4] Not so the writers in the original Book of Job, who are neither gentle nor cynical. For them the fact that wickedness usurps the place of justice, and "where the righteous should have been, the wicked was"[5] constitutes the most serious problem of life, since it involves the possibility that at the head of the universe stands a blind and cruel fate in place of a loving Father of mankind. The questioner scans the heavens and finds the supposed throne of mercy without an occupant; and the discovery bears heavily on his disturbed soul.

This, then, must constitute our point of departure in any endeavor to penetrate into the meaning of the philosophic poem in its earliest form, that its spirit is skeptical. The Book of Job arose out of a circle which was not content with the conventional answer

---
[3] Ecclesiastes 7, 15.
[4] Ecclesiastes 3, 12.
[5] Ecclesiastes 3, 16.

to the question why the innocent suffer in this strange world. Hence the manifest sympathy of the writers to whom we owe the Symposium (chapters 3-27) with Job. The three "friends" introduced as participants in the discourse are merely foils to press home the arguments of Job against the assumptions of the prevailing orthodoxy. Job is the Alpha and Omega in the situation, the climax and the anti-climax.

But the objection may be interposed, why designate Job as a book that questions the current view that suffering is for a good cause, when we have the speeches of the three companions who in answer to Job's complaints uphold the orthodox point of view? Besides there are the discourses of Elihu (chapters 32-37) in defence of orthodoxy, and the magnificent series of poems (chapters 38-41), put into the mouth of God Himself. Is not the orthodox point of view triumphant? Does not Job repent and only after his repentance is rewarded for his sufferings by having health, wealth and happiness restored to him? Why not judge the book from this angle? Such indeed was the prevailing view taken of Job till the advent of modern Biblical criticism, and even among the critical students there are at present some—and in the former generation there were more—who look upon the Book of Job as written for the purpose of vindicating the story of Job, instead of questioning the basis on which that story rests.

If we take the book as it stands in our ordinary Bible translations, there is no escape from the conclusion that Job is a powerful argument for the maintenance of Jewish orthodoxy of post-exilic days, but the

THE BOOK OF JOB

fatal objection to the conclusion is that we *cannot* take the book as it stands. As we have it, the production is far removed from its original draft. It is not a unit composition, as little as is the Book of Koheleth. It is composite not to the same degree as the Pentateuch is a gradual growth, but of the same order. It consists of a trunk on which branches have been grafted. In the course of its growth from the first draft to its final form it covers a considerable period, just as the compilation of the five books into which the Psalms are divided stretches over several centuries. It received in the course of its growth large additions the purpose of which was to *counteract* the tendency of the original draft, precisely as was the purpose of the additions to Koheleth.[6]

II

THE ORIGIN OF THE LITERARY SYMPOSIUM

Now in order to establish this, let us try to make clear to ourselves how a Symposium such as we have in Job[7] based on the story of Job may have arisen. We must take as our starting-point not an individual author—for there were no authors in any real sense of the word among the Hebrews till some time after the contact with Greek culture[8]—but rather a circle in which the problem suggested by the folktale would form the subject of discussion. Some thinker in such a circle, gifted with insight into human nature and an

---

[6] See the author's *A Gentle Cynic*, p. 71, *seq.*
[7] Consisting at one time of chapters 3–21 only; then enlarged by a third series of speeches, chapters 22–27, with chapters 29–31 to form a supplement to the original book and chapter 28 as a separate insertion. See further p. 67 *seq.*
[8] See *A Gentle Cynic*, p. 31 *seq.*

THE BOOK OF JOB

observer of what was happening in the world around him, raised the question whether such a story as that of Job was a true one, that is, in the sense of representing what would really happen if misfortune should overtake a thoroughly good and virtuous and God-fearing man. Would such a man act in the manner indicated in the folktale, like Job accept the evil in the same spirit as the good and bow his head in silent resignation? The third chapter in which Job begins by cursing the day on which he was born, and ends by complaining that God will not grant release to those who long for death more than for hidden treasures,

"Who rejoice at the thought of the mound,"

furnishes the answer. "There you have the real Job," exclaims the thinker. That is the way in which a man who feels keenly the injustice of being made a butt of misfortune would feel. To be deprived of family possessions and station and finally to be tortured with loathsome disease would change the pious and God-fearing man into a violent accuser of the Deity. Throughout the Symposium, Job is represented as protesting against his cruel and unjustifiable treatment. He wrings our soul with pity by his bitter outcries. Those who write the speeches which they put into his mouth visualize for us the sufferings of Job beyond human endurance. Ever and again he breaks out in his anguish and indulges in indictments against Divine injustice that know no bounds.

A second question put by our thinker, who analyzes the story that was repeated from generation to generation, was even more pertinent. What about

God? What an awful Deity to permit a man "perfect and removed from evil" (1, 2) to be thus wracked on the wheel! The introduction of the scene between Yahweh and Satan only enhances the callousness of the former in heaping misfortunes on an innocent head, just for the satisfaction of winning a wager. What a shocking and immoral story, we can fancy the thinker saying, to tell children and to impress upon their elders. Even if Job had acted as he is represented in the folktale, what is there to be said in justification of God? The good "Sunday School" story is thus transformed under the searching test of those who approach it from a more critical angle, into a most objectionable tale. Its supposed lesson to suffer without murmuring is punctured by the two questions thus raised in regard to it, the one of a psychological nature, the other of a theological order. How can one reconcile the conduct of Yahweh in the story with the conception of God taught by the Hebrew prophets of the century and a half preceding the downfall of Jerusalem (586 B. C.), as a Being ruling the world and the destinies of mankind by laws of justice, tinctured with mercy? That is the problem as it appeared to the circle within which at some time a thinker arose, who put his two questions and who stimulated his fellow thinkers to discuss the theme involved in what on the surface appeared to be an altogether proper and impressive folktale.

The Symposium in which arguments and counter arguments are exchanged by Job and his friends is the outcome of these discussions. The purpose of the Symposium is not to elaborate the story, but to illuminate the religious problem which may, in other words, be briefly defined as the search for the reason of suffering and evil in a world created by a supposedly merciful, just and loving Creator. One must enlarge the problem to one of suffering *and* evil, for the one implies the other. The counterpart to Job, the innocent sufferer, is the wicked man who escapes punishment. Our thinker is unsparing in his search, for no less typical than Job's case of what is happening daily is the concurrent instance of the wrongdoer who eludes the fate that is his due. The one who heaps up ill-gotten gain enjoys his wealth without even a twinge of conscience at forcing others to tread the mill, so that he may acquire substance. The tyrant on the throne, the thief who robs his fellow, the murderer who mounts over the prostrate body of his victim, the dishonest dealer who defrauds his customers by false scales, the brutal employer who grinds the faces of the poor—are they not all around us, happy and prosperous while the weak and defenseless perish? Such is the terrible indictment that we encounter in the utterances put into the mouth of Job. Here is a problem indeed, well worthy of discussion. Where is God while innocent suffering and terrible injustice is going on in His world? Is a solution possible?

III

THE DATE OF THE SYMPOSIUM

The circle in which the problem thus extended into a general discussion of the reason for suffering and evil in the world was tossed to and fro must have

THE BOOK OF JOB

consisted of bold thinkers who had freed themselves from the shackles of traditional views to plunge fearlessly into the maelstrom of doubt and rationalism. They knew of the counter arguments that would be brought forward in orthodox circles against the position taken by Job. In order to illuminate the problem from all sides, the three friends of the folktale are introduced as the representatives of the prevailing orthodoxy, but it is evident throughout the Symposium that although the speeches put into the mouth of Eliphaz, Bildad and Zophar are from the literary point of view fully as impressive as those of Job, the sympathy of the writers is on the side of Job. It is only when we come to the four speeches of a fifth personage—Elihu—that we obtain compositions in which the attempt is made to divert our sympathy, but Elihu takes no part in the Symposium proper.

We are led to a post-exilic date for the existence of such a circle of free thinkers, sufficiently bold and advanced to tackle the most perplexing problem that arises when religion passes from the earlier stages in which the chief attribute of the gods is strength, arbitrarily exercised, to the highest level in which ethical motives enter into the conception of the Divine government of the universe. With the appearance of the great series of prophets, about the middle of the ninth century, B. C. the Hebrews definitely advance to this level, for the burden of the teachings of Amos, Hosea, Micah and Isaiah is that Yahweh, the national deity of the Hebrews, is a Power "making for righteousness." He does not act arbitrarily, but rewards or punishes according to the good or bad deeds

THE BOOK OF JOB

of his people. The obedience that He exacts is to dictates of justice. He knows no favorites and cannot be bribed by sacrifices or homage to divert just punishment from wrongdoers. The pre-exilic prophets do not stress the universal sway of Yahweh. For them Yahweh is still, or at least primarily, the God of the Hebrews. In this sense the Hebrews are His chosen people, but the corollary that a God of justice and righteousness must be a unifying force, in control of the universe and exercising His sway over all nature and all mankind, was in due time drawn, though it is not until the exilic period that a genuine ethical monotheism was preached by the successors of the earlier prophets, by Ezekiel, by the anonymous prophets whose utterances are embodied in the second part of Isaiah,[9] by Zephaniah and Zechariah.

We must descend well into the fifth century before Judaism, as we know it, became part and parcel of the life of the people. In the Symposium God is viewed as a power of universal scope. There is no longer any trace of the former nationalistic limitations; and it is just because the doctrine of the prophets involved the rule by this universal Power of the destinies of mankind by self-imposed laws of righteousness and justice, that the problem as to the cause of innocent suffering and unchecked evil in the world becomes real and intense. For religions of the older type, the difficulty did not exist. The gods were arbitrary. They could not be held to account. It was man's sole endeavor to keep them in good humor and

---
[9] Chapters 40–66, with some scattered utterances also in the first 35 chapters.

THE BOOK OF JOB

favorably disposed by doing what would please them. If despite gifts and homage, the gods were disposed to manifest their anger by sending disease, by catastrophes and miseries of all kinds, there was nothing to be done but to wait until their displeasure had passed away. The circle from which the Book of Job emanated could therefore not have arisen in Palestine, where the book originated, before the fifth century, B. C. and scholars are generally agreed to proceed far into this century for the first draft of our book. The discussions on the vital problem may have gone on orally for some time before the thought rose of giving a written form to them, and we are probably safe in fixing upon 400 B. C. as the approximate date for the Symposium.

The problem of the Book of Job is thus one which directly arises out of the basic doctrine of post-exilic Judaism; and it was inevitable that the question would some time be raised, whether what the prophets taught of the nature of God which the people accepted as guidance in their lives was compatible with the facts of experience. Is there a just and loving Providence at the helm of the universe? If so, why does man live in a vale of sorrow? As the Psalmist asks:

"Why standest Thou afar off, O Yahweh,
 Why hidest Thou Thyself in times of trouble?" (Ps. 10, 1).

The questioning spirit arises in the circles of the orthodox and pious quite as much as among those who boldly challenge conventional views, but the significance of the Symposium consists in the thorough manner in which for the first time the problem is

THE BOOK OF JOB

discussed in the light of a particularly significant example of a contrast between what *ought* to be in a world that is supposed to be ruled by justice, and what *is*. Occasionally in other literatures of the ancient East, the problem is touched upon. So, for example, in a remarkable Babylonian poem of a king of Nippur[10], who despite his piety is smitten with disease. Tabi-utul-Enlil, as the king is called, is represented as indulging in reflections on the prevalence of suffering in the world.

> "I had reached and passed the allotted time of life.
> Whithersoever I turned—evil upon evil;
> Misery had increased, justice had disappeared."

But under the limitation of the Babylonian conception of the gods, who although not insensible to justice, yet exercise their power according to their pleasure and in arbitrary fashion, the poem goes no farther than to suggest that the ways of the gods are unfathomable, and that without apparent cause man's fate is subject to constant change.

> "What, however, seems good to oneself, to a god is displeasing,
> What is spurned by oneself finds favor with a god;
> Who is there that can grasp the will of the gods in heaven?
> The plan of a god full of power (?)—who can understand it?
> How can mortals learn the way of a god?
> He who was alive yesterday is dead to-day.
> In an instant he is cast into grief,
> Of a sudden he is crushed.
> For a moment he sings in joy;
> In a twinkling he wails like a mourner.
> Like opening and closing, their (*i. e.* mankind's) spirit changes;
> If they are hungry, they are like corpses;

---
[10] See below, p. 48.

THE BOOK OF JOB

Have they had enough, they consider themselves equal to their god.
If things go well, they prate of mounting to heaven;
If they are in distress, they speak of descending into Irkalla.[11]

In the Upanishads of ancient India, from about the seventh and following centuries,[12] the tragedy of life is the constant theme, and the spirit in which life is viewed is preëminently philosophical, but we have sporadic reflections rather than a genuine attempt to get at the core of the problem. In this respect the Symposium of Job is unique. Its philosophy is not academic but intensely human. It brings the problem home to us in a way that betrays its origin in a circle which responded sympathetically to the hard experiences of life from which few escape, a circle that was alive to the consciousness of frequent failure, despite all endeavors to follow the dictates of an ethical code of life and that grasped the bitterness of seeing wrong triumphant while virtue is trampled under foot. The Symposium is all the more remarkable because despite its rebellious tone, its boldness is kept within the limits of an honest search for truth, undertaken in a profoundly serious frame of mind. Its pessimism is free from any tinge of cynicism or frivolity; its skepticism is never offensive, because it keeps close to intense sympathy for suffering mankind as typified by Job. The Symposium, quite apart from its literary qualities, stands out for these reasons in the world's literature as one of the boldest attempts to attack a problem which to-day, after two thousand years and more, still baffles religious minds.

---
[11] One of the names of the lower world, wherein the dead are huddled.
[12] See Macdonnell *Sanskrit Literature*, page 226.

THE BOOK OF JOB

IV

THE TWO JOBS

A further condition for a proper understanding of the book that follows from what has just been set forth, is the separation of the story of Job from the philosophical discussion occasioned by the story; and here we touch upon the most significant of misunderstandings in regard to our book which is still widely prevalent. To the average person who has been accustomed to think of the Book of Job as a unit composition, written by one person as a book generally is in our days, there is only *one* Job. In reality there are two, the Job of the story and the Job in the discussions with his three companions. The only connection between the two Jobs is the similarity in the name.

An uncritical tradition is responsible for the confusion, for the compilers of the book in its original form did all that lay in their power to distinguish between the two. Even externally the Job of the story is separated from the Job in the discussions. The story of the pious, patient, taciturn Job is told in prose,[13] whereas the other Job who is impatient, and rebellious, voluble in the denunciation of the cruel fate meted out to him, and blasphemous in his charges of injustice against the Creator of the universe in control of the destinies of mankind is made to speak in poetry, as are his friends. Apart from this, the Job

---

[13] Chapters 1 and 2 and the conclusion of the story (though modified from its original form) chapter 42, 7-17. The distinction is made evident in the Revised Version, as in other modern translations.

THE BOOK OF JOB

who when misfortunes follow upon disasters in close succession exclaims—

"Yahweh has given, and Yahweh has taken,
Blessed be the name of Yahweh." (2, 21).

cannot possibly be the same as the one who at the outset of the Symposium between him and his companions gives vent to his embittered soul in the most vehement terms:

"Perish the day on which I was born,
And the night when a male was conceived." (3, 3.)

Can there be a more striking contrast than between the Job in the story who, when called upon by his unsympathetic wife to do away with himself and thus put an end to his sufferings, asks:

"Should we indeed receive the good from God, but the evil we should not receive"? (2, 10.)

and the Job in the discussion, whose piercing cry of despair resounds through the ages:

"Why did I not die at the womb,
Come forth from the lap and perish?
Why did knees receive me?
And why were there breasts to give me suck?" (3, 11-12.)

One must admire the persistency of the uncritical tradition which thus succeeded in confusing the two Jobs, in the face of the contradiction between the one as not "sinning with his lips,"(2, 10) despite all that he had to endure, and the unbridled blasphemy of the other Job who exclaims to God,

"I will not restrain my mouth;
I will give voice to my despair.

* * * * * * *

I prefer strangling of my soul,
Death rather than my pains.
I refuse to live any longer;
Cease, for my days are vanity." (7, 11 and 15–16.)

Nor does the Job of the discussion stop short of accusing God of deliberate injustice. He goes so far as to suggest that it is God's nature to be cruel, to take pleasure in seeing the innocent suffer:

"If I were in the right, my mouth [14] would condemn me;
If I were entirely right, He would twist the verdict.

* * * * * * *

The guiltless and the wicked He destroys.
If a scourge should suddenly strike one dead,
He would laugh at the death of the innocent." (9, 20–23.)

Can a denial of a *merciful* Providence go further? The Job of the story has sublime faith in God's justice, despite all appearances to the contrary. The Job of the discussions conceives of God as strong and powerful, but as arbitrary and without a sense of justice. Such are the two Jobs, the one as far removed from the other as heaven is from earth—

"Look here, upon this picture, and on this."

V

THE FRIENDS IN THE FOLKTALE AND IN THE SYMPOSIUM

The contrast between the story and the setting in the discussion extends to the portrayal of the three friends and to the conception of God. In the story, as told in the opening two chapters, the friends are intensely sympathetic. They are shocked at the

---

[14] *i.e.*, my complaints against fate.

THE BOOK OF JOB

appearance of Job; they are so deeply moved by the misfortunes that have overwhelmed him and by the sufferings that he endures as to be incapable of speech. Their sympathy is expressed by their silence. But note the contrast when we come to the Symposium. Their sympathy changes to harshness in a steadily ascending scale. Eliphaz, the first to speak, begins, to be sure, in an apologetic strain, excusing himself as it were for venturing to offer a suggestion to Job as to the cause of his suffering, but only to advance to a rebuke that is none the less stinging for being put in the form of a question:

"Can man be more righteous than God?
Can a man be purer than his Maker?" (4, 17.)

The implication is clear, and with subtle skill Eliphaz advances to a more direct charge that Job must have committed some great wrong which brought on his hard fate.

"I have seen the foolish take root;
But his habitation of a sudden is swept away.
His sons far from salvation,
And crushed, with none to save [them]." (5, 3-4.)

Eliphaz uses the milder term "foolish," but he means "wicked;" and he wishes to leave no doubt in Job's mind that his only hope is to confess his guilt and to throw himself on the mercy of God.

If Eliphaz in his first speech is somewhat restrained, not so Bildad and Zophar, who introduce their arguments with sharp invectives, and whose example is followed by Eliphaz in his subsequent speeches. There is no trace of friendly sympathy in Bildad's greeting:

THE BOOK OF JOB

"How long wilt thou babble thus?
Thy words are a mighty wind." (8, 1.)

and there is downright hostility in Zophar's opening taunt:

"Should one full of words remain unanswered?
Should a babbler be acquitted?" (11, 1.)

The friends in the story of Job become the accusers in the discussion. One after the other declares that Job—in flagrant contradiction to the assumption throughout the story—is a wicked sinner whose punishment is merited because of his unrepentant nature, which manifests itself in the charges of injustice that he hurls against the Almighty as the cause of his ills and woes. We almost lose sight of the main discussion in the great variety of the taunts, rebukes and charges brought by the three companions against Job.

VI

THE TWO CONCEPTIONS OF GOD

There are also two conceptions of God. The Yahweh of the story is a different being from the Elohim [15] in the discussions. Yahweh is proud of Job's piety and has supreme confidence that His "servant Job" will endure the test to which he is put

---

[15] Elohim, varying with El, is a generic designation like our "God" or "Deity," in contrast to Yahweh, the name of the old national deity of the Hebrews. So personal was the name Yahweh that it became customary to avoid the pronunciation and to substitute for it "Adonai" meaning "Master," "Lord." The substitute was not due to the holiness of the name Yahweh, as the later tradition assumed, but on the contrary to its distasteful association with a deity limited in scope to one people and restricted in jurisdiction to the territory controlled by that people. The later documents in the Pentateuchal compilation use "Elohim," *i.e.*, Deity, which is impersonal, just as we might to-day prefer "Almighty" to the term "God," because of the strong implication of personality in the current use of God. See further the note to the translation of chapter 12, 9.

THE BOOK OF JOB

at the instigation of Satan. Yahweh boasts of Job as one might take pride in a fine achievement.

"Hast thou observed my servant Job? There is none like him in the earth—pious and upright."

"There's a fine fellow," Yahweh says to Satan. See what a splendid creature I have made of him! One is tempted to say that the dialogue between Yahweh and Satan has a touch of bonhomie in it that is in refreshing contrast to the severe and forbidding picture we receive of the Deity in the philosophical poem. Goethe in the prologue to Faust, based on the two introductory chapters of Job, has caught this spirit in the scene between the Almighty and Mephistopheles, though he has also intensified it by a thorough modernization of the scene itself.[16]

The use of a generic designation of the Deity like Elohim to avoid the personal quality involved in the more specific name Yahweh—is intentional; and similarly, El, Eloah and Shaddai are employed as synonyms of Elohim, because they conjure up the picture of a Being of universal scope and power whom one approaches in awe, and whose decision once made is unchangeable. The God portrayed by the friends is stern and unbending, while for Job He becomes a cold tyrant, indifferent to appeals for mercy even when they come from those whose lips are clean and whose hearts are pure.

How, then, are we to account for the two Jobs, the two varying portrayals of the three companions and the two conceptions of God? It is only necessary

---

[16] Eckermann's *Conversations with Goethe* under date of January, 1825.

THE BOOK OF JOB

to put the question in order to show the obviousness of the answer that the story of Job is *independent* of the philosophical poem; and if independent also older. Three passages in Ezekiel [17] come to our aid in establishing the existence in early days of a current tradition about a man of great piety whose name was Job. The prophet, in order to drive home his doctrine that, on the one hand, God does not punish His people without cause, and that, on the other, punishment for wrongs and crimes cannot be averted by the existence of some righteous members of the community —as in the case of Abraham's plea to save Sodom and Gomorrah for the sake of the few righteous in the multitude of sinners,—declares that even if such men as Noah, Daniel and Job were living in the midst of the sinful nation, their virtues would only secure their own deliverance from the four scourges—the sword, famine, evil beasts and pestilence—decreed for Jerusalem. The juxtaposition with Noah and Daniel shows that Job, like these two men, had come to be regarded as a model and *type* of piety and human excellence. Ezekiel, is anterior to the Book of Job, as he is by four centuries earlier than the Book of Daniel, in which the traditional Daniel is utilized as a medium for encouraging pious Jews, suffering under the tyranny of Antiochus Epiphanes (175-164 B. C.), to remain steadfast in their faith. [18] The tradition about Job survives, however, the composition of the book which is called by his name, for in the Epistle of

---

[17] Ezekiel 14, 14; 16, 18 and 20.
[18] That this is the aim of the various sections into which the Book of Daniel may be divided is now the generally accepted view of scholars. See *e.g.*, Driver, *Commentary on Daniel*, p. lxv *seq*.

THE BOOK OF JOB

James (5, 11), Job is incidentally referred to as an example of piety and patience. As late as the days of Theodore of Mopsuestia, (died c. 428 A. D.) whom we have already had occasion to mention,[19] the story of the patient Job who becomes in the popular conception a holy prophet was still current in a form which suggests to Theodore that the author of the Book of Job had taken some undue liberties with the original tale. The Arabs have preserved traditions about Job,[20] which point to the growth of the popular tale even after it had been given a literary form among the Hebrews.

We are, therefore, justified in concluding that from an early age, Job had become a popular figure among the Hebrews. In accordance with the tendency of folktales the story received additions from time to time, and it also shared the fate of popular tales in being carried from one people to another.

VII

THE NON-HEBRAIC ORIGIN OF THE STORY OF JOB

It does not follow that the tale of the pious man who became the prototype for the virtuous man not to be moved from his position by any misfortunes that might sweep over him originated among the Hebrews. Indeed, the name Job—for which there is no satisfactory Hebrew etymology and which we do not encounter elsewhere in the Old Testament—points to a foreign origin; and if, as we may properly assume, the statement in the prologue to the Book of Job that

---
[19] Above, p. 25.
[20] In the "Stories of the Prophets" by Thala'abi (d. 1035 A.D.). A translation by Prof. D. B. Macdonald will be found in the American Journal of Semitic Languages, Vol. 14, pp. 145-161.

THE BOOK OF JOB

he lived in the land of Uz, which lies to the east of Palestine, was part of the popular tale as it circulated among the Hebrews, it becomes even more definite that Job was not a Hebrew, as little as the three companions were Hebrews.[21] The entire setting of the story is in fact non-Hebraic. Job is described as "greater than any of the sons of the East," (1, 3) in a manner to suggest that he belongs to that vague region known as "East," but without any suggestion of a connection with the "sons of Israel"; and it is rather surprising that in the adaptation of the tale to the purposes of the discussion, which we must perforce assume, a more Hebraic atmosphere should not have been given to it. In the dialogue between God and Satan, the specific Hebraic name Yahweh is introduced, but Job himself is represented as using the general name Elohim, (1, 5 and 2, 10) as is also his wife (2, 9.) It is only in his pious submission to the Divine will, that the name Yahweh is introduced in what is probably a quotation from a "Yahweh" prayer. That such a touch as Job himself bringing sacrifices without the mediation of a priest, as demanded by the Pentateuchal codes, should have been retained in the adaptation may be taken as a further proof of the unconscious influence exerted by the non-Hebraic origin of the tale—an influence strong enough to have kept out of it any reference to specific Hebraic rites or customs.[22]

---

[21] Shown by the names and by the statement of their homes in parts of Arabia. See the note to the translation of 2, 11.

[22] The term used for sacrifices is the most general that could have been selected. The annual festival that brings Job's family together (1, 4–5) is similarly of a most general character—without any warrant in any of the Pentateuchal codes.

THE BOOK OF JOB

We are thus led to the conclusion that the story of Job was a tale that became current in ancient Palestine and wandered, as tales do from place to place, subject to modification as it passed down the ages, altered to some extent in its adaptation to different localities, but retaining enough traces of its origin to preserve its distinctive character as a general illustration of the spirit in which misfortunes and sufferings should be received and endured. The story of a pious man who maintains his firm faith and his simple piety under most distressing circumstances, who bore all trials in patience was what we would nowadays call a good "Sunday School" tale—one that might be told with profit to encourage the young and to edify their elders. Tales of this character are common enough in antiquity. The "good man" is a type in folktales as common as is his counterpart—the "bad man." It is not surprising, therefore, to encounter "Jobs" elsewhere, as, for example, in India where we have the tale of an "upright king" who loses his possessions and sells his boy, his wife and finally himself in order to carry on his works of charity, and to whom all is restored in the end because he had endured the burdens of misfortunes in patience and without complaint.[23]

Similarly, in the story of the pious king of Nippur above referred to,[24] who, like Job, is smitten with sore disease and is finally restored to health through the intervention of the gods, there are analogies with

---

[23] Maive Stokes, *Indian Fairy Tales*, Calcutta, 1879, pp. 68–72.
[24] Page 37. See an article by the writer, "A Babylonian Job," in the Journal of Biblical Literature, Vol. 25, pp. 125–191 and Barton, *Archæology of the Bible*, pp. 392–97.

the philosophical discussions in Job that are most suggestive, but even such literary analogies furnish no warrant for assuming a direct influence from the outside on our Biblical book. The problem suggested by the sufferings of Job is a perfectly natural one, so that if we find it discussed elsewhere it would merely point to a stage of intellectual development in which people—or at least the choice spirits—were no longer entirely satisfied with the conventional view that sufferings are due to sin.

VIII

ORAL TRANSMISSION *VERSUS* LITERARY PRODUCTION

It is not necessary to assume that a definite literary form was given to the tale among the Hebrews before it was incorporated into the Book of Job, though, on the other hand, one cannot dogmatically assert that this could not have been the case. Stories in the ancient East, as to a large extent still in the East of today, are recited, not read. Our specifically Western attitude towards mental productivity can hardly conceive of literature except as embodied in a definite written form, whereas until the East came under the influence of the West through contact with Greek civilization in the second half of the fourth century B. C., the oral transmission without a definite literary form was the regular mould of literature to which the written form, if it existed at all, was entirely secondary and incidental—memoranda to serve as a prop in the further oral transmission. Under such

THE BOOK OF JOB

conditions a story or even a book might have existed for ages before it received what we would call a book form. One of the chief reasons why the modern critical study of the Bible aroused such hostility when its results began to be disseminated among the lay public and why it is still eyed with suspicion in many circles, is because we thoughtlessly—almost unconsciously—apply our modern and Western conceptions of literary composition to an age to which they do not apply. As I have pointed out elsewhere,[25] we can hardly conceive of a book without a title and an author, whereas these two features are precisely the ones which are lacking in ancient compositions until we reach the age of Greek literature, which may be said to have invented the author.

The written form, when it arose in the ancient Orient, was not due to the promptings of the literary instinct, or to an ambition on the part of certain individuals to be known as authors, but purely as a preservative method to prevent tales and traditions that no longer enjoyed a full spontaneous existence among the people from perishing or from being distorted. Writing begins when genuine production comes to an end. As long as a tale retained its full popularity, as long as a tradition formed, as it were, part and parcel of the life of the people there was no urgent necessity to give the tale or tradition a written form. It lived in the minds and the hearts of the people. And so with the exhortations of a prophet, with the decisions of a lawgiver, or even with the

---

[25] *A Gentle Cynic*, pp. 31–41.

THE BOOK OF JOB

prayers of a Psalmist, giving expression to emotions shared by the entire group. There was no occasion for the definite written form until with the advent of a new age with new interests and new problems, the tale no longer made its appeal, the tradition was no longer living, the exhortation was in danger of becoming a memory, the law needed reinforcement, and the prayer through the development of the cult was embodied into a fixed ritual.

It is also immaterial whether such a man as Job ever existed, just as it is of no consequence whether there was such a man as Noah or Daniel. A rabbi of the Talmudic age, [26] betraying a critical spirit which is quite exceptional, declares in one place that Job is a product of popular fancy; and it is at all events clear that he as well as Noah and Daniel, as likewise Abraham, became a mere *type* of steadfast piety, just as to a later age David and Solomon, despite the historical character of much—though far from everything—that is told of them become types, David of the pious king to whom an unhistorical tradition subsequently ascribed the Psalms, and Solomon of the wise king to whom Biblical productions embodying the wisdom of the age were assigned.[27] This tendency to transform traditional or historical personages into types is a by-product of the spirit peculiar to the ancient East, which only gradually reaches the point where the individual stands out in sharp outline from his surroundings.

---

[26] Talmud Babli, Baba Bathra 15ᵃ.
[27] See further on this "*A Gentle Cynic*" p. 52 *seq.*

THE BOOK OF JOB

IX
THE MODIFICATIONS IN THE FOLKTALE
THE FIGURE OF SATAN

We are now prepared to face the question, whether we have the story of Job entirely in its original form in the prologue, or whether there are some features which are due to its adaptation to the purpose of a philosophical discussion! The story being of non-Jewish origin, as has been made probable, the introduction of the name Yahweh in the prologue is obviously a natural consequence of its adoption by the Hebrews. The scene in heaven in which likewise the name of Yahweh is used with, however, the attendants or ministers of Yahweh spoken of as the *benê Elohim* "Sons of God," does not strike one as a popular feature. Particularly through the introduction of the figure of Satan does the scene receive a theological admixture that reflects a more sophisticated age than the one in which the story arose. One can in fact cut out the scene in heaven without detriment to the essence of the story, and some scholars see in the scene an interpolation subsequent to the completion of the book. This, however, is most unlikely. For not only is the dramatic effect of the tale heightened by the test to which Job is put by the agreement between God and Satan, but the intent to show that Job is really innocent and is condemned to suffering by a deliberate and quite arbitrary decision of Yahweh is in accord with the main theme of the Symposium that sufferings in this world are not *always* due to just causes, that the Divine power which controls the destinies of nature and of mankind does not work under the inflexible law of ethical standards.

We conclude, then, that the dialogues in heaven between Yahweh and Satan represent modifications of the folktale that may represent the contribution of those to whom we owe the thought of making the story the vehicle of a discussion of human suffering. There is a certain callousness in the readiness with which Yahweh is willing to accede to the suggestion of Satan to put Job to the test, that betokens the questioning spirit. The popular tale everywhere is marked by naïveté; it is free from self-consciousness, and above all it is without a skeptical taint. Even a touch of skepticism would vitiate the flavor of the tale. It would discountenance its single import, to show how a pious and good man would act under the blows of misfortune. The folktale of Job starts from the common experience of changeable fate in the fortunes of men. Its lesson is that man must endure patiently and in resignation, and must not be swerved from the line of righteous conduct by life's hard experiences. The naïveté of both the tale and its lesson disappears the moment we are told that the sufferings of Job are due to a wager. The mystery of suffering which is its chief claim to popular attention is dissolved.

The figure of Satan, as he appears in the prologue, arrests our attention. The term connotes an "adversary," and it is not infrequently used in the Old Testament for a human "opponent" [28] as the abstract term derived from it, *sitnāh*, means "hostility."[29]

---

[28] *e.g.*, a number of times to designate adversaries of Solomon, I Kings, 11, 14. 23–25.
[29] A late term occurring in the memoirs of Ezra (4, 6).

THE BOOK OF JOB

The Satan in the story of Job is an evil spirit, but of a different character from the demons and *jinns*, the mischievous sprites of popular belief, to which the Hebrews in common with all people of antiquity—and for that matter of modern times—clung, whose presence in the human body manifested itself as disease, and to whom also the minor ills and the many accidents of life were ascribed. Such demons were supposed to act at the behest of the gods, or they were under the control of human sorcerers and witches. Satan in the prologue to Job is a semi-divine being, placed on a par with the "Sons of God," though occupying an independent position. He has not yet advanced to the position of the "accuser" as which he appears in Zechariah, (3, 1-2) but he is on the road to assuming the general role of an enemy of man—the one who tempts man towards evil. The development of the conception stops short in the Old Testament as the one to whom evil thoughts are ascribed in an age which found it distasteful to associate such a rule with God himself. The comparison of II Sam. 24, 1 with the parallel passage I Chron. 21, 1 is instructive in this respect. In the earlier compilation it is God's anger enkindled against Israel that is set down as inducing David to sin by planning a census of the people, whereas by the time that Chronicles came to be compiled—in the third century B. C.—such an explanation was regarded as not in accord with the conception of a spiritual Power at the head of the universe. God is replaced by Satan, acting apparently independently. It is not, however, till New Testament times that Satan becomes the full-

THE BOOK OF JOB

fledged tempter, assuming the guise of a serpent in the famous third chapter of Genesis, which becomes the basis of St. Paul's Christology.

In the scene of the heavenly court, as depicted in the Book of Job, there is not as yet any inherent opposition between God as the source of good, and Satan as the cause of evil, such as we encounter in Zoroastrianism where the control of the destinies of the universe is divided between Ahuramazda, the good power, and Ahriman, the evil one. [30] In the passage quoted from the prophet Zechariah and which belongs to the Persian period of Hebrew history, *i. e.*, after the sixth century, scholars are inclined to recognize the influence of Persian dualism, but hardly in the person of Satan as depicted in the prologue to Job, unless it be the personification of the figure as a semi-independent being. For, be it noted, Satan cannot afflict Job without the express permission of Yahweh, and he must keep the affliction heaped upon Job within the bounds assigned by Yahweh (1, 12; 2, 6). He is, as the name Satan indicates, still essentially an "adversary." He is a cynic who belittles the character of man, and his cynical attitude towards human virtues is admirably and adroitly displayed in the two opening chapters. Instead of sharing the universal admiration for Job, he suggests that Job is worldly-wise in being a model of goodness and piety. It pays him to be virtuous. We can picture him asking with a shrug of the shoulder:

"Is Job God-fearing for nought?" (1, 9.)

---
[30] See the section on "Zoroastrianism and the Book of Job" below in chapter V.

Why should he not be good, since God is so good to him? When Job endures the first test of losing his wealth, his family and his household, Satan still questions the sincerity of Job, and with aggravated cynicism suggests that the pious man is so wrapt up in selfishness that he will endure every loss as long as it does not touch his own life. "There is a skin beneath the skin"—(2, 4). Only the outer epidermis has been touched by the misfortunes that have come to Job. Prick the inner skin—the man himself—and see what happens? "All that a man has will he give for his life." The subtlety of Satan, as here portrayed, is sufficient to show that the scene is not part of a genuine folktale, but the product of a more advanced age, intent upon giving the story a special turn.

X
"THE SONS OF GOD"

But, it may be objected, do not the "Sons of God," occurring in the scene that describes the Divine court, grouped around God, point to a primitive conception? Assuredly, for the phrase must be brought into connection with the strange semi-mythological tale in the sixth chapter of Genesis, where as part of the general conception of the universe the "Sons of God" are portrayed as attracted by the beauty of the daughters of men, and by commingling with them, producing a brood of giants. The story was originally told to explain the tradition, so common among peoples of antiquity, of a once mightier race that disappeared. Its original purpose was not derogatory either to mankind or to the Divine beings who thus helped to produce the giants of old. To the stern moralist, however, who puts his own interpretation on the popular tradition of a destructive deluge—originally a nature myth to symbolize the annual change from the dry to the wet season—the giants become a band of wicked tyrants whose superhuman strength is traced to an unnatural and therefore immoral union between gods and men. To him the union with the "Sons of God," is rape committed on the daughters of men. The writer in Genesis uses the primitive conception of "Sons of God" to point the moral of the tale, and similarly, the one to whom we owe the prologue in Job inserts in the scene the old conception of "Sons of God,"—which must have been particularly distasteful to the strict monotheist—because it added picturesqueness and heightened the dramatic effect of the dialogue between God and Satan, taking place in an assemblage of all the semi-divine beings gathered like courtiers around the Divine throne.

It is, of course, possible that in some version of the popular tale of Job, the praises of Job's piety were celebrated by a chorus of minor gods or semi-divine beings in illustration of the exceptional position which he had acquired through his blameless and happy life. The popular fancy would naturally ascribe Job's good fortune to the favor of the Deity as a reward for his piety. It is, therefore, conceivable that some popular "reciter"—as in the modern Arabic world we still encounter such story-tellers, adding new touches to the adventures of the popular hero Antar, or to some

THE BOOK OF JOB

scene from the Thousand and One Nights [31]—should have introduced an incident which the writer of the prologue further embellished with traits that are distinctly not of popular origin. It is foolish to be dogmatic on such suppositions which in the nature of things can neither be established nor disproved, though we may go so far as to place the probability on the side of the hypothesis that the tale was popularly expanded to include a scene in which the "Sons of God" joined Yahweh in singing the praises of Job. The point is of comparatively little importance as against the main conclusion that in its present form the scene between God and Satan serves a purpose foreign to the entire spirit of the original tale. That story, however much it may have been embellished by touches to heighten the effect, must have retained its simplicity by laying the sole stress on the character of Job as supremely good, on the rewards granted to him because of his piety, and on the variety and severity of his subsequent sufferings which he bore in model patience. Details in the description of Job's goodness as exemplified in his life and of the variety of his possessions may have been added endlessly, but all such variations and embellishments would keep to the main purpose and trend of the folktale. The wager between God and Satan robs the story of its flavor, by affording an *explanation* of Job's sufferings, whereas the feature of the story which gives it its charm is that Job suffers without any apparent cause. He seeks for no explanation of his sufferings.

---

[31] See the interesting chapters on modern reciters in the East, in Lane, *Manners and Customs of the Modern Egyptians*, Vol. I, chapters viii–x.

THE BOOK OF JOB

He takes evil as he receives good, because of his supreme faith and because of the firmness of his character that remains unaffected by the changing winds of fortune. He is like a mighty oak that gratefully raises its head to receive the sunshine and that bends to the storm without being moved from its place. The folk spirit would have instinctively rejected the suggestion that Job's fate was merely prompted by a cynical suspicion that Job's goodness was calculated selfishness, and that Yahweh in order to prove that He was right and Satan wrong was willing to impose cruel sufferings on an innocent man. Cut out the dialogue and substitute for it, if you will, a scene in heaven with the Sons of God joining Yahweh in praising Job, somewhat like the fancy embodied in one of the Rabbinical legends [32] in which the good Angels sing the praises of creation and urge God to create man despite the failings that he will show, whereas others less kindly disposed urge that he be not created, and you have a much finer story from the folktale point of view as well as a truer one. For the purpose, however, of the philosophical discussion, the dialogue between Yahweh and Satan is not without significance, for it anticipates as has been suggested one of the main thoughts of the Symposium that the Divine will does not always act from deep set motives of right and justice.

XI
THE FOUR EPILOGUES TO THE BOOK OF JOB

But, how stands the case with the three friends who come to comfort Job and end by rebuking him?

---

[32] See Ginzburg, *Legends of the Jews* I, pp. 52–54.

THE BOOK OF JOB

The names of the three and the districts from which they come vouch for their forming part of the original tale. They hear of his sad fate and hasten to his side to help him bear his heavy burden, but when they see him writhing in pain, words fail them.

"Then they sat down with him on the ground seven days and seven nights, without speaking a word to him, because they saw how very great was his pain." (2, 13.)

There you have the folktale in its genuine form—charming in its simplicity and impressive by its naïveté. It is inconceivable that such sympathizers, feeling Job's grief as though it were their own, could under any provocation become "sorry comforters" (16, 2) as Job in the course of the discussion calls them, just as the high intellectual plane of the philosophical discussions is entirely beyond the reach of the simple-minded friends portrayed in the prologue. If in the folktale any discussions were introduced after the seven days of silence—and this was possibly the case in one of the versions that floated about—we may feel quite certain that, true to their original role, the three friends endeavored to encourage Job to retain his patience in the assurance that God will listen to his entreaties and have pity on his sad condition. The atmosphere of simple, child-like faith and of calm sweetness must have been retained in the folktale and, therefore, we may assert with considerable confidence that the epilogue of the story (42, 7-17), as told (in prose like the prologue) at the close of the philosophical book, has been modified to make it accord with the purpose of the discussion superimposed on the story itself.

THE BOOK OF JOB

In its present form, the epilogue makes Yahweh manifest his displeasure with the three friends, for they did not speak "What was proper as my servant Job did." (42, 7.) They are directed to bring burnt offerings as an atonement and Job is to intercede in their behalf so as to prevent their just punishment from being meted out to them. Such a conclusion presupposes the discussions between Job and his companions, and moreover points to the triumph of Job and to the discomfiture of the three participants in the Symposium. It reflects the point of view of those who entirely sympathized with the situation unfolded in the course of the Symposium by the speeches of Job; it is, therefore, in direct contradiction to the words— in poetic form—put into the mouth of Job (42, 6), just before the prose conclusion:

"Therefore, I recall and repent,
In utter worthlessness." [33]

Similarly, the other draft of Job's final words (40, 4-5), likewise poetical in form:

"I am entirely unworthy to answer Thee;
My hand I lay upon my mouth.
Once I have spoken, but never again;
Twice, but now no more,"

is entirely out of keeping with what must have been the *original* close of the story, which we clearly have in 42, 10-17, beginning

"And Yahweh turned the fortune of Job, and Yahweh restored everything to Job in double amount."

---

[33] See for this translation of the phrase "dust and ashes" the note to 42, 6.

THE BOOK OF JOB

Such further details as the rejoicing of the entire family of the patient sufferer at the happy ending, the congratulatory gifts [34] and the praise of the beauty of Job's daughters show that in these verses we are again dealing with the naïve folktale. In the prose conclusion we must, therefore, separate 42, 7-9, which belongs to the Symposium from 42, 10-17, which is the *original* conclusion to the folktale, describing how all ended happily because the pious man endured in faith and in silent resignation to the Divine will. We thus have no less than four conclusions to the book, two in prose (1) 42, 10-17, (2) 42, 7-9 and two in poetic form (3) 40, 1-14 [35] and (4) 42, 1-6.

But the further contradiction involved between the prose conclusion (42, 7-9) added by those who regarded Job as justified in his argument against his friends, and the two poetical epilogues in which Job is clearly portrayed as in the wrong and, therefore, repenting in deep humility and in consciousness of his guilt, needs to be explained.

The attempts of commentators to reconcile these opposite points of view involve them in subtleties that border on sophistry. Surely, the humbled and repentant Job cannot be also described as the one who spoke what was "proper." (42, 7) Nor can the companions who rebuke Job for his charges of injustice preferred against God be held up as "having kindled Yahweh's anger," since their rebukes are reinforced

---

[34] Namely, the piece of money and the golden ring (42, 11), reflecting some ancient custom of bestowing congratulatory gifts upon recovery from disease.

[35] See the notes to the translation which will show that an "Introduction" has been combined with this epilogue.

THE BOOK OF JOB

by God himself when He is introduced in the closing chapters:
> "Who is this that darkens counsel,
> By words without knowledge?" (38, 2.)

not to speak of the interposed speeches of Elihu (chapters 32–37), which are likewise intended to disprove Job's contentions and to hold him up to scorn for his audacity.

There is only one way out of the difficulty, to wit, to regard the varying conclusions of the story as independent of one another. The one in which Job is represented as being justified while his friends are rebuked was added to the Symposium in its *original* form, the two in which Job confesses that he was wrong belong to the Book of Job in a form *amplified* to controvert the aim of the older book. This process of amplification, involving many hands and extending over a considerable period, found its crowning point in the addition of the two poetical prologues to the two prose ones.

This leads us directly to the composite character of the present Book of Job.

CHAPTER II
THE THREE STRATA IN THE BOOK OF JOB
I
COLLECTIVE AND ANONYMOUS AUTHORSHIP

What has been said in regard to the gradual manner in which the folktale of Job took on a literary form and was transformed in this process to adapt itself as a prologue to the discussion of the philosophical problem applies to the Symposium (chapters 3-27) with its supplements (chapters 28 to 31), as to the two appendices (a), the speeches of Elihu (chapters 32-37), and (b) the speeches placed in the mouth of Yahweh (chapter 38-41). These natural divisions into which the Book of Job falls represent the three main strata of the literary masterpiece. The evidence is overwhelming that these three divisions are not the production of one mind or of one time; and to those who followed what was set forth in detail in a previous publication [36] as to the profound difference between literary composition in ancient times and in our days, it will no longer come as a surprise to be told that books produced in the ancient Orient do not come down to us in their original form, but enlarged, modified and not infrequently distorted through additions and changes of all kinds—actual supplements, comments,

---
[36] See the author's "*A Gentle Cynic,*" pp. 71-101 the reading of which sections is essential to an understanding of the view here taken of the composition of the Book of Job.

answers to views set forth and even intentional changes to controvert unconventional or otherwise objectionable views. The spoken word in the ancient Orient enjoyed greater authority than the written one. What a man said was apt to be orally transmitted with considerable care, but when something was written down it became, as it were, public property and could be augmented and modified *ad libitum*, without any realization that such a process trespassed upon the prerogatives of the one who gave to a literary production its first draft. Instead of individual authorship we have composite and anonymous production. The difference between ancient Oriental and modern Western literary composition may be summed up in the statement that with us the finished book begins its life, whereas in the ancient Orient the final form of a composition represents a dead book—one that had ceased to arouse sufficient interest to warrant further additions being made to it.

It is significant as illustrating the persistence of the Oriental conception of literary composition that despite the late date, c. 90 A. D., when the canon of the Old Testament was definitely fixed, the Book of Job as well as Lamentations and Ruth and even still later productions like Daniel (c. 165 B. C.) and Esther—perhaps as late as 100 B. C.—have come down to us without any author's name attached. When we find authors named as in the headings to Ecclesiastes, Song of Songs and to most of the Psalms—though by no means to all [37]—it is due to very late editorship, at a time

---
[37] See further on this "*A Gentle Cynic,*" p. 57, note 22.

THE BOOK OF JOB

when anonymous and collective authorship had yielded under the influence of the Greek conception of individual authorship to the disposition to seek for an author to compositions that had after a longer or shorter literary process received their definite and final form.[38] The Talmud, in a passage[39] embodying a list of "traditional" authors for Biblical books, names Moses as the author of Job. It is led to do so apparently because Job is described as a patriarch, and therefore belonging to the patriarchal period portrayed in the Book of Genesis. Since Genesis as part of the Pentateuch was of Mosaic origin, according to the Rabbinical tradition, the Book of Job was likewise assigned to Moses. The fanciful character of the assumption appears to have been recognized even by those who put it forward, for it did not acquire sufficient force to lead to the name of Moses being attached as a heading to the book, which plunges at once in *medias res* by the statement:

"There was a man in the land of Uz, whose name was Job."

The anonymity of the book thus preserved lightens the task of the investigator in his endeavor to distinguish the three strata to be discerned in the gradual growth of the book.

---

[38] See *A Gentle Cynic*, pp. 52 *seq.*, for the details of this "traditional authorship" which ascribed the Pentateuch to Moses, the Books of Joshua and Samuel to the individuals whose names they bore, the Books of Kings and Lamentations to Jeremiah, the prophetical books to those whose utterances they contained, despite the fact that the pre-exilic prophets did not write but merely spoke.
[39] Talmud Babli, Baba Bathra 15ª.

THE BOOK OF JOB

II

THE ORIGINAL BOOK OF JOB AND THE SUPPLEMENTS TO IT

The final editors of the Book of Job have curiously enough preserved the proof that the book at one time terminated with the thirty-first chapter, where we actually read:

> "The words of Job are ended."

Now, to be sure, exegetes bent upon maintaining the assumption of unity in the composition of the book, explain these words as referring to the close of the speeches of Job, but apart from the fact that there would be no special reason for mentioning this, Job is actually introduced again as speaking in 40, 3-4 and a second time in 42, 1-6.[40] Taking the words as they stand, they are clearly as definite as our "finis," which we place at the end of a composition. The "Words of Job" would constitute an appropriate title for the book, corresponding to the heading "The Words of Koheleth" as the title of Ecclesiastes. Moreover, the editorial comment at the beginning of chapter 32,

> "And these three men ceased answering Job"

bears out the obvious interpretation that the book closed at one time with Job's insistence (31, 35-37) upon the justice of his case against God.[41]

---

[40] On these two epilogues, see above, p. 61 *seq.*
[41] Forming originally the close of Job's answer to Bildad's third speech. See the note to chapter 25, 1. Verses 38-40 of chapter 31 are misplaced; they belong after 31, 12. See further in the translation of this 31st chapter.

THE BOOK OF JOB

"O that there were some one to hear me!
Here is my brief—let Shaddai refute me.
Aye, I will lift it on my shoulder;
I will wear it as my crown.
With steady gait, I will confront him;
[And] as a prince approach Him."

Could there be a more effective close than this defiant speech, throwing down the challenge to God as Job's final answer to the arguments of his companions and to their endeavor to force him to confess wrongs that he did not commit? What more was there to be said? No wonder that an editor added that the three friends had no answer to make, and we may go a step further and suggest that in place of the statement that the three friends had nothing more to say,

"because he was justified in his eyes"

the text originally read "in their eyes."[42] This would accord with the entire tenor of the discussions, for they reveal throughout—barring additions made in the interests of orthodoxy—the sympathy of the editor with Job.

But even in this older book we can distinguish traces of a gradual growth. Look at chapters 29-31, put as speeches into the mouth of Job, and, apart from their inordinate length, they will be seen to be of a totally different character from any of the preceding eight speeches, for in all of these Job, after answering the rebukes of his friends, complains of his sufferings and brings forward the injustice and cruelty of the fate meted out to him. In all he protests his innocence

---

[42] So the Greek and Syriac translations actually read, as well as some Hebrew manuscripts.

THE BOOK OF JOB

and hurls charges at God in bold defiance, or in reply to the false pictures drawn by his friends of the punishment of the wicked, he argues that in this world the wicked are generally happy, while it is the innocent and virtuous who suffer. In these three chapters, however, Job does not argue at all. He does not refer to his friends nor to their contentions or rebukes, and he merely refers to his present condition [43] by way of contrast to his former state. In all of the previous speeches the position of Job before misfortunes overwhelmed him is assumed on the basis of the folktale. Not only his happiness but his superior wealth and rank "greater than any of the sons of the East" (1, 3) is part and parcel of the story. What need, therefore, for Job to dwell as he does in those chapters upon the distinction that he once enjoyed, how all honored and stood in awe of him, how when he spoke the nobles remained silent, how the poor, the orphan and the widow blessed him?

The three chapters are entirely out of harmony with the other speeches, and to clinch the argument that they are supplemental to the book in its older form, we have an entirely different kind of heading:

"And Job again took up his speech" [44]

instead of the conventional:

"And Job in answer said"

which marks the speeches from chapters 3 to 26. Chapters 29-31 represent, as a matter of fact two sup-

---

[43] 30, 26–31. The other section (30, 16–24) in which he gives voice to his sufferings, is in the style of the earlier speeches and belongs after 27, 6. See below in the notes to the rearrangement of chapters 25–31.

[44] 29, 1. Repeated from here at 27, 1 where it is not in place. See on the word used for "speech" the note to the passage in the translation.

THE BOOK OF JOB

plemental speeches of Job, added by someone or by various writers, who wished to try their hand in putting speeches of a different character into the mouth of Job.

A further proof that chapters 29-31 are supplementary is to be found in the circumstance that they follow upon chapter 28, which is clearly an addition to the original book, since its contents have no connecttion whatsoever with the theme of the Symposium. The chapter is indeed one of the most impressive bits of literature in the entire Old Testament collection, but it is an entirely independent composition setting forth man's vain search for wisdom. Some editor came across it and fortunately preserved it for us by attaching it to the original Book of Job. Its purpose is to show that wisdom is with God and not accessible to man.

III

THE THIRD SERIES OF SPEECHES OF JOB AND HIS FRIENDS

We thus have four chapters which are supplemental to the original book, but even with these lopped off we have not reached the original core. Chapters 3 to 21 contain two series of speeches (a) chapters 3-14 and (b) chapters 15-21. In each series we have the three friends replying to Job, who in turn replies to each of his friends; and since Job inaugurates the Symposium, we have seven speeches by the great sufferer and two each by the three friends—thirteen in all. The third series begins with chapter 22. According to the present arrangement, there is a speech

THE BOOK OF JOB

of Eliphaz chapter 22, an answer by Job chapters 23-24, a short speech by Bildad chapter 25, and a supposed reply by Job extending over two chapters 26-27. Zophar's third speech and Job's reply are missing. Apparently, then, the third series is incomplete. But a closer examination [45] reveals that we actually have a portion of Bildad's third speech (namely, 26, 5-14) and Zophar's third speech (27, 7-23 and 30, 2-8) *put into the mouth of Job*. This rearrangement was made by later editors with the intention of assigning to Job orthodox sentiments such as would naturally emanate from Bildad and Zophar.

It was hoped that in this way the unfavorable impression made by Job's earlier speeches, so objectionable from the orthodox point of view, might be removed. Accepting the proper arrangement of chapters 25-27, the third series becomes almost complete, for all that is now lacking is Job's reply to Zophar. Perhaps there was no reply, or it was suppressed and its place taken by the supplementary chapters 29-31, added by those who were bent on having Job bring his discourses to a conclusion by a more conciliatory tone than could have been the case in his reply to Zophar.

The book in its older form thus consists of the prologue and the two series of speeches to which subsequently was added (1) a third series of speeches—these 27 chapters forming the original Book of Job (2) an entirely independent chapter on the search for wisdom (chapter 28) and (3) the supplemental speeches of Job (chapters 29-31) which would complete

---

[45] See further below and in the notes to the translation of chapters 25-31.

THE BOOK OF JOB

the third series, though in a spirit entirely out of keeping with chapters 3-27.

The question will naturally be raised whether we should not go further and reduce the first draft of the Book of Job to the prologue and to a *single* series of speeches of which the second series would be an imitation and amplification produced at a subsequent date. The question is not irrelevant, for in fact all the arguments of the friends and the counter arguments of Job are presented in the first series comprising chapters 3-14. Contrary to the still current view there is no *progressive* development of the theme of the Symposium; there are merely variations on a few melodies. The literary superiority of the book lies, next to its superb style and its splendid poetry, precisely in the skillful manner in which these variations are handled. The arguments are in reality few in number. They may be reduced to four on the part of the three friends.

(1) That God is just, (2) that Job must have committed some wrong, (3) that when suffering comes, one must throw one's self upon the mercy of God, (4) that the wicked may flourish for a while, but always in the end meet their doom. Job has only four counter arguments to bring forward: (1) that, as the popular story shows, he was not wicked but on the contrary supremely virtuous and pious, (2) that God is arbitrary, (3) that one cannot bring one's case before God without thereby already impugning Divine justice, (4) that the wicked are not punished.

These few arguments are all introduced in the first series, and the one or the other of them is elaborated in the six speeches of the second series. So, for example, Eliphaz in his second speech (15, 7-16) enlarges upon the impossibility of penetrating to the essence of things, which Bildad (11, 7-9) had already emphasized. The second speech of Eliphaz even contains a quotation from the first.[46] Bildad in his second speech (chapter 18) sets forth at length the punishment in store for the wicked which was already suggested more briefly in his first speech (chapter 8, 11-20), as well as by Zophar (11, 20). Job brings forward his strongest argument that one cannot carry one's case before God in the speech replying to Bildad (chapters 9-10), and he repeats it in the speeches of the second series (*e. g.*, 16, 20-21 and 19, 6-11). In his reply to Bildad (9, 20-24) he suggests that God is callous to merit, that the innocent and wicked are treated alike, aye, that

"The earth is given into the hand of the wicked."

It is, therefore, merely an elaboration of the thought, when in a speech in the second series (chapter 21) he launches into a most detailed picture of this topsy-turvy world in which the wicked grow fat, are not troubled with remorse and escape even when a general calamity ensues.

For all that, we have no *decisive* data to warrant us in saying that a Book of Job once existed with only one series of speeches. A group of writers might easily be led to indulge in variations upon a single theme; and the circumstance that the second series is entirely in the style of the first is another reason for assuming that

---

[46] Cf. 15, 14-15 with 4, 17-18.

THE BOOK OF JOB

the elaboration and even the repetition of the arguments and counter arguments were part of the Book of Job in its earliest form. There is just enough independence in the manner of treating the theme and of presenting the arguments to warrant us in asserting that, despite the general similarity of the speeches to one another, the second series forms an integral part of the oldest written draft so far as we can trace it; far more so than is the case in the third series of speeches which betrays' in various ways its supplemental character, though not to the extent of modifying the thesis that chapters 3-27 form a harmonious whole and represent the original Symposium in its *completed* form.

IV

THE TWO APPENDICES TO THE ORIGINAL BOOK OF JOB

Now, how can we be so certain that the first twenty-seven chapters of the book with the prose epilogue 42, 7-9 form an original Book of Job? Look at the second division of the book in its present form, which consists of chapters 32-37, containing the speeches of Elihu. We are transported at once to an entirely different scene, with a different environment and a different atmosphere. The Symposium is at an end, as the introduction to the speeches of Elihu specifically tells us. The three friends had nothing more to say. A new character appears on the scene who, in contrast to Job and his three friends, bears a Hebrew name. His father's name Barachel is also Hebraic, and he is represented as a descendant of one of the Hebrew clans.[47] The four separate discourses into which the six chapters may be divided are of an entirely different character from the speeches in the Symposium. Elihu approaches the problem from a different angle, though one can also see some borrowings from the Symposium proper, [48] due perhaps to later editors who wished to connect these chapters with the original book. The two arguments urged by Elihu are (a) that God warns man of his fate by dreams and visions and also by chastisement and that (b) whether one is wicked or righteous, one neither takes anything from God nor gives anything to him. Clearly, the purpose of these six chapters is to complement the Symposium, by suggesting other points of view from which the problem might be attacked.

The language also in these supplementary chapters is different, though this point must not be stressed, because there was a conscious imitation on the part of later amplifiers of the book of the style adopted in the earlier sections. Here again the absence of distinctly individual authorship favors the rise of a large number of amplifiers of a book, interested in the problem and expressing schools of thought rather than individual points of view, men who by deliberate imitation could write much in the same style as their predecessors. Such a collection as the Psalms, the

---

[47] He is called "the Buzite of the family of Ram." The prophet Ezekiel's father bears the name of Buzi (Ez. 1, 3), and Ram is the name of a Judean clan (Ruth 4, 19).

[48] *e.g.*, 34, 3 is taken from 12, 11; 35, 5 from 22, 12 and harks back also to 7, 20. Besides, in 33, 9–10; 34, 5–6 and 35, 2–3 he quotes utterances of Job in the original book.

THE BOOK OF JOB

work of many hands and yet in which so many Psalms bear a close resemblance to one another, furnishes an illustration of how much great literature can be steadily produced by this process of imitation on the part of those who belong to the same school of religious thought, and who live in the same congenial atmosphere. The same applies to the Proverbs, showing an *apparent* unity through the influence of the factor of collective and imitative authorship. The restraint upon imitation in our days of literary production, marked by the intense desire to express one's own personality, acts as a deterrent in producing literature of a certain even grade.

The speeches of Elihu are followed by a second appendix, consisting of chapters 38 to 41 and purporting to be speeches addressed by Yahweh to Job. In reality these four chapters constitute a series of nature poems intended to illustrate the manifestations of the Divine will in the creation of the world, in the movements in the heavens, and in the phenomena of the rain and snow. From such subjects the little anthology passes on to a description of animal life, illustrative again of God's forethought in providing for his creation, while the powerful beasts introduced in the poems, such as the hippopotamus and the crocodile, suggest by contrast man's insignificant stature and his physical weakness. The problem that forms the central theme in the original Book of Job is not touched upon; and if it were not for the attachment of this magnificent series of poems to the Book of Job, no reader would for a moment have associated the poems with the theme suggested by Job's experience.

THE BOOK OF JOB

Moreover, in the case of these four chapters the criterion of language can be used with even greater assurance than in the case of the speeches of Elihu to reinforce the view of the independent origin of this collection of nature poems. The style deviates entirely from that of the Symposium. Chapters 38 to 41, therefore, constitute the third stratum of the book. The present Book of Job is therefore not only a composite production but one of gradual growth; and this gradual growth is to be further discerned within each division. We have seen that the original Book of Job is not of one piece, and we must now test the thesis for the discourses of Elihu and for the anthology of nature poems.

V

THE COMPOSITE CHARACTER OF THE SPEECHES OF ELIHU

The four speeches of Elihu represent the endeavors of orthodox circles to find a satisfactory solution for the problem which in the Symposium the friends gave up as hopeless, with a confession that "Job was justified in their eyes." [49] A glance at their arrangement (chapters 32-37) shows their composite character. Chapter 32 is taken up entirely with a series of introductions, and it is not until chapter 33 that we reach the first speech. We first have five editorial introductory notes (32, 1-5) then another introduction with a separate heading (32, 6-10), followed by a second introduction (32, 11-17) which

---
[49] See above, p. 68.

repeats the substance of the preceding one, after which a third introduction—in an ironical vein (32, 18-22)—is added which brings us to the close of the chapter. Evidently some one has put together a series of drafts of introductions which he came across, and true to the Oriental mode of literary composition, attached them as the preliminary material to the speeches themselves.

Now the existence of a series of drafts of introductions[50] of itself points to various independent speeches, just as the presence of four epilogues to the book furnishes testimony to the composite character of the book to which they are attached. This supposition is confirmed when we come to the speeches themselves. We note in the first place that the first and third speeches (chapters 33 and 35) are addressed to Job, whereas the second speech (chapter 34) is addressed to "wise men" in general with Job referred to in the third person (34, 5, 7; 35, 36), and the fourth speech is clearly supplemental, for as indicated by the introduction (36, 2) it is not addressed to any one in particular. It is the work of some one who felt, as he said, that "there were still things to be said for God" and proceeds to set forth his defense of the orthodox doctrine as to the cause and meaning of human suffering. The writer of this speech is not as original in his thought as he perhaps fancied, for he takes up the argument of the first speech which emphasizes suffering as a warning to man against slipping into a wrong path, but gives the thought a new turn by laying the

---

[50] We have still another draft of an introduction (33, 31-33) which an editor inserted at the end of the first speech, or which he intended as an alternate introduction to the second speech.

THE BOOK OF JOB

stress on suffering as a discipline (36, 10) as well as a warning. In this chapter, moreover, we have as a further proof of both its supplemental and composite character, the insertion of a separate and most impressive little poem, descriptive of God's majesty as seen in a storm. [51] One must read this splendid description in full and separate it from its present environment to appreciate its beauty. The purpose of this poem, which takes us still further away from the theme of the book, is to pave the way for the second large appendix—the nature and animal poems forming the third stratum of the book. The insertion thus appears to have been made by some one who already had this second appendix (chapters 38-41) before him and who, finding the poem, dovetailed it into a supplemental speech, put into the mouth of Elihu.

We have a similar case of the dovetailing of an independent composition into a speech of Elihu in the 34th chapter—forming the second speech of Elihu. This speech, as already suggested, steps entirely out of the frame of the others by being addressed to "wise men" and not to Job, who is spoken of in the third person. Surely if all four speeches were written by one and the same individual, there would be no reason for such a strange and unnecessary deviation. In the middle of the 34th chapter (v. 16) we suddenly encounter a new heading and strangely enough with an abrupt change from an address in the plural to one in the singular,

"If there be understanding, hear this."

---
[51] 36, 24 to 37, 13 and verses 21–22 as the close of the poem. See the translation of the poem after chapter 36.

THE BOOK OF JOB

An entirely new subject is introduced. Up to this point the writer is concerned with repeating the argument, so familiar to us from the Symposium, that God is not wicked, that it is "far from Shaddai to commit iniquity" (v. 10), that He requites man according to his deeds, with the supplementary thought that man is dependent upon the favor of God, as the whole earth is in His sole charge. Without any premonition, a totally different theme is now taken up—the punishment of unworthy rulers. This poem, which is clearly again an independent composition, is inserted into the chapter [52] because some editor thought it appropriate to the general theme. As a matter of fact its departure from the central theme is so complete as to be a disturbing factor, though we should be grateful to the one who thought of preserving the little poem, which is also valuable as an illustration of how far those were willing to go who placed the attribute of absolute and impartial justice as the primary quality of Divine government. God is no respecter of persons.

"He says to a King, 'Thou worthless one,'
'Thou wicked one' to nobles.
He pays no regard to princes,
And favors not rich against poor.
For all in a moment die;
In the middle of the night are shaken off."
(34, 18–20.)

But all this has no bearing on the central theme, except as a further rebuke to Job who questions the justice of God. This method of dovetailing two com-

---
[52] Verses 16–20 and 24–27 with v. 30 as a summary. See the translation of this inserted poem after the fourth speech of Elihu.

positions into one another seems strange and irrelevant, but one must bear in mind that it is the common procedure in Biblical books. It is the regular method followed by the compilers of the Pentateuch, who when they find two versions of a story—as of the Deluge and of many incidents in the lives of the patriarchs—combine them, even at the risk of thus putting contradictory details together. Similarly in the historical books proper—Joshua, Judges, Samuel and Kings—various originally independent compositions are dovetailed into one another. The editor or compiler who inserted the two poems in chapters 34 and 36, therefore, follows the traditional method to fit in the independent compositions as best he could by distributing the single verses in sections through the chapter, so as to give at least a semblance of unity to each of the speeches.

Again, chapter 35 consisting of only sixteen verses, is clearly a draft of some speech which attempts to answer the assertions of Job in 9, 21 and 7, 20. The former passage is quoted almost verbatim in 35, 2; the latter in 35, 3. The writer taking up Job's complaint that even if he had sinned, he has not injured God,

"What have I done to Thee, guardian of man?
Why hast Thou made me a mark?" (7, 20.)

argues that in truth when men do wrong, they do not injure God, as little as when they are virtuous they benefit God.

The conclusion that our writer draws is that since righteousness or wrongdoing affects only mortals, God should not be held responsible for sufferings

THE BOOK OF JOB

which are due to the actions of man. The point urged in the third speech evades the problem by relieving God of responsibility for wickedness in His world. The one who wrote the first speech could never have thought of introducing an argument so little in keeping with his entire attitude towards the problem. We see, therefore, that the four speeches are separate compositions, each representing an endeavor to find a solution that might save the day for orthodoxy.

VI

A COLLECTION OF NATURE POEMS AS THE THIRD STRATUM

Is it possible to establish for chapters 38-41—the speeches put into the mouth of Yahweh—the thesis which we have seen to apply to the four speeches of Elihu, to wit, that they consist of a series of independent compositions, representing various attempts to describe the manifestation of the Divine in the universe, which is the theme throughout? To this question an affirmative answer can be given with an assurance derived from the repetitions to be found within these chapters and from the abrupt transitions from one theme to the other. We have in the first place two large divisions, (1) chapters 38 and 39 with its separate conclusion, 40, 1-5 and (2) chapter 40, 6 to the end of chapter 41 with its conclusion 42, 1-6. That the second division is supplementary to the first and presumably by a different author follows from the repetition of the challenge to Job:

THE BOOK OF JOB

> "Gird up thy loins like a warrior,
> That I may ask thee to tell me." (38, 3.)

which is found again with a slightly different wording at the beginning of the second speech 40, 7. The separate editorial headings (38, 1 and 40, 6) to each of the two divisions,

> "Then Yahweh answered Job as follows"

with the words "out of the storm" added because of the description of the storm in chapter 37 [53] are, therefore, justified. Within the first division we have (1) The Paean of Creation (38, 4-18), (2) The Phenomena of the Heavens (38, 19-38), after which there is an abrupt transition to a different theme—the manifestation of Divine power in the animal world, which is viewed from two angles, (a) the strength shown by certain animals which makes them superior to any attempt on the part of man to tame them and (b) the provision made for animals by God, and which likewise lies beyond human comprehension.

Now it would, of course, be carrying the analysis too far to divide up the two broad divisions into which the four chapters fall into as many subdivisions as the subjects of the poems! While it may well be that the animal poems, treating eleven different animals (38, 39—39, 30), are not by one writer, yet they are all of the same general character with the single exception of the poem on the ostrich and stork (39, 13-18) which is not in question form as are the others, and in other respects deviates from the style of the other animal poems. This little section does not emphasize God's provi-

---
[53] See above, p. 79.

dence as do the poems on the lion, raven, mountain goat, wild ox and horse, but on the contrary stresses the cruel and senseless habits of the ostrich and stork in deserting her young, because "God has deprived her of wisdom." On the other hand, the description of the hippopotamus (40, 15-24) is clearly of a totally different character than the other animal poems, and so is likewise the very detailed description of the crocodile (40, 25–41, 26).[54] Both poems are to be regarded as further endeavors on the part of writers to illustrate the general theme of God's power as seen in the animal world. In these poems on the hippopotamus and the crocodile it is the huge size and strength that is emphasized. The circumstance that the description of these two largest and most powerful of all huge beasts are put forward as a second speech in the mouth of Yahweh is a further proof of their supplementary character. A compiler in the ancient Oriental manner would have no hesitation in thus putting together a series of poems, each of independent origin, though all presumably emanating from some common circle of writers who strove to emulate one another in describing the glories and marvels of inanimate nature and of the animal world. The description of the hippopotamus, consisting of ten verses, is a single composition, but the much longer poem on the crocodile consisting of 34 verses is just as clearly a combination of three separate compositions.[55] Of

---

[54] Or according to the enumeration in the AV and RV (following the example of the Greek text which begins chapter 41 with the description of the crocodile) 41, 1–34.

[55] The first extending from 40, 25 to 41, 4 (or 41, 1–12 according to the enumeration in the AV and RV), the second from 41, 5–13 (or 41, 13–21) and the third from 41, 14–26 (or 41, 22–34).

THE BOOK OF JOB

these three poems, the second is sharply separated from the first by the reflection (41, 1-4 or 41, 9-12) added as a summary to the description of the overwhelming strength of the crocodile, while we are justified in making a second break at 41, 13, (or 41, 21) because in what follows we have in part a repetition of what has already been said in the two preceding poems.[56]

What we have, therefore, in this second appendix is an anthology of nature and animal poems, which may well represent a selection from an extensive literature of this character that was produced in Palestine during the three or four centuries before this era. I say a selection, for there is no reason to suppose that our editor, who attached chapters 38 to 41 to the Book of Job exhausted the material of this character at his disposal. There are sections within many of the Psalms that impress one as extracts from just such poems of which we have specimens in our third stratum. Some of these nature poems embodied in the Psalms, like 18, 8-16; 29, 3-9; 77, 17-20 are marvellous descriptions of storms or of violent upheavals, based on the earlier conception of Yahweh as a storm-god, and are probably older than any of the nature poems in Job as well as cruder in their symbolism. Others like Psalms 19, 2-7 and 93, 3-4, attached to a glorification of the law, breathe the same spirit as the chapters in Job. In some, like 8, 4-9; 65, 10-14 and 97, 2-6 there is the same delicate association of nature's way with God's forethought as in our little

---
[56] 41, 15-16 express the same thought as 41, 7-9; 41, 18-21 suggest 40, 31; and 41, 22-23 recall 41, 10-12.

THE BOOK OF JOB

anthology, while such a Psalm as the 104th, embracing the various aspects of creation and of God's witnesses to the Divine in phenomena on earth and in the heavens, and in the waters, might just as well have been attached to the Book of Job as to have been placed among the Psalms. Conversely, except for the fact that they are put into the mouth of Yahweh by editors who in this way connected them with the Book of Job, we might just as well call these four chapters Psalms.

VII
THE MESSAGE OF THE NATURE POEMS

These additional four chapters are even more extraneous to the theme of the original Book of Job than are the discourses of Elihu. To the obvious question, what have these magnificent poems to do with Job's complaints and his arguments to show that there is injustice and innocent suffering in the world, the only reasonable answer is—nothing at all. Couched in question form, they ask whether man can perform the marvels of Nature which bear the stamp of Divine power? It is only in the editorial introduction (38, 1-3 which is repeated 40, 6-7) [57] and in the two epilogues that Job is introduced. There is no reference to him or to his sufferings or to his arguments in any of these poems. The questions are just as effective if we assume them to have been addressed to man in general.

---
[57] The second verse of chapter 38:
"Who is he that darkens counsel
By words without knowledge"
has accidentally been inserted as a reflection in the wrong place, 42, 3a. It should have been placed after 40, 6. See note 65 in the translation of the second epilogue.

THE BOOK OF JOB

The purpose in adding this precious anthology to the Symposium was clearly to direct the attention of the reader to the majesty and power of the universal Creator, so as further to counteract the baneful implications of the Symposium itself. The nature poems were intended to preach the lesson of a becoming humility in the face of the overpowering achievements of the Almighty, but it is inconceivable that the same group of writers who, sympathizing with Job, declare that in his vehement denunciations of the cruelty of his fate and in his serious indictments against the arbitrariness of the Divine will, Job spoke what was "proper" (42, 7), could also represent Job as confessing his audacity in uttering that which he did not "understand" (42, 3^b). To accuse a writer of thus blowing hot and cold at the same time is to deprive him of all claim to serious consideration. One need only state the proposition thus baldly to clinch the conclusion that the nature poems represent a later amplification of the book conceived in a totally different spirit from that which pervades the Symposium.

Job had repeatedly complained that he was unable to appeal directly to God, that the mere thought of bringing his case before God would be regarded as involving an impious charge against God. Very well, say those who collected these nature poems, we will show you what God would say to you. He would silence you by the demonstration of His boundless power in contrast to your insignificance; He would crush your haughty spirit and compel you to bow humbly to His superior, aye, to His infinite majesty.

CHAPTER III
CHANGES AND ADDITIONS WITHIN THE ORIGINAL BOOK OF JOB

I

JEWISH ORTHODOXY *VERSUS* SKEPTICISM

The Book of Job thus enlarged by the four speeches of Elihu and the poems placed in the mouth of the Deity Himself would naturally serve to counterbalance the skeptical trend of the original book. By their very length these two appendices would profoundly impress the reader, in an uncritical age, which would fail to separate the earlier from the later strata. The confession of Job at the conclusion of each of the two speeches of Yahweh of his unworthiness,[53] setting forth his repentance for his audacious utterances in the original portion of the book would suffice to remove the impression made by these utterances and quiet the soul of the pious simple-minded reader. For the irreconcilable contrast between the patient and submissive Job of the story and the impatient and rebellious Job of the Symposium, such a reader would find the explanation ready at hand, that under trying circumstances even such a model of piety as Job might forget himself and be prompted to sin by complaining of his bitter fate. He could by way of confirmation point to such Psalms

---
[53] At the close of the first series of poems, 40, 3–5 and at the close of the poems on the hippopotamus and crocodile 42, 3. 5–6.

as the 22nd, beginning with a cry of anguish from a distressed soul,

> "My God, My God, why hast Thou forsaken me,
> And art far from my help at the words of my cry?"

or to the 88th, wholly taken up with complaint, not unlike the manner of Job,

> "Thou hast laid me in the nethermost pit;
> In the darkest place in the deep.
> Thy wrath presses hard upon me,
> And all thy waves afflict me.
> Thou hast removed my acquaintances from me,
> And hast made me an abomination unto them.
> I am shut in, I cannot come forth."

And since in the Psalms such outbursts are followed or counterbalanced by expressions of faith abiding in the midst of despair:

> "In Thee did our Fathers trust;
> They trusted and Thou didst deliver them.
> Unto Thee they cried and were set free;
> In Thee did they trust, and were not put to shame." (22, 5-6.)

the analogy with the Book of Job would be complete.

For all that some doubts must have remained in the minds of more inquiring readers, whether the spirit of the Symposium, clearly revealing the author's sympathy with Job's outbursts as well as with his arguments, could be reconciled with the tone of the speeches of Elihu and with the implications of the impressive nature poems. Job's charges against God in permitting the innocent to suffer in this world would remain in all their force. They were too serious to be dismissed by a mere glorification of the marvels of Nature. The picture drawn by Job of the happiness and security of the wicked (chapters 21 and 24) was

THE BOOK OF JOB

too severe an indictment to be set aside by an irrelevant emphasis on the doctrine of punishment as a test of one's faith and as a warning to return to God. How could Job's despair at being unable to *find* God despite his earnest search (9, 11, and 23, 8-9) be reconciled with teachings that emphasized that "God is near to all who call upon Him" (Psalm 145, 18). Supplements and appendices alone could not save the book from being regarded as an essentially unsatisfactory work. To make the task of converting an unorthodox production into a bulwark of faith, it was necessary to attack the original book as well. By additions here and there, by pious comments inserted at appropriate places, by enlarging upon the counter arguments presented by the three friends of Job, by giving a turn to some of Job's utterances different from the one that he had in mind, and also by the more radical procedure of putting utterances into Job's mouth which would have a meaning only if spoken by one of the friends, since they directly contradict the fundamental position assumed by Job—such means had to be employed in order to give a flavor of orthodoxy *also* to the original book. This flavor, while strong enough to satisfy an age not accustomed to too critical a scrutiny and which still lacked a complete sense of personal authorship in a composition, was however not strong enough to endure the test of the critical method in the study of the Old Testament that set in at the close of the eighteenth century and that reached its climax in our own days.

Before passing on to some illustrations of the additions and insertions in the original book and of

THE BOOK OF JOB

other attempts to modify its tone and character, a word of warning is in place, lest we misconceive the spirit in which this deliberate endeavor to save the reader from the skepticism of the book was undertaken. There was on the part of pious commentators no *intention* to deceive. Nothing was farther from the minds of those who felt free to give any turn that they pleased to a literary production that was regarded as common property. In the ancient Orient plagiarism belongs to the virtues, and the quotation mark had not yet been discovered. The modifications that a book underwent were an indication of the interest it had aroused. Moreover, the character of the revision to which a literary production in the ancient Orient was subject would vary according to the point of view of the individual or the circle that would be attracted to the task. A book like the original Job would have its sympathizers and its opponents; and we can trace in the insertions and in the additions the work of both classes of commentators or amplifiers as they might be called, while at times one may recognize the purely literary desire to try one's hand at improving a speech of Job's or of one of his friends. Again, in many cases the desire to make an utterance clearer leads to the addition of an explanatory gloss or phrase. There were no footnotes in ancient codices, and where the margin was used for variants, comments, explanations and additions, the next copyist who came along might embody all these modifications in the text, leaving it to the reader, if he felt so inclined, to differentiate between the original and the supplementary matter. The study of an ancient

THE BOOK OF JOB

literary production thus assumes a very complicated aspect, and it has been one of the chief tasks of modern Bible study to develop a critical method for distinguishing the various strata in the case of a Biblical book, to trace the dovetailing of originally independent documents in the compilation of traditions and historical narratives, to show in the case of the Pentateuchal Codes and of the historical books their gradual expansion, to separate original material from later supplements in the collections of the utterances of the prophets, and to follow the growth of more purely literary productions like Proverbs, Psalms, Ecclesiastes and Job, in all their ramifications. For the Book of Ecclesiastes I have shown [59] how by additions through pious commentators, anxious to furnish the antidote to Koheleth's cynicism, and by the insertions of ethical maxims and popular sayings as a further means of weakening the effect of unorthodox teachings, a different turn was given to the original book. In the case of the much larger Book of Job the process of growth and modifications is far more intricate, and it will not be possible, without exhausting the patience of the general reader to do more than offer a number of illustrations of the manner in which the original Book of Job was modified throughout.

II

VARYING VERSIONS OF THE HEBREW TEXT

A comparison of the Hebrew text with the various Greek translations made of it is more than suffi-

---
[59] *A Gentle Cynic*, p. 29.

THE BOOK OF JOB

cient to show that there was no fixed original as late as the second century B. C. when the oldest of these translations, commonly known as the Septuagint, appears to have been made. According to the Church Father Origen (185–254 A. D.) who compiled a comparative table of the variations in no less than six versions, [60] the Septuagint recension was about one-sixth shorter than our present Hebrew text, which means that instead of 1070 verses or about 2200 lines, it contained only about 890 verses or about 1830 lines. The missing portions were supplied chiefly from a version made by Theodotion towards the end of the second century A. D. Origen distinguished these additions by an asterisk and there are some codices in which these asterisks still appear, though in most codices of the Greek translation the additions have been incorporated into the text without any distinguishing mark.[61]

As a further witness to the existence of a translation of Job differing considerably from the Hebrew text, we have a version made during the second century A. D. from Greek into the Sahidic dialect [62] and which was found in the Library of the Museum Borghianum in Rome in 1883 and published in 1889.[63] This version actually contains about 400 lines less than the full text. It confirms, therefore, the exis-

---
[60] The standard edition of what is preserved of Origen's comprehensive work is by Frederick Field, *Origenis Hexaplorum quæ supersunt* (2 vols., Oxford, 1875).
[61] See for details Budde's introduction to his commentary on Job, 2nd edition, p. lvii *seq.*
[62] Sahidic is a dialect of Coptic, which was spoken in Upper Egypt.
[63] By A Ciasca, *Sacrorum Bibliorum Fragmenta Copto-Sahidica Musei Borgiani.*

THE BOOK OF JOB

tence at one time of a much shorter Book of Job than our present one. To be sure, there are many scholars who are inclined to explain the omissions in the original Greek translation on the assumption that the translator in many cases intentionally abbreviated the Hebrew original, and in others omitted lines which he did not understand. The former supposition is most unlikely in view of the sacred character of the books of the Old Testament, which would deter a translator from taking such liberties with the model before him. He might, if not in sympathy with the original purport of the book, be tempted to add to it but not to curtail it. Furthermore, it is noticeable that the omissions in the Sahidic version become more numerous as we proceed from the first series to the second and third series of speeches. In chapters 3 to 6 (Job's first speech, the answer of Eliphaz and part of Job's reply) there are no omissions; in chapters 7 to 11 (conclusion of Job's reply, the first speech of Bildad, Job's reply and Zophar's first speech) only eleven lines are omitted, whereas in Job's reply (chapters 12 to 14), we find as many as 17 lines left out. The obvious conclusion is not that the translator grew tired of his task and proceeded to curtail, but that only a portion of the Symposium had as yet reached its final stage, that additions continued to be made even to the first series of speeches, and that still greater liberties continued to be taken with the later series and with the supplements and appendices to the book.

Nor is it at all plausible, as some scholars assume, that omissions in the original Greek translation were due to the difficulties of the original text which the translator evaded by the simple method of leaving them untranslated. That was not the disposition of ancient translators, who would be disposed to make a guess at a translation rather than to omit anything of what was before them. Throughout the Old Testament the Greek version varies considerably from the Hebrew original; in some of the books more, in some less. These variations in thousands of instances rest upon a different text which can frequently be reconstructed. The difference of one letter or at times a different vocalization of the consonantal framework of the Hebrew original often accounts for the varying translation, though in a larger number of cases a more radical variation in the text must be assumed, while in many hundreds of instances the Greek translation represents a *guess* in order to get some meaning out of a difficult or a corrupt text. It does not, of course, follow that the reading upon which the Greek version rests is more acceptable than the Hebrew text, though this is very often the case, but the variant reading is under all circumstances an important witness to the absence of a standardized text of the Old Testament as late as the second century B. C. It is a sufficient answer to the assumption that omissions in the original Greek translation are due to evasions of difficulties to point out that the omissions occur as frequently—if not more so—in passages in which the Hebrew text is perfectly clear as in such cases where difficulties exist. Furthermore, in the older Greek versions as in that of Theodotion, there are not only omissions but also numerous additions not found in the

THE BOOK OF JOB

Hebrew Text, which confirm the position here taken of the incompleteness of the book until close to the threshold of our era and perhaps indeed beyond this limit.

It is interesting as well as significant to note in this connection that even after a standard Hebrew text of the Old Testament had been established, at the end of the first century A. D., the Jewish Church did not object to its expansion on the part of those who made a rendering of the collection into the current Aramaic speech [64] so that the uneducated classes might also share in the benefits of the sacred collection. The Aramaic rendering, known as the Targum,[65] is a combination of a translation with amplifying comments not distinguished from the text. Often the amplification is limited to a few words, but very frequently it is extended to a little homily on the text. It was customary for the expounder first to read a verse in Hebrew and then to give an Aramaic rendering which might be literal, but which would also furnish him with the occasion to expand it at will. The point to be born in mind is that in this expansion no separation was made between text and comment. The expansion of the text led in the course of time to the elaboration of Biblical traditions and narratives which developed into an extensive Midrashic literature embodying further legends entwined around the patriarchs and around such types as Moses, Aaron,

---

[64] Hebrew ceased to be the current speech in Palestine after the sixth century B.C. and was gradually replaced by Aramaic which had spread also through Mesopotamia and Syria.

[65] Meaning "translation" or perhaps more accurately "interpretation." The underlying stem is the same as in *dragoman*, *i.e.*, targeman.

THE BOOK OF JOB

Joshua, Samuel, Elijah, David and Solomon.[66] Biblical books thus became the starting-point of a literature that is the outcome of a process of continuous expansion of an original text by comments, variants, additions, illustrations and the like.

III

ADDITIONS TO THE TEXT OF AN EXPLANATORY CHARACTER

Perhaps we can best approach our task of showing the method followed in making the original Book of Job more palatable to orthodox tastes by some illustrations of additions made with an explanatory purpose, or which represent variant readings embodied into the original text instead of being relegated to footnotes as we would do in the case of a modern text. From these we can then pass on to additions and modifications introduced with the specific purpose of toning down some particularly objectionable utterance or of giving a different turn to Job's thought.

Even in the prose prologue we find evidence of the hand of commentators engaged in making additions to the text. In chapter 2, 1 the phrase "to gather around Yahweh" appears twice. The repetition is unnecessary and is not found in the original Greek version or in some of the later ones. The addition was made by some commentator who wished to emphasize

---

[66] A large collection of these *Legends of the Jews* in English translation was made by Dr. L. Ginsburg and published by the American Jewish Publication Society (*Legends of the Jews*, 4 volumes, Philadelphia, 1909-13).

THE BOOK OF JOB

that Satan came *with* the "Sons of God," and not alone, that he was at God's service and not an independent being. Again towards the close of the chapter, the words "toward heaven" are added to the statement that the three friends as a sign of grief at Job's distress "tore their upper garments and sprinkled dust over their heads." This was done in order to explain that the dust after being placed on the head was thrown into the air, though it is doubtful whether this explanation is correct. The words are again missing in the Greek version.

Of a different character but pointing to an intentional change in the text is the substitution of "bless" for "curse" in no less than four places in the prologue (1, 5 and 11; 2, 5 and 9) in order to avoid a word of ill omen, as in English "darned" came into use in place of "damned." To a sensitive age it seemed objectionable to find Job saying in a sacred book that his sons may have "cursed" God (1, 5) or Satan intimating that Job might "curse God" (1, 11 and 2, 5) or even that Job's unsympathetic wife should call upon her husband to "curse God and die." In all these cases the word "bless" was substituted with intent. [67] In the prose epilogue (42, 7-17) there are likewise late additions, partly to add picturesque touches and in part with a more serious intent. So *e. g.* is the closing statement (42, 17)

"So Job died, old and full of days"

which is missing in the original Greek version. In re-

---
[67] The Church Father Ambrosian already recognized that the avoidance of the word "curse" was intentional.

THE BOOK OF JOB

turn, the Greek version of Theodotion has a long supplementary notice [68] about Job and his friends which is not in the Hebrew text.

When we come to the Symposium, we have a valuable index for detecting comments and variants in the practically uniform character of the stanza of four lines [69] and a further index in the length of each line—with three beats in each line—for while to be sure there is no absolute uniformity, yet when we find an inordinately long line, we may properly suspect some addition as a comment or gloss.[70] Let us take up these two points. Without entering into details of Hebrew poetry which would carry us too far, [71] there is general agreement among scholars that the two striking features of this poetry are the *parellelismus membrorum*, *i. e.*, an agreement in thought with some progression in the thought, dividing a stanza into two halves and within each stanza an agreement in regard to the number of beats in corresponding lines. There is no rhyme in Hebrew poetry but there is rhythm which rests upon an equal number of beats, irrespective of the number of syllables beyond certain limits, which would obviously interfere with the regularity of the beats. When, therefore, we find a disproportion between two lines that form the first or second half of a stanza, we are

---

[68] See below at the close of the translation for this supplementary statement which is very elaborate and clearly based on a Hebrew or Aramaic original.
[69] See Duhm's discussion, *Hiob*, p. 17.
[70] Occasionally we find shorter lines with two beats and frequently long lines with four beats, but in all such cases the variation raises a suspicion whether the line in question is not defective, or whether the superfluous word or words belong to the original text.
[71] See for a general survey, G. B. Gray, *Forms of Hebrew Poetry* (London, 1915).

justified in suspecting some addition. So, *e. g.*, in 7, 9 which reads

"The cloud dissolves and is gone;
So the one who goes down to Sheol does not come up."

The second line in the original Hebrew is halting because of its length. If we remove the word "Sheol," this difficulty disappears and the poetic quality is improved. Some commentator added "Sheol" to indicate what was meant. In 10, 12 the word "life" does not accord with the verb used which is literally "made." The combination is un-Hebraic. The line is improved in its proportions by making it read:

"Grace Thou didst grant me"

and by regarding "life" as a comment or gloss. Not infrequently the excess word or phrase in a line has been inserted as a comment or gloss into the wrong place, which suggests that it may originally have been placed on the margin of a scroll, and then misplaced by a copyist who wished to embody the comment in the text. An example of such a misplaced gloss is to be found in 5, 4 where the words "in the gate" (in Hebrew one word) are clearly out of place. The two lines should read:

"His sons far from salvation,
And crushed, with none to save them."

Transpose the phrase "in the gate" to the first line of the preceding distich,

"I have seen the foolish take root in the gate"

and you get a comment that is reasonable, the phrase "in the gate" being idiomatically used for the place where people gather. A still clearer case of an entire

THE BOOK OF JOB

line forming a variant and inserted at the wrong place is to be found 15, 30,

> "He shall not escape from the darkness."

A glance shows that it does not fit in with the context, neither with what precedes nor with what follows. If, however, one transfers it to v. 22, the first half of which reads:

> "He has no hope to escape from darkness,"

we have an intelligible variant, which some commentator presumably placed on the margin of his copy and which a copyist inserted at the wrong place. Again 17, 12 is a distich that interrupts the context. It is omitted in the original Greek version, and can best be explained as consisting of two glosses,

> (a) "Night they change to day"
> (b) "Light is preferable to darkness"

added by way of comment to 18, 5-6, beginning:

> "Surely, the light of the wicked is put out"

The first gloss is intended to suggest that the wicked ply their trade at night, and the second is to furnish the reason for the emphasis on light, spark and lamp in 18, 5-6. Such comments need not necessarily reveal the true explanation; and in this case the commentator mistakes the force of the metaphors, by taking them too literally. In the same way 22, 8 which properly translated reads:

> "The man of might—to him is the earth;
> And the exalted dwells therein,"

interrupts Eliphaz's accusations against Job that he refused charity to the poor (v. 7) and neglected widows

THE BOOK OF JOB

and orphans (v. 9). The distich clearly belongs to Job's indictment of injustice in the world with which chapter 21 is taken up. It would be appropriate after 21, 31. The two lines impress one as a popular saying which some reader added on the margin of his copy, and which thence crept into another copy prepared by some scribe.

We have quite a number of such maxims introduced into Job, just as many were interspersed throughout Ecclesiastes by later manipulators of the text. At times they are appropriate, but often they interrupt the context in a somewhat unfortunate manner.

So in Eliphaz's first speech (chapter 4) we have a popular maxim introduced in v. 10:

> "The lion may roar and the fierce one howl,
> But the teeth of the young lions are broken."

with the following verse added by way of amplification:

> "The old lion perishes for lack of prey,
> And the whelps of the lioness are scattered."

The two verses do not stand in close relation to what precedes, and appear to have been inserted by some commentator as an illustration of one's reaping what one sows (v. 8^b). Chapter 17, 5 which should be translated as follows:

> "Among friends one divides one's fortune,
> While one's own sons languish"

is evidently a popular saying to illustrate a foolish kind of generosity, which, to be sure, is not particularly appropriate at its present place. The first half is missing in the original Greek version, which in-

THE BOOK OF JOB

creases the suspicion of its being a later insertion—perhaps again at an entirely wrong place.

A clear case of a popular saying is 20, 16:

"He who sucks the poison of asps,
The tongue of the viper shall kill him,"

It was suggested by the reference to "gall of asps" in v. 14, though the maxim has no bearing on the argument that ill-gotten gain will not endure. Again, it is to be noted that in the original Greek version only a part of the verse is found.

Referring the reader to the translation for further examples of such introduced sayings as well as little comments and glosses—of which there are several hundred scattered throughout the original book and the supplements—let us take up a few examples of superfluous lines added to the conventional stanza of four lines, and which will be found to be either an amplification of the text or must be regarded as a variant line, either orally transmitted or taken over from some codex.

IV

SUPERFLUOUS LINES

In Eliphaz's first speech, we encounter a superfluous line, 4, 19 where

"Whose foundation is in the dust"

is evidently a comment to "clay houses" in the line reading:

"How much more in those who live in clay houses."

In the same speech the fifth verse of chapter 5 has occasioned endless difficulties to modern exegetes.

If we remove the superfluous line (5, 5ᵇ) we obtain a distich

"What they gather, the hungry eat;
And the thirsty (?) drain their substance,"

while the additional line by a textual change gives us

"Gathering it into granaries"

as a comment to the verse.

In Job's reply to Eliphaz we find in 6, 4 a superfluous line,

"Whose poison drains my spirit,"

which is an explanation to

"The arrows of Shaddai are within me."

An instance of a superfluous line suggested by a parallel passage occurs 13, 27 where

"Thou keepest guard over all my ways"

is taken over from 33, 11, just as in 7, 11

"I will speak in the anguish of my spirit"

occurs again 10, 1 [72] and is evidently there taken over from our passage.

In chapter 24, we have a superfluous line in each of four successive verses (12-15). The close of v. 12 which should be rendered

"But God does not hear (their) prayer"

is a gloss on the part of a reader or commentator who sympathized with Job's argument. At the end of v. 13 the line

"They do not know its ways"

---

[72] Except that a synonym "soul" is used for spirit.

THE BOOK OF JOB

is a comment (reminding one of Ps. 2, 2) or a variant line to the second half:
> "They sit not in its paths."

In v. 14
> "He kills the poor and the needy"

is a comment to the first half of the distich, and again in v. 15, the superfluous line
> "Saying, no eye sees me,"

is an explanatory comment to
> "The eye of the adulterer waits for the daylight?"

These examples justify us in removing the large number of superfluous lines, scattered throughout the original Book of Job, as well as through the supplement and appendices and to regard them as comments or variants. By thus restoring the four line stanza, [73] we obtain a uniform poetic form, with a resultant greater force in many cases where the superfluous line makes the style turgid.

As a final proof of the liberties taken with the text in expanding it by comments, variants and glosses, we may instance the many cases in which an entire verse or several verses appear to be later insertions, with a view of clarifying the thought or for other reasons amplifying it. A few illustrations will suffice. The fourth verse of chapter 8, reading
> "If thy children had sinned against Him, He would give them up because of their transgression"

---

[73] First consistently carried out by Bickell, *Das Buch Hiob* (Vienna 1894), though on the basis of a metric theory which does not commend itself. Duhm (*Hiob*, p. 17) likewise assumes a four-line stanza throughout and Beer (*Text des Buches Hiob*, p. viii) inclines towards this view, as does Gray (American Journal of Semitic Languages, vol. 36, p. 95), though the latter assumes some exceptions.

THE BOOK OF JOB

is an interruption of the context, and moreover prosaic in form. Verse 3 reading:

"Does God pervert judgment?
Does Shaddai pervert right?"

joins directly to v. 5, promising God's grace if only Job would seek out God and provided he were really pure and upright. The inserted verse is the reflection of some reader who thought to answer the question asked in v. 3, by suggesting that since Job would expect his children to be punished in case they had sinned—why should that not be the explanation in his case?

Similarly, in chapter 13, verse 10 reading:
"He would surely rebuke you, if you secretly showed favor"
is an inserted answer in prose form to the question asked in v. 9 and which is continued in v. 11,

Again in chapter 14, verse 11, reading:

"Waters drain the sea,
And the stream dries up"

interrupts the context and may be regarded as a reflection inserted by some reader or commentator, on the inevitableness of death as set forth in verses 10 and 12. It appears to be a quotation from Isaiah 19, 5.

In chapter 22, verse 24 is missing in the original Greek version which confirms the suspicion that

"Gold ore will be regarded as dust,
And Ophir [74] gold as the rock of the valleys."

is a later insertion which interprets the metaphor in v. 25 literally:

"Shaddai will be thy gold mine,
And silver in superabundance to thee."

---
[74] Name of the region whence specially fine gold was procured.

THE BOOK OF JOB

The aggregate of these additions is considerable. By removing superfluous lines, briefer comments and glosses, the text is reduced by several hundred verses, so that we can now understand how a version of the Hebrew text should have existed in the second century B. C. so much shorter than our present one and from which the first Greek translation was made. How foolish in view of this to make a fetish of the authorized Hebrew text as finally fixed by the Jewish church, and to regard it as an infringement on the sanctity of Biblical books to apply the canons of textual criticism to Job or to any other book of the sacred collection.

As a matter of fact, quite apart from the evidence brought forward to prove the liberties taken both with the original book and with the supplements and appendices by readers or commentators, the Hebrew text of Job teems with all kinds of errors due to careless or ignorant copyists. In many cases the correct text can be restored, often through the substitution of a single letter for a wrong one. At times the Greek version helps us to detect the errors of Hebrew copyists, just as in return the Hebrew text occasionally permits us to recognize an error made by a Greek copyist. Often—very often indeed—a more radical procedure is necessary to enable us to restore the text at least approximately to what it must have been, and sometimes we must confess ourselves baffled by a hopeless corruption—hopeless beyond recovery except through the employment of an arbitrary method which the best Biblical scholarship has never countenanced. It is impossible to penetrate the meaning of

THE BOOK OF JOB

hundreds upon hundreds of passages in the Book of Job without resorting to a critical method in the study of the text. Our English versions which aim to translate the book as it stands are the proof for this assertion. Excluding the prologue and epilogue, it is rare to find ten *consecutive* verses which can be regarded as correct renderings, and not infrequently more than half of the verses in a chapter in the ordinary translation stand in need of greater or smaller revision in order to reproduce what once stood in the original. The need, therefore, of an entirely revised translation, based upon a critical study with a utilization of the results reached by other scholars who have toiled over the Book of Job, is too obvious to require further justification. This need becomes even more obvious when we turn to additions made to the original book in the interest of Jewish orthodoxy, in the hope of converting a skeptical work into a support for conventional views against which the writers of Job in its original form entered a protest.

CHAPTER IV

HOW A SKEPTICAL BOOK WAS TRANSFORMED INTO A BULWARK OF ORTHODOXY

I

CHANGES IN THE ORIGINAL BOOK OF JOB MADE IN THE INTERESTS OF JEWISH ORTHODOXY

We have already had occasion to point out how the word "bless" was substituted for "curse" in four places in the prologue, because to the final editors it seemed objectionable even to suggest that any one should "curse" God. The same spirit prompted pious commentators to change the third person "He" when it referred to God to "I," in order to tone down a too audacious challenge on the part of Job. So at the close of chapter 9, the ordinary translation:

"For I am not so with myself"

is meaningless and stands in no connection with the preceding line in which Job says that if God would only remove His rod and not startle him by terror—meaning his sufferings—

"I would declare without fear of Him"

Now if in the following line we change the "I" to "He" and take the word translated "so" in the sense of "fair" or "just" which is obviously meant here,[75]

---
[75] First suggested by Ehrlich (*Randglossen* 6, p. 220). The Hebrew word is *ken* which means "just," though the same two consonants also form an adverb "so."

THE BOOK OF JOB

we obtain at once a proper parallel and a logical continuation of the thought:

"That He is not fair to me."

In the same chapter, the bold challenge of Job in the 19th verse was toned down by changing "Him" to "me" and by a different vocalization of the final root, so as to make the line read:

"And if of justice, who will appoint me a time?"

The line as it stands is meaningless. Job in his bitter revolt against his fate says that he is willing to admit God's superior strength, but what he asks is justice. The distich should read:

"If it is a test of strength—He is surely superior,
But if it is [a question of] justice—who can arraign Him? [76]

The two lines emphasize the dilemma which is the theme of chapter 9 that no one can bring a suit against God, because God is the judge before whom the suit would have to be brought.

Similarly, as already pointed out, the reading at the beginning of chapter 32 that Job regarded himself as justified in "his own eyes" is an intentional change, so as to avoid the implication that Job had completely triumphed by answering his friends. The Greek version shows that the original reading was that

"Job was justified in their eyes."

Such an assertion which would put an end to all

---
[76] The Greek and Syriac versions preserve the original reading "Him."

THE BOOK OF JOB

further discussion could not be tolerated, and so by a slight change the final verdict in favor of Job was changed into a rebuke for his conceit, none the less severe for being put in an indirect manner. It is with the same intent of increasing the severity of Zophar's rebuke to Job because he regards himself as innocent that prompted a pious commentator to change what Zophar said to Job;

"Thou art pure in thine eyes." (11, 4.)

into a direct assertion on the part of Job:

"I am pure in His eyes" [77]

implying that God knew that Job was innocent but was wilfully cruel toward him.

By way of contrast to a change made with such intent, we have instances of others that might be characterized as introduced *ad majorem gloriam Dei*. So, for example, in the description of the strength of the crocodile, a pious reader thought that it would heighten the effect to change the obviously correct reading:

"Who could stand up against him?
Who could attack him and come out whole?" (41, 2.) [78]

into a reference to God's superior power by reading in both lines "me" for "him." A glance at the context suffices to show that the change entirely spoils the climax to the stirring and impressive description of the huge beast against whom no one can stand up.

---

[77] *i.e.*, in God's eyes. So the Greek version. We might also retain "Thine eyes" (with a capital T) and refer it to God. So the translation of the American Jewish Publication Society.

[78] Or 41, 10 according to the enumeration in the AV and RV.

THE BOOK OF JOB

The Greek version, as usual in the case of such intentional changes, preserves the correct reading.[79]

II
ADDITIONS BY PIOUS COMMENTATORS

As long as Job confined himself to complaints, as he does in his first two speeches, pious commentators allowed them to pass, bitter though those complaints were. Nor did they feel prompted to intervene when Job, enlarging upon his theme, generalizes on the hard fate of man which he pathetically describes as service like that of a hireling thirsting for the evening shade (7, 1-2) when he will be released from his task, but when in his third speech, (chapters 9-10) he reaches his main argument that one who feels himself to be suffering without just cause cannot bring his case before God for investigation without by so doing offending the Deity by the implied suspicion of injustice, the pious commentators felt that it was time to step in. Job, in reply to the insistence of Eliphaz on God's power, admits this and proceeds to give illustrations of the destructive and terrifying manifestation of Divine power—how God overturns mountains in His wrath and shakes the earth, hides the sun and seals up the stars (9, 2-7). In this same strain he continues,

"He goes by me without my seeing Him;
He passes on without my knowing." (9, 11.)

but just before this, two verses are inserted to give a different turn to Job's thought by emphasizing, as

---

[79] Not infrequently, however, one of the later Greek versions itself tries to tone down the unorthodox utterances of Job by giving them a different turn. Example will be found in the notes to 9, 21 and 11, 3.

THE BOOK OF JOB

Eliphaz does, the marvels of God that are majestic *without* being destructive or terrifying. Clearly verses 8–10 of this ninth chapter reading:

> "Who by Himself stretches out the heavens,
> And treads their heights,
> Who makes the Aldebaran, and Orion,
> The Pleiades and the constellations of the South.
> Who does great things past finding out,
> And wonders without number,"

are a later insertion, introduced with intent to make Job speak as Eliphaz has done. If any further proof were needed, it would be found in the last distich which is a quotation from Eliphaz's speech (5, 9).

In this fourth speech (chapters 12–14), the extraordinary length of which raises the suspicion that it has been amplified, Job begins by bringing forth his charge that the wicked prosper while the innocent are laughed to scorn. Such is also the burden of his four following speeches by the side of the ever-recurring complaint of his sad plight. This affords the pious commentators the desired opportunity to intersperse their orthodox reflections, so as to take off as it were the sharp edge of the severe indictment of Divine justice. So in 12, 6 after Job has declared that

> "The tents of the robbers prosper,
> And there is security for those who provoke God"

Our pious commentator adds:

> "Whom God holds in His power."

Job continues and says that the beasts, the birds of heaven and what crawls on the earth and the fish

of the sea know that all nature is a struggle in which one fails to see justice at work,
> "Who does not know all these things?"

Knows what? To the assurance:
> "That the hand of Yahweh has done this,

Our pious commentator adds:
> "In whose hand is the soul of every living being and the breath of all mankind." (12, 10.)

The prose form reveals the insertion, the evident intent of which is to give Job's thought a different direction from the one towards which it was moving. The introduction of the name Yahweh, which is not used in the poetic discussions, is a further proof that some other hand than that of the original compiler has been at work. The following verse (12, 11):
> "Cannot the ear test words
> And the palate taste for itself?"

is a quotation from Elihu's second speech (34, 3), merely changed into a question form, while v. 12 reading:
> ["Not] with grey beards is wisdom,
> Nor understanding with the aged."

was suggested by another utterance of Elihu (32, 9). Furthermore, verse 13
> "With Him is wisdom and might;
> With Him is counsel and intelligence."

is a reflection that clearly betrays the same pious commentator who added verse 10. Omitting these verses, we find v. 14 forming the continuation to the question:
> "Who does not know all these things?"

THE BOOK OF JOB

Job recurs (vv. 14-25) to his admission that God *is* powerful, but powerful in destroying and terrifying.

We may likewise suspect the hand of the orthodox amplifier in the last verse (v. 25) of the chapter:

"So that they grope in the darkness without light,
And He makes them stagger like a drunken man."

Our pious commentator is thinking of the overthrow of worthless guides of the people, and therefore pictures them like the wicked stumbling in the darkness that surrounds them. Job, however, has in mind merely the terrifying manifestation of God's power in setting aside earthly rulers, no matter how high their station. Nobles, princes, judges, priests—are all swept away whenever God chooses to do so. He is supreme—that is Job's thought. But is His superiority exercised with justice? That is the question which torments the writers in the original Book of Job.

Removing these numerous additions the length of the chapter is reduced by almost one-half. The process of amplification is continued in the following two chapters (13-14.) Job, reflecting on the brevity of life and its fullness of care, says:

"Man is born of woman,
Few of days and full of trouble,
He comes forth like a flower and withers;
Fleeing as a disappearing shadow." (14, 1-2.)

He then asks:

"Hast Thou, indeed, considered this,
In bringing him to judgment?"

The pious commentator (verse 4), conscious of man's sinful nature, answers by the reflection,

"Can one bring clean out of unclean? Not one"

THE BOOK OF JOB

i.e., the unrepentant sinner who is none other than Job himself ever remains unclean and cannot expect to be pardoned for his misdoings.

Consistent with what we have seen to be the practice of the pious commentators, Job is permitted in his fifth speech (chapters 16–17) to rebuke his friends, to recall his sufferings and to pass on to a description of the hostile forces arrayed against him—all without interruption. Only when towards the close of chapter 16, he reaches a climax of bitterness in appealing to the earth not to allow his blood to be shed in vain,

> "Earth, do not cover up my blood,[80]
> That there be no occasion for my outcry."

a pious commentator intervenes to give the assurance;

> "Even now my witness is in heaven.[81] (16, 19.)

How could Job in one and the same breath complain of Divine injustice, and then declare his faith in a heavenly witness. So far from God vouching for him, Job implies in the verses immediately following that his appeals are *not* heard:

> "On high my thoughts are my intercessors;
> To God my eye makes the appeal;
> That mortal may secure justice from God,
> As between a man and his fellow." (16, 20–21.)

—but all to no avail. God is callous to the cry of anguish. It is precisely in order to counterbalance the extreme bitterness of such outbursts that a pious reflection about the "witness in heaven" is inserted.

---
[80] The covering up of the blood means concealing the crime. See the note to the passage.
[81] See further in the notes to the translation of 16, 19–20.

THE BOOK OF JOB

In chapter 17, our pious commentator has another opportunity of adding a reflection (v. 9):

"The righteous clings to his way,"
And the clean of hand increases in strength."

to counterbalance Job's ironical exclamation that the "upright must rejoice" at his having become a byword of the people and that "the innocent will be aroused against the impious"—meaning himself. What bitter irony! Job speaks of himself as "impious," knowing that this is what those who do not understand him think. His awful fate will cause rejoicing among the godly, because he is looked upon as a sinner. Could rebellion against the Divine order of things go further? No wonder that the pious commentator felt called upon to step in.

In Job's seventh speech (chapter 21) he replies to the second series of speeches of the three friends who have tried to outdo one another in portraying the fate that overtakes the wicked. The burden of these speeches is that though the evildoers may seem to flourish for a while, inevitable punishment through God's wrath overtakes them. Says Eliphaz (15, 20):

"All his days the wicked is in terror,
And the number of his years are limited."

Says Bildad (18, 17–18):

"His remembrance shall perish from the earth;
And nowhere will there be a memorial of him.
They shall drive him from light into darkness;
And out of the earth they shall chase him."

Says Zophar (20, 27):

"The heavens shall reveal his iniquity,
And the earth shall rise up against him."

THE BOOK OF JOB

Job's patience—or rather what is left of it—is exhausted by this three-fold repetition of an utterly false account of what really happens in this world. With a violence surpassing all previous utterances Job proceeds to paint a true picture of the world in which we live.

"When I think of it, I am dismayed,
And horror takes hold of me.
Why do the wicked flourish,
Grow old and even wax mighty?" (21, 6-7.)

That is the keynote to the chapter, which rings the changes on the theme that happiness and success crown the activities of those who ride roughshod over all ethical restraints in seeking their goal.

The indictment becomes terrible as Job describes the merriment that abounds in the homes of the wicked, how everything goes well, how all ventures succeed, how they pass their lives without any thought of God, how they are spared when calamity overtakes others, and how, when satiated with happiness, they sink quietly into the grave, the bier is followed by a large concourse of mourners.

"The clods of the valley seem sweet to him,
As the whole population draws after him.
How then can you comfort me with vanity,
Since your arguments are a tissue of falsehood?"(21, 33.)

What can the pious commentator do in the face of such an indictment? He tones down the bitterness of the chapter by two pious reflections. When Job portrays the indifference of the wicked to the commands of God,

"To God they say, 'Away from us;
We desire not the knowledge of Thy ways.'" (21, 14.)

THE BOOK OF JOB

our commentator, wishing us to conclude that Job speaks thus (v. 16), adds:

"Ah, there is no happiness in their hand;
The counsel of the wicked be far from me."

The reflection would be in place if one of the friends had made it, and we actually find the second line inserted in a speech of Eliphaz (22, 18^b), but Job whose whole point is that the wicked *are* happy could not so flagrantly contradict himself. Again, when Job rises to the height of bitterness in answering the contention of his friends that even if the wicked is not punished in his lifetime, his sons are made to suffer. What does he care, asks Job, what happens to others as long as he escapes.

"Let Him (*i.e.*, God) requite him that *he* may know it.
* * * * * *
What is his concern in his house *after* him,
When the number of his months is completed?" (21, 19–21.)

This audacity was too much for our pious commentator who therefore adds:

"Shall one presume to teach God,
Him who judges on high?" (21, 22.)

These examples will suffice to show how throughout the original book the attempt was made to weaken the skeptical trend by insertions and reflections that in an uncritical age would not fail to make their appeal. The insertions would counterbalance the genuine passages in which Job passed beyond all bounds in the vehemence of his charges against God and in the denunciation of the cruel fate that so often overtakes those who have led virtuous and pious lives. One could point to these pious exclama-

THE BOOK OF JOB

tions, thus liberally interspersed throughout the speeches of Job, in reply to those who might have been troubled by the large number of sentiments expressed by Job that were anything but pious. The rebellious and impatient Job, according to this explanation, represents a passing mood; the true Job is revealed in the pious utterances; and so the contradictions between evident insertions and the genuine passages were allowed to stand until the advent of modern criticism.

A traditional interpretation of the original Book of Job thus arose that made it consistent with the genuine Jewish orthodoxy as taught in the speeches of Elihu and in the collection of nature poems; and tradition as it grows apace is apt to warp the critical instinct to such an extent that after the lapse of time even manifest contradictions fail to arrest one's attention.

III

THE TRANSFORMATION OF CRUCIAL PASSAGES

Comments and variants and changes tending to tone down objectionable utterances did not exhaust the resources of those who were bent on showing that the Job of the Symposium was as patient and as God-fearing as the Job of the popular tale. Pious commentators, in addition to adding their reflections which came to be looked upon as integral parts of Job's speeches, did not hesitate to go a step further and by apparently innocent changes in the text itself before it became rigidly fixed, succeeded in giving to crucial passages an entirely different mean-

THE BOOK OF JOB

ing from the one originally intended. Let us take up as illustrations the two most famous passages in the Book of Job, still popularly regarded as proving the staunch piety of the central figure in the Symposium. The first of these occurs in the thirteenth chapter and is familiar to everyone in the traditional rendering:

"Though He slay me, yet will I trust in Him." (13, 15.)

Modern scholarship has shown that the verse must be translated:

"Aye, though He slay me, I tremble not," [82]

as the following line, furnishing the parallel required by poetry, conclusively proves;

"For all that, I will maintain His [83] course to His face."

The correct translation is adopted by the Revised Version and by all modern translators with a single exception.[84] Now how did the erroneous translation arise? Simply by a marginal reading "Him" in the Hebrew text in place of "not," [85] and by taking the word "tremble" (or possibly "hope") through a different vocalization to mean "trust." There can be no doubt that the marginal reading "Him" is an intentional change made by some commentator *after* the text had been fixed. Convinced that the Book

---

[82] Or possibly, "I have no hope." The translation of the American Baptist Publication Society renders: "Behold, he will slay me, I may not hope." See the note to the passage in the translation.

[83] Text has "my"—likewise an intentional change, to diminish the audacity of the challenge.

[84] The translation issued by the American Jewish Publication Society retains the traditional, but entirely untenable rendering.

[85] Involving a very slight change, both words having the same sound in Hebrew. See the note to the passage.

THE BOOK OF JOB

of Job as it stood was a unit and determined to make it a defense of orthodox Judaism, he could not reconcile himself to the thought that Job could give utterance to such a defiant challenge, as

"Though He slay me, I tremble not."

That was going too far. The pious, patient, model Job *could* not have said that, and so he was made to say the very contrary that he would retain his faith in God, even though God should decide to put him to death—innocently. This intentional but unwarranted change is an interesting illustration of the difficulties felt by the later Jewish theologians in giving to Job an orthodox character, even after pious commentators and the amplifiers of the book had done their work. They therefore continued the process of changing the spirit of Job's speeches as best they could. After the text had been fixed by the Jewish rabbis of the first century A.D., no further additions were permitted, but codices still differed somewhat in their readings, and therefore the rabbis felt free to introduce marginal readings of their own, when they felt that in doing so they could obtain a reading more satisfactory to them. When marginal readings failed, a twist could be given by a subtle exegesis to passages in which the text was corrupt—perhaps, indeed, in some cases *intentionally* corrupted, so as to obscure the objectionable original.

A single passage, thus given an entirely different interpretation from the one intended by the author, would not fail of effect; and, particularly a verse that

THE BOOK OF JOB

could by its striking admission of profound faith serve to counterbalance many other utterances calculated to arouse suspicion of Job's faith. What could be stronger than the assertion

"Though He slay me, yet will I trust in Him?"

A Job who could say that in the midst of his sufferings was, forsooth, the model of piety, as he is pictured in the popular tale. Accordingly, up to our own days this famous passage occurs to the average Bible reader as characteristic of Job. The beauty and simplicity of the verse has stuck in the popular mind; and even the critic must feel a pang of regret at being forced to point out its incorrectness. Job *ought* to have said it, but unfortunately he said just the contrary, that though God crushes his life, yet he will maintain his innocence without fear—"I trust in Him" was a sentiment appropriate to the meek Job of the folktale, but not to the rebellious character in the Symposium.

If we assume that the verse in its original form was regarded as a bold challenge, we can understand why a pious commentator felt it necessary to insert, as a further means of removing the unfavorable impression, the following verse, revealed as an insertion by its prose form:

"Aye, this will be my salvation that the impious will not come before Him." (13, 16.)

That is precisely what Job in his defiant mood could not and would not say.

Our second illustration of an intentional distortion of a crucial passage is the utterance of Job which

THE BOOK OF JOB

has become the most famous of all in the entire book (19, 25-27). According to the view still current, the sufferer voices his firm faith:

"I know that my Redeemer liveth"

and goes on to express his belief that he will yet be justified—according to the older traditional interpretation—"in the flesh" in a future world when he will see God for himself, or according to a later though also orthodox view "out of the flesh."

The entire passage has occasioned endless difficulties to exegetes, particularly v. 26, which, as it stands, is syntactically almost impossible.[86] The ordinary translation:

"And when after my skin this is destroyed,
Then without my flesh shall I see God"[87]

cannot be correct, for the thought of a meeting with God after this earthly life is *over* is entirely contrary to the belief of Job as set forth in his speeches. In his very first speech (chapter 3), in which he expresses the wish that he had never been born, he speaks of Sheol as the general gathering place where all distinctions of rank disappear and where inactivity reigns. There is not the slightest suggestion of any thought of retribution or justification. When in subsequent speeches Job longs for death, it is as a release from his sufferings. He sighs for the "place of no return" (7, 8), where he will be safely hidden—

---
[86] See the commentaries of Budde, Duhm and Barton for details which are too technical to be introduced at this point.
[87] So the rendering in the translation of the American Jewish Publication Society, following the AV.

even from God. Throughout the speeches [88] Job's point of view, as is also that of Koheleth writing about two centuries later, is the older general Semitic conception of continuing consciousness after death, but minus all activity and without any punishment for wrongs done in this world or compensation for endured sufferings. If, therefore, such a doctrine is put forth in the 26th verse of chapter 19, it is only because the text has been manipulated in such a way by pious commentators as to permit of such an interpretation under the sway of an ungrammatical exegesis. The comparison of the Hebrew text with the Greek version of this verse bears out this contention.[89] The Hebrew of v. 26 begins with "after my skin" (or "under my skin," which is preferable), but the Greek version omits "after." To maintain that this phrase means "after death" either within one's skin or out of one's skin is quite impossible. Nor can the following words be rendered "this is destroyed," for the sufficient reason that in the Hebrew text subject (sing.) and verb (plural) do not agree. We must take the context as our point of departure for a correct interpretation. Job has asked his tormentors:

"Why do you pursue me like a stag" [90]

since he is so worn with disease that his flesh would not suffice for a meal. Realizing that his friends are utterly lacking in sympathy, he exclaims that if

---

[88] See especially the passage 14, 7–12.
[89] See the full discussion of the point in Beer, *Text des Buches Hiob*, pp. 124–126.
[90] For this reading instead of "God," see the note to the passage.

THE BOOK OF JOB

only his words were hewn into the rock, like an inscription that would remain for all times, he would be certain that a defender would arise some day. It is in this sense that he uses the old Semitic term *goël* as the one on whom the obligation rests to seek redress for a wrong done to a kinsman.[91] The *goël* is the avenger, the justifier the vindicator—the redeemer, if you choose, but in the literal sense as the one who *redeems* a wrong committed. A human "redeemer" is meant,[92] one who will act as a justifier or better still as a "defender," which would be the modern term corresponding closest to the ancient one. What Job therefore says is:

"Oh that my words could be inscribed,[93]
Graven for all times in the rock![94]
Then I would know that my defender will arise,
Even though he should rise up in the distant future."

This being the thought demanded by the context, what follows must be in accord with this hope.

We owe to Ehrlich[95] the suggestion that v. 26 embodies the lament that unfortunately Job *alone* knows of his sufferings. They are inscribed merely on his person,

"Under my skin this (*i.e.*, the record of his sufferings) is indited."

---

[91] See further the note on the word, in the translation of the chapter.

[92] Credit should be given to a Jewish commentator Saadia, living in the ninth century A.D., who recognized that redeemer could not refer to God, but his is a single voice.

[93] A commentator paraphrases this by adding "Oh that one might inscribe in a book," to point out that recording on a soft material like papyrus or skin had taken the place of the earlier incision on a hard substance like stone, metal or rock.

[94] A glossator adds prosaically "and with an iron stylus and lead." See further for the justification of my translation, the notes to 19, 23-29.

[95] *Randglossen*, 6, p. 257.

He alone sees the evidence of his tortures which are hidden from others. He will be forgotten and his sufferings with him. Therefore, he adds:

"And within my flesh do I see these [words]" [96]

The following verse (v. 27) appears to be an amplification, added by some commentator who felt the obscurity of the passage;

"I alone can see it (*i.e.*, the record of tortures) for myself;
Mine eyes see it, but not another's."

In justification of this interpretation, that Job is here referring to his sufferings and not to any sight of God after death, we have another comment added;

"My reins are consumed within me" [97]

which is merely another way of saying that he alone is conscious of all that he is forced to endure. His friends are estranged from him. They are blind to his condition. They have no understanding for his state of mind. He alone sees the record of his endurance, written clearly on his own person—in the emaciated form and in the features distorted with pain.

The loneliness in his grief adds to the poignancy of his martyrdom. That is the thought which the author wishes to bring out in a passage that has been completely distorted by a deliberate endeavor to twist its meaning, both before the text became fixed and even after this period. The passage in the interpretation given to it by a false exegesis has become crucial for the traditional interpretation of the Book

---

[96] Which he would like to have inscribed on a rock so that *all* may see the record for *all* times.

[97] If we follow the traditional translation, this line remains suspended in the air.

of Job. The utterance in the mouth of Job "I know that my Redeemer liveth" outweighs the impression made by his bitter complaints. By the side of the equally erroneous rendering "Though He slay me, yet will I trust in Him" and the assertion "Even now my witness is in heaven," Job's faith in his justification in a future life—for that also was read into this passage—appeared to be established beyond all question. However utterances that seemed to contradict these assurances of a pious and trusting soul were to be explained, here were three utterances whose testimony seemed to be unimpeachable. In this way the Job of the Symposium was brought into accord with the Job of the folktale. Both Jobs endured the test. Both remained pious and God-fearing under the severest trials ever imposed upon man. The cause of Jewish orthodoxy was saved. For an uncritical age the three passages sufficed to win the day for the doctrine of Divine government as taught by the prophets, and which became the corner stone of post-exilic Judaism.

It is not a pleasant task for the critic thus to hold up as erroneous passages in the original book which have not only made their way into the Church and Synagogue service, but which by their beauty and impressiveness have been a source of consolation to countless myriads these two milleniums, sustaining them in sorrow and helping them to bear the ills and burdens of life. The critic must forego popularity. He lays himself open to the suspicion of being wilfully destructive of hallowed traditions and of long-existing conventions. If he is serious minded—and the critic is not genuine unless he feels the responsibility of his task—he may himself share the regret of thus being forced to abandon an interpretation of the Book of Job to which in common with his non-critical fellows he had clung. He must console himself by the deeper penetration that he gains into the spirit of Biblical literature and the clearer view of the evolution of religious thought and practice among the Hebrews from lowly beginnings to an advanced stage —a stage higher than that reached by any other people of antiquity and which culminated in a temporary climax in the commingling of Hebrew and Greek spirituality in early Christianity.

Applying this to the original Book of Job, is there not a decided compensation for the abandonment of the traditional view of significant passages that have always been associated with the popular conception of the book, in the recognition that the *main* aim of the writers of the remarkable Symposium was precisely to depict this struggle involved in the attempt to penetrate the mystery by which we are surrounded—the mystery of all mysteries, life itself with its burdens and sorrows that seem to be the heritage of mankind? The writers shrink from the task of solving the mystery, which they frankly regard to be beyond human reach, but they wish to arouse our sympathy for the distressed soul, for the sufferer who typifies for them man universal, wringing his hands in anguish and crying—why and how long? Why—this burden of sorrow too heavy to be born? How long this torture, imposed for no good apparent reason? Job's case *is* of general application, just because it is an extreme instance. The problem of human suffering is intensified by the example of a really pious and God-fearing man doomed to pain and misery. The original Book of Job as a consistent expression of the questioning spirit is a greater masterpiece than Job as an awkward combination of contradictory points of view, brought about through the conscious endeavor to change the original drift of the book.

IV

ORTHODOX SENTIMENTS PLACED IN THE MOUTH OF JOB

We now approach the boldest stroke on the part of those who aimed to convert the original Book of Job into a support for the orthodox point of view. The confusion existing in the third series of speeches (chapters 25 to 31) to which attention has been called [98] has long been recognized by scholars. Various explanations have from time to time been brought forward to account for the brief speech of Bildad (chapter 25) consisting of only six verses, and the long utterances of Job, covering the remaining six chapters. The absence of any third speech of Zophar had also been noticed, but only a few even of modern scholars[99] have recognized the need of a radical method in

[98] Above, p. 71. See the details in the notes to the translation of Chapters 25-31.
[99] Barton is among those who have realized the need of a radical rearrangement of the chapters in question. (*Journal of Biblical Literature*, vol. 30, pp. 66-77) though I differ from his restoration in some important points. Siegfried in his critical text of the Book of Job (ed. Haupt, Leipzig, 1893) gives a correct reconstruction of chapters 25-26 but fails to reconstruct Zophar's speech and introduces rather arbitrary transposition of verses within chapter 29, instead of recognizing that 29, 21-25 is an independent fragment which has been inserted into Job's first supplementary speech. He also fails to recognize that 30, 16-24 is part of Job's reply to Bildad and that 31, 35-37 must represent the close of this reply, or possibly the close of Job's missing reply to Zophar.

THE BOOK OF JOB

getting order out of a seemingly hopeless chaos. Referring the reader to the translation for the rearrangement of these chapters, it is sufficient for our purposes here to recall once more that the six chapters (22 to 27), represent further discussions of the problem that emanate from the same circle which produced the first two series of speeches.

Chapters 22 to 24, containing a speech of Eliphaz and Job's reply, add nothing to the arguments already presented by both sides, except the *direct* charge of lack of charity and mercy levelled at Job and for which his sufferings, it is claimed, are a just retribution. The absurdity of Eliphaz saying to Job:

> "Surely, thy wickedness must be great,
> And there can be no end to thy iniquities." (22, 5.)

is so patent that one can only explain the introduction as deliberate, in order to put a weapon into the hands of Job which he wields with force in his reply. Eliphaz then once more unrolls the false picture of the punishment of the wicked (verses 15–20) and, again as in previous speeches, calls upon Job to return to God and all will be well. Job in reply (chapter 23) once more brings forth his plea that he cannot bring his case before God, adding with special emphasis that he cannot find God, no matter how intensely he searches for Him. In chapter 24, he sets forth in detail all the crimes committed by the wicked. In powerful language, he describes the oppression and misery of the poor, forced to go about naked, drenched by the rain and clinging to rocks for shelter, as the result of the ruthlessness against which they are powerless. All this is clearly an amplification of what Job has already dwelt upon in chapter 21. There is no reply in these two chapters to Eliphaz and it is, therefore, evident that the speech of Eliphaz is, as already suggested, another draft of the argument of this speaker put forth in previous speeches, while Job's speech is similarly an imitation and amplification of former utterances—likewise an independent draft by some hand which tried to set forth what Job *might* have said.

Suddenly, however, we find Job speaking as the friends do. Instead of picturing the success of the wiles of the wicked as he did in chapter 21, we find him foretelling their doom. Beginning with v. 18 of chapter 24 in which a pious commentator inserts the reflection:

"Their portion is cursed in the earth."

we find Job telling us of the wicked (v. 20):

"The womb forgets him;
Worms feed (?) on him.
He is no longer remembered;
Iniquity is crushed like a tree,"

and again v. 24:

"They are exalted for a while and brought low;
And as the tips of the grain they wither."

Such reflections, entirely contradicting what Job had previously said, are interspersed in this supplementary speech with the deliberate intent of taking off the edge of the skepticism and cynicism in Job's utterances. The closing verse of the chapter:

"If it is not so, who will prove me to be a liar,
And nullify my speech?"

would only be in place if Job were denouncing the success of the wicked. This verse clinches the argument in favor of v. 18^b, 20 and 24 as insertions by a pious commentator.

But those interested in toning down the skeptical implications in Job's speeches did not stop short here in their endeavor to change the original character of the book. In chapter 27, some one was bold enough to place a more detailed description (27, 7-23) of the awful doom in store for the evildoer into the mouth of Job. It is manifestly inconceivable that the Job who speaks so bitterly in chapter 22 of the way in which evildoers escape the consequences of their deeds should now say of the wicked:

"Though he heap up silver as dust,
And provide garments as clay;
He may provide, but the righteous will put on,
And the innocent shall divide the silver.
  *   *   *   *   *   *
He lies down rich, but it will not endure;
He opens his eyes, and it is gone.
Terrors overtake him by day;
The tempest removes him by night." (27, 16-20.)

Job is actually represented as quoting from a speech of Zophar (20, 29):

"Such is the portion of the wicked from God,
And the heritage of the oppressors from Shaddai." (27, 13.)

What has happened? Clearly, a portion of a third speech of Zophar—in imitation of his second one—has been deliberately added to 27, 1-6 which is a genuine utterance of Job, protesting his innocence and which is entirely out of keeping with 27, 7-23. Not content with this, some other commentator,

THE BOOK OF JOB

intent upon representing Job as God-fearing and acknowledging the merciful providence of God, took a piece of Bildad's third speech 26, 5-14, detached it from its connection (25, 1-6) and tacked it on to the introduction of Job's answer to Bildad (26, 1-4.)[100] There is no connection whatsoever between Job's rebuke of his friends (26, 1-4) and the sudden transition to the power and providence of God (26, 5-14) beginning:

> "The shades below are in terror;
> The waters and their inhabitants"

and ending with:

> "These are but the outskirts of his ways,
> And a mere whisper that penetrates to us."

It is claimed by some scholars that this confusion between Job's utterances and those of his friends is accidental, due to a confusion of separate leaves of a codex. This can hardly be, for it is difficult to see how it could happen *accidentally* that by such confusion only orthodox sentiments should have been put into the mouth of Job. At all events, exegetes permitted the confusion to remain to the threshold of modern Biblical study, and even at the present time there are defenders of the present arrangement who point to it in their desperate effort to prove that the original Book of Job ended in an orthodox strain. Our modern translators of the Bible have done nothing to enlighten the lay reader as to the *real* situation. Translations of the Book of Job continue

---

[100] This answer of Job thus consists of 26, 1-4, followed by 27, 2-6 and 30, 16-24, with 31, 35-37 as the probable conclusion.

THE BOOK OF JOB

to be printed in strict obedience to the indications of the Hebrew text, and the reader is left to solve the enigma as best he can, how Job can say one thing in one place and directly contradict himself in another. Surely, respect for the Bible is not increased by thus hiding the truth.

V
THE "SEARCH FOR WISDOM"

The natural upshot, however, of the manifest confusion was to strengthen the case for Job's orthodoxy. The pious commentators and editors secured the triumph for which they yearned, but at the expense of eschewing criticism and of producing a work full of contradictions. The same spirit of saving the book for orthodoxy which prompted the insertion of pious reflections to counterbalance Job's audacious charges and indictments, which led to the distortion of passages from their original meaning and which prompted later editors deliberately to remove sections from speeches of one of the friends and give them to Job, also superinduced the insertion of chapter 28—the "Search for Wisdom" which is without any connection whatsoever with the Symposium, and without any bearings on the arguments of the friends of Job. Superb in its diction and of the highest order of literary excellence, this description of the search for wisdom which is hidden from man betrays the same point of view as that found in the first nine chapters of Proverbs, constituting the first main division of this book.[101] It reflects a highly

---

[101] Though not the oldest section. See Toy, *Critical and Exegetical Commentary on the Book of Proverbs*, p. xviii seq.

THE BOOK OF JOB

intellectual age in which knowledge was exalted above all other possessions, but an age which had already begun to experience the disappointment due to the impossibility of solving through knowledge the mystery by which man is surrounded.

The writer of this chapter (or possibly some later amplifier) [102] agrees with Proverbs in placing wisdom above all treasures, but he is an agnostic when it comes to securing wisdom.

"Wisdom whence cometh she?"

rings as a refrain through the chapter. The answer to the question is impressive but discouraging.

"God knows the way to her;
And He knows her place." (28, 23.)

God—but not man. And then in a passage of unsurpassed eloquence, which likewise finds a parallel in Proverbs 8, 22–30, the writer exclaims that when God created the world;

"When He gave a weight for the wind,
And measured out the waters;
When He assigned a law for the rain,
And a path for the thunderbolt;
He saw her and proclaimed her;
Established her, aye, singled her out." (28, 25–27.)

Our author furnishes, as it were, a commentary to the original Book of Job by suggesting the reason for the unsatisfactory conclusion which the author of Job reaches. Wisdom is with God—not with man! How, then, can man hope to understand the ways of God? Orthodox circles, ignoring the agnostic

---

[102] Verses 15–19 of the chapter may be later additions taken over from Proverbs 3, 14–15; 8, 11 and 18–19. See the notes to the translation.

THE BOOK OF JOB

implications of the chapter, would welcome this production as a strong support for their cause. They would be only too eager to have Job confess that man cannot by human wisdom penetrate the secrets of God's universe, created by Him through His wisdom which God alone can "proclaim and single out." It was, therefore, an editor acting in the interest of orthodoxy who attached this splendid bit of literature at the close of the supplemental third series of speeches to form an appropriate finale to the Symposium, before another supplement, consisting of the two speeches of Job in chapters 29–31, was added. By the addition of the little word "for" at the beginning of chapter 28, the production was made to appear to be a continuation of the orthodox sentiments concerning the punishment of the wicked, deliberately put into the mouth of Job (27, 7–23), though, as we have seen, they originally formed part of Zophar's third speech.

VI
THE VIRTUES OF JOB

The further supplement to the original book, embodied in chapters 29 to 31 is from the literary point of view most impressive, even though the chapters strike a note entirely inconsistent with Job as presented in the three series of speeches. In these series, Job complains of his condition but never boasts of his virtues. Not so chapters 29–31 covering two independent speeches [103] plus a supplement to

---

[103] For the arrangement of these two speeches, see the notes to the translation of Chapters 25–31.

THE BOOK OF JOB

the first,[104] one detailing in a direct manner his virtuous conduct and the esteem in which as a consequence he was held, the other setting forth in equal detail what he avoided doing. One would prefer to have had others say of Job that he delivered the poor and rejoiced the heart of the widow, that he clothed himself in righteousness and put on justice as a diadem (29, 12-14). The impression one receives of Job in the Symposium is spoiled by having him sing his own praises:

"Eyes was I to the blind;
And feet to the lame.
A father I to the needy;
And I searched out the cause of the unknown." (29, 15-16.)

It is in equally poor taste to find him in the second speech commending himself in somewhat unctuous fashion for keeping himself free from violation of a virgin and from adultery. As he proceeds with the long catalogue of vices and wrongs which he avoided, the tone becomes more and more patronizing, at times offensively so. The self-praise reaches its climax of self-satisfaction in a little section (31, 5-8) which may be an independent fragment that has slipped in at an inappropriate place.

"If I had ever followed falseness,
And my foot had hastened to deceit;
If my step had turned out of the right path,
And my mind had followed after my eyes;
Let me sow and another eat,
And let my produce be rooted out."

The two speeches were, no doubt, added to heighten our sympathy with Job, but it is difficult

---
[104] 29, 21-25.

THE BOOK OF JOB

to suppose that the writers of the original Book of Job should have allowed their hero thus to lay himself open to the charge of pharisaical self-esteem and smug self-glorification. This picture of the self-satisfied boastful Job is due to others who did not in their imagination pass through Job's experiences. Those who wrote those speeches approach the subject from the outside. They give us a view of Job as he must have appeared to others, though the picture is spoiled by having Job draw it himself. The writers in the Symposium proper approach the subject from the inside. They feel for Job so intensely that they identify themselves with their subject. They make Job speak as we feel that the real and human Job *must* have spoken. Not so with the supplementary speeches which are in the nature of literary exercises, superb and admirable as such, but lacking the fervor and strength of the preceding eight speeches.

For those, however, who were intent upon making the Book of Job appear to be a support for orthodoxy these added chapters accomplished the object which they had in view. If the book was to make its appeal as a production in accord with the prevailing orthodoxy, it was necessary to leave no question in the minds of any that Job not only was supremely virtuous and pious as in the folktale, but remained so even *after* his discussion with his friends. How could this better be done than by attaching to the Symposium such a detailed picture of all the generous deeds of the hero, and then supplement this by an equally detailed picture of all the temptations that he resisted? Here was testimony out of Job's own mouth, which none could gainsay; and in order to heighten the impression of the genuineness of these speeches a compiler inserted a section (30, 16–24) which is precisely in the style of the Job of the Symposium proper, and as a matter of fact has been removed from its correct place (after 27, 2–6),[105] for the very purpose of creating the impression that these three chapters in their entirety belong to the Symposium.

VII

THE TWO APPENDICES AS THE COPING TO THE STRUCTURE OF JEWISH ORTHODOXY

To complete the task of converting an originally skeptical book into a bulwark of orthodoxy, the two appendices were added to the enlarged Book of Job, the one embodying the four speeches put into the mouth of a fifth personage who represents himself as a defender of the faith of better calibre than the three friends, the other in the form of two speeches assigned to God himself. The two features that stand out preëminently in these appendices, which, it is plausible to assume, were added at about 300 B.C., are in the first place, the need that was felt by the circles of staunch believers to make a further defense of the orthodox position, and secondly, the scale on which this defense was carried out.

The Symposium must have fallen like a bombshell into the orthodox camp, the effect of which was all the greater because the book was not the product of a single mind as a book is in our days, but represents the combined effort of a circle that, even

---
[105] See further the notes to the translation of chapters 25–31.

THE BOOK OF JOB

though it may not have been excessively large, was powerful because it contained those who were determined to think for themselves and who were unwilling to accept ready-made opinions without questioning their basis. "He thinks too much," says Cæsar,[106] voicing his suspicion of Cassius. "Such men are dangerous." It is not necessary to go so far as to assume that the circle which produced the Book of Job was regarded as dangerous to the prevailing faith, but the Symposium must at all events have created a feeling of discomfort among those who in their honest zeal for the cause of orthodoxy felt that the movement in the direction of free thought must be checked by a reinforcement of the orthodox point of view. The Symposium was a symptom of the intellectual unrest which at the close of the third century found a further and still more objectionable expression in the cynicism of the writer who hid his personality beneath the *nom de plume* of Koheleth.[107] It is quite possible that other books of the same calibre as Job and Koheleth were produced that have not come down to us, because they failed to be received into the sacred canon. However this may be, these two productions suffice as evidence of a reaction that set in towards the close of the fifth century against the fundamental assumptions that had grown up around the teachings of the pre-exilic and post-exilic prophets. The upholders of orthodoxy were challenged to prove their position, and we may see in the speeches of Elihu and in those placed in the mouth of God the answer to this challenge.

---
[106] Act I, 2, 215.   [107] See *A Gentle Cynic*, page 62 *seq.*

THE BOOK OF JOB

The circumstance that four separate speeches of Elihu were embodied, each, as we have seen, of independent origin, may be taken as a further indication of the seriousness with which the situation was viewed. Their accumulative weight, it was hoped, would effectually silence all doubters in a just and merciful Providence. The editorial introductions to the speeches of Elihu [108] are of special interest in this connection, because of the admission involved that the arguments of the three friends as representative of Jewish orthodoxy were not regarded as convincing. Had it been possible to ignore the original book, we may feel quite sure that this would have been done, just as the original words of Koheleth would have been passed over in silence had they not made too profound an impression to admit of such a procedure.

A still bolder stroke was represented by the introduction of God himself to pronounce, through a series of magnificent poems, the final verdict on the discussion. We have seen that these poems are in reality productions of poets stirred by the love of nature and inspired by the contemplation of marvels in animal life. The editorial work of those who utilized them for the reinforcement of orthodoxy was limited to the collection of the poems, to the two poetic epilogues attached and to the introductory sentences representing the poems as two speeches addressed by God to Job, though we have seen that there is nothing in the poems themselves to suggest such an address. Here again the circumstance that it was thought

---

[108] See above, page 77 *seq.*

necessary thus to introduce Yahweh in order to reduce Job to humble silence and to bring him to a proper state of repentance for his audacious utterances in the Symposium is the significant feature. A further decisive blow had to be struck at the growing menace of independent thought away from conventional lines; and since Elihu begins his fourth speech by the assertion that there are "still things to be said for God," it was a natural device to supplement the discourses of Elihu by summoning, as it were, God himself to take part in the discussion.

This assumes that the nature poems were attached to the Book of Job *after* the speeches of Elihu. Strangely enough most scholars, while recognizing the independent character of the Elihu chapters, are yet disposed to regard chapters 38–41 as an integral part of the book, which would reverse the position here taken and make the inserted speeches of Elihu a later production than the closing four chapters. The weakness of this view lies in its failure to assign a good reason for introducing six chapters within what would be the body of the book, the orthodoxy of which, moreover, would have been sufficiently assured by the introduction of Yahweh himself as a participant in the Symposium. *After* Yahweh has spoken, Elihu is an entirely superfluous personage. Moreover, the view fails to take into account the sharp demarcation between the trend of the Symposium and that of chapters 38–41. The reader who has followed my exposition will be able to see for himself how inconceivable it is that one writer or one group of writers belonging to the same circle should

THE BOOK OF JOB

have produced the Symposium, and then also thought of assigning to God the nature poems in defense of Jewish orthodoxy. We fail to understand the book unless we recognize the three different strata of which it is formed; and the most natural sequence for these strata is to assume that the present arrangement follows the order of growth of the original draft of the book to its present complete form.[109]

Now the two appendices constitute more than one-third of the entire book. An addition on so large a scale, while not unusual in the case of literary productions of the ancient Orient subject to steady growth, is yet significant in this instance because the branches grafted on are so completely at variance with the character of the original trunk. The speeches of Elihu, though bringing forth new arguments in reply to Job's disturbing contentions, could not have been regarded as completely satisfactory. The problem continued to occupy the minds of believers and doubters alike, and we must look upon the device of placing the collection of nature poems in the mouth of Yahweh and of adding them as a last word on the vital subject as further evidence of the need for a defense of the orthodox position.

The supplements to the Symposium and the two appendices saved the original production from being lost, for the Symposium by itself would never have been included in the sacred canon, as little as the original "Words of Koheleth" would have secured

---
[109] One might also urge that the insertion of the words "out of the storm" in the heading to chapter 38 which is (repeated in 40, 6), clearly suggested by the storm poem inserted in chapters 36–37 (see above, p. 79), *assumes* the existence of the Elihu speeches at the time when the nature poems were added as the third stratum.

THE BOOK OF JOB

admittance. The new Job led to the preservation of the old Job, as a modified Koheleth, obscuring its irreverent cynicism, rescued the genuine Koheleth from probable oblivion.[110] We must, therefore, feel grateful to those who thus labored to change the original trend of the book, even though they also hoped that the apparent unity given to the elaborate compilation might remain unquestioned for all times. Nor should we after completing our task of undoing the work of zealots, exchange our gratitude for condemnation of the uncritical spirit betrayed by those who thus tried to cover the naked skepticism of the original book with an orthodox garb. An age that has not developed the full sense of individual authorship necessarily lacks the critical attitude towards a literary production. *We* can see the intent in the manipulations to which the text was subjected, but those who were engaged in the endeavor saw only a perfectly obvious method of furnishing their superimposed interpretation of a problem that was left in an unsatisfactory state by predecessors who had tried their hand at solving it; and they no doubt sincerely believed that they were improving the original production. What we would differentiate as text and commentary, as argument and answer, as original draft and later amplification, are, in an ancient composition, produced at a time when a literary product was regarded as common property to be modified and enlarged at will, thrown together. When in the course of such literary process contradictions result that are *too* glaring to be overlooked,

---
[110] See *A Gentle Cynic*, p. 119.

the difficulties are overcome in a naïve but sincere spirit by balancing an objectionable utterance with a pious reflection deliberately introduced.

The naïveté which marks what we of a modern day would regard as unwarranted interference with a literary work is further illustrated by the additions through later editors and amplifiers even in these two appendices. In chapters 32–42 we likewise encounter superfluous lines, pointing to variants, comments or deliberate additions. There are reflections by pious commentators, desirous of enforcing the orthodox teachings of Elihu, and likewise numerous passages the text of which needs to be corrected in order to yield an intelligible sense and sequence.[111] Without bewildering the reader with more examples, suffice it to say that the endeavor was consistently made throughout the entire book to create the impression that despite the many audacious sentiments of Job remaining in the original portion, the trend of the book was towards orthodoxy, that the skepticism was on the surface, whereas its deeper aim was to furnish a support for the conventional and generally accepted beliefs of the day.

It may well seem startling to the ordinary reader, accustomed to look upon the Book of Job as a unity, an authentic composition of one writer, which is supposed to have come down to us in the form given to it by this writer, to be asked to cast all preconceived views aside and to regard the book from an entirely different angle, as a gradual growth with an original

---

[111] All such passages as well as all additions will be indicated in each instance in the notes attached to the translation.

THE BOOK OF JOB

trunk to which branches were added from time to time; and in addition to this to cut out hundreds of comments, variants and glosses and superfluous lines. It is not surprising to find such a demand, when first made, arousing a feeling akin to resentment. The alternative, however, would be to accept the book as a tissue of contradictions, full of abrupt transitions, lacking an orderly arrangement of themes, to an extent that would reflect most seriously on the mentality of those who could produce such a confusing work. In short, we have the choice on the one hand between clinging to the traditional view of the book which has been shown to be untenable, which is contrary to the literary method of antiquity, which rests on a corrupt text and leads to translations of crucial passages and many hundreds of other passages that cannot endure the test of criticism, and on the other hand in being willing to revise our attitude towards the book on the basis of a corrected and rearranged text, freed from all subsequent additions, in the hope of thus obtaining a clear in place of a hopelessly confused view of one of the world's masterpieces of literature. The realization of this hope must be the final test for the justification of the application of the critical method to the study of the Book of Job.

In assuming that the book as we have it has passed through many hands, each one of which left its trace upon it, we recognize that the book itself had an eventful history before it received its final form. The critical method asserts that we cannot understand the book without following its history.

CHAPTER V

THE BOOK OF JOB AS PHILOSOPHY AND AS LITERATURE

I

THE INSOLUBLE PROBLEM

If, as I have tried to show elsewhere,[112] we must picture the author of the original "Words of Koheleth" as an old man who has advanced to old age gracefully, for whom the storms of life are over and who has become mellow by his varied experiences, disposed to take things as they are in this world not too seriously, we must imagine the group who first conceived of the idea to give a written form to the oral discussions on the problem of human suffering as they took place in the circle to which they belonged, as intensely serious, rather inclined to austerity, and of a rebellious disposition as they contemplated the hardships frequently endured by those who lead pure and decent lives, as against the better fortune of those who were callous to ethical standards. The group would correspond to a circle of independent thinkers at the present time, fearless and independent but whose spirit while rebellious would not necessarily be destructive. If they oppose conventional beliefs it is because they are earnestly seeking for a firm foundation for their faith in a guiding Providence

---

[112] *A Gentle Cynic*, p. 194.

THE BOOK OF JOB

which they have not abandoned. They are seekers after truth and as such we must picture them—struggling souls groping for the light.

Only men in the vigor of life, still engaged in the struggle from which few escape, could express themselves so forcibly, so pathetically, aye, so violently as in the speeches put by them in the mouth of Job. Old men do not talk that way. The writer of the original draft of Job and his successors hold the mirror up to nature and paint the reflection in bold colors. They have the courage to look at things as they are. At the same time, while their outlook on life is anything but cheerful, it would hardly be fair to call them pessimists. That overworked term is not quite appropriate, for the pessimist suggests a sullen and bitterly resigned thinker, whose personal disappointments make him incline towards cynicism. There is scarcely a trace of cynicism in the original Book of Job, which in this respect presents such a contrast to Koheleth, albeit that the cynicism of the latter is gentle and free from the sting which frequently accompanies the cynical attitude. Koheleth, the old man, smiles as he thinks of this topsy-turvy world. The writers in Job, young and impatient, frown; and the frown grows deeper as they proceed in their ungrateful task of showing the untenability of the current views regarding the rule in this world of a merciful and just Providence. "Why worry?" asks Koheleth. Take things as they are. You cannot improve them. Try to get as much joy out of life as you can and in order not to grow weary of *mere* enjoyment, work so that joy may be your recrea-

THE BOOK OF JOB

tion from your toil. Don't imagine that everything is going to perdition, for things are not worse than they were; they were always bad. Such is not the mood of the writers in Job. They are terribly in earnest, but always out of intense sympathy with the sad lot of mankind in being condemned to suffer without cause. If at times one of the group seems to clinch his fist in bitter revolt against things as they are, it is a bitterness born of a profound realization of the tragedy of life. Nor are the writers unbelievers. Doubt as to the existence of God never enters their minds, but they boldly ask whether the prophets were right in picturing the Deity as merciful and just? For them the two horns of the dilemma are that either God is indifferent to human suffering in which case He would not be merciful, or as the source of good and evil He doles out both without judging the acts of man, in which case He would not be just. Neither cold rationalism nor apathetic stoicism could satisfy a group of writers whose religious fervor shows itself in such a passage, descriptive of God's tender care for mankind as the following:

"Thy hands moulded and fashioned me.

* * * * * *

Didst Thou not pour me out as milk,
And like cheese didst curdle me? [113]
Clothed me with skin and flesh
And knitted me together with bones and sinews?
Grace Thou didst grant me;
And Thy providence watched over my spirit."

(10, 10–12.)

---

[113] Referring to the growth of the fœtus from the semen.

THE BOOK OF JOB

Only one of strong religious bent could write such a passage; and we must perforce assume that the impressive description of God's marvels in nature which occur in the speeches of the friends [114] found a response in the hearts of those who, nevertheless, ranged themselves on the side of Job. If the writers in Job could have reconciled themselves to the hypothesis of God's callousness to man, the dilemma would not have seemed so terrible that a watchful Providence should also be cruel enough to lay in store tortures for His creatures.

"And yet such things didst Thou hide in Thy mind.
I *know* that this is Thy way." (10, 13.)

With this problem the writers in Job strive long and earnestly, and in a deeply religious spirit, only to reach the negative conclusion that one cannot argue with God, because one cannot bring one's case before Him. To think of doing so already involves the questioning of Divine justice. Job's plight being regarded as typical, the problem of human suffering thus remains suspended in the air. The give and take in the debate between Job and his friends leads by sheer necessity to no issue. The Symposium becomes merely a play of tossing the conundrum like a ball forwards and backwards. There is no further progress in the discussion after Job has once gone so far as to declare,

"How can a man win a suit against God?" (9, 2.)

The arguments of the friends are weak and futile against this obstacle to further discussion. They are

---
[114] *e.g.*, Eliphaz (5, 9–10) Zophar (11, 7–9).

THE BOOK OF JOB

like waves dashing themselves against a breakwater that hurls them back with still greater force. Of what use is it for Eliphaz to argue (4, 7-8) that no innocent ever perished and that those who sow iniquity perish by the breath of God, when the assumption in Job's case is that he *is* innocent? Of what avail is it for Bildad to assure Job that those who forget the paths of God are doomed to destruction, and that if Job will only turn to God all will be well (8, 22), when the point is that God is deaf or indifferent to Job's cries of anguish. How bootless for Zophar to ring the changes on the threadbare argument that if Job will confess his guilt his sufferings will come to an end (11, 11-15), in the face of the undeniable fact that the innocent *do* suffer and that the wicked are *not* punished in this world. Indeed the rebellious spirit goes so far as to suggest in the chapter which marks one of the climaxes in the Symposium (chapter 21) that the friends of Job *know* that the picture of the doom of the wicked as drawn by them is false,[115] and that in this topsy-turvy world fates are meted out without reference to merit or demerit.

Throughout the Symposium, therefore, there is a consistent rebellious spirit. The aim of the original Book of Job is not to deny Providence, but to enter a protest against the Prophets' assurance of the government of the universe by a Power acting according to the dictation of justice and mercy. That is the gist of the philosophy in Job—a protest.

---

[115] Eliphaz (chapter 15, 17-35). Bildad (chapter 18), Zophar (chapter 20).

THE BOOK OF JOB

II

THE RELIGIOUS STRAIN IN THE ORIGINAL BOOK OF JOB

And yet we miss the real meaning of the book if we conceive of this protest as irreligious. It is the protest of profoundly religious spirits who seek to unravel the mysteries of life and decline to content themselves with the repetition of meaningless phrases, or to be lulled to rest by a false view of actual conditions. Job's philosophy harks back in a measure to the earlier conception of Yahweh as a nature Power, exerting its force irrespective of ethical motives. Just here is the crux of the attitude towards life assumed by the writers in the Symposium. The position reached by independent inquiry is superlatively painful, because the choice lies between an ethical view of Divine rule and a non-ethical Power, representing a force of nature to whom no appeal for either justice or mercy is possible. The gods of the older period could at least be bribed and flattered by sacrifices and homage. The God of Job is a blind force.

"The guiltless and the wicked He destroys.
If a scourge should suddenly strike one,
He would merely laugh at the death of the innocent."
(9, 22–23.)

We must not, to be sure, stress the implication of cruelty involved in this outburst too hard. Job's concern is with the *absence* of evidence for a just rule interfering in the affairs of man. Even if a pious man by virtue of his strong faith endures the test of

THE BOOK OF JOB

innocent suffering, the conception underlying this faith cannot endure the test of the plain fact that in this world the wicked frequently escape the merited punishment for their deeds. The value of the Book of Job in its original form lies precisely in this sharp formulation of the situation—either a God who is cruel, or a blind force. The prophets of the pre-exilic period could develop and press their ethical theory of Divine government, because the evidence was overwhelming that the people had sinned by falling away from the old national protector Yahweh, through the adoption of rites that were foreign to Him. Political corruption and social injustice reinforced the position of the religious leaders, who could thus maintain the doctrine of just retribution as the main attribute of Yahweh. But the very acceptance of the doctrine by the Jews of the post-exilic period who regulated their lives and their worship according to the teachings of the prophets created the problem with which Job is pictured as wrestling. The Israel of the pre-exilic period had sinned and had suffered punishment. The chastened Israel of the post-exilic period was justified in looking forward to Divine favor and grace, but things went on just the same. Suffering was not diminished, wrong continued to be triumphant, and the hoped for independence was not realized, despite the growing piety of the people. The fate of Job thus became in a special sense typical of the disappointment encountered by the people as a whole. The post-exilic prophets reflect this disappointment, and there is a close affiliation between the figure of the suffering servant of Yahweh in the post-exilic sections

THE BOOK OF JOB

of the Book of Isaiah [116] and the figure of Job, just as we have echoes in Psalms dating from about the same period as the Book of Job, of the pathetic complaint at God's apparent indifference to undeserved distress and misfortune.[117]

The problem of human suffering was thus directly suggested by the political and social conditions prevailing in the fifth century B.C. The writers in Job lived in a questioning age, and the spirit affected both those who maintained a strong faith in the "Guardian of Israel," of whom it was felt that despite appearances to the contrary He "neither slumbers nor sleeps" (Psalm 121, 3), and those whose questioning went beyond prescribed limits. A struggle between accepted beliefs and their apparent incompatibility to explain the facts—the fate of the people and the fate of individuals—was inevitable. It is from this point of view that we must judge the attitude towards life reflected in the original Book of Job. The skepticism of the writers is revealed not merely in raising the problem of human suffering; but even more in the abandonment of the problem at the close of the Symposium as an apparently hopeless conundrum. The individual aspect of the problem was inseparable from the larger national point of view and is to be regarded as an outcome of the general feeling of depression that set in in the post-exilic period and became accentuated with each succeeding century.

---

[116] See especially chapters 42, 44, 49 and 53.
[117] Above, p. 36.

THE BOOK OF JOB

III

INDIVIDUALISM IN RELIGION

While Israel, the suffering servant of Yahweh, and Job the suffering individual are merely two aspects of one and the same problem, the significant feature of the philosophy in the Book of Job lies, however, in the application of the problem to the individual. The Book of Job thus transports us to an age in which religion was no longer exclusively an affair of the group, as is the case everywhere in early stages of culture and which survives as the underlying theory of the cult even in advanced civilizations of antiquity. As long as Yahweh was merely the national protector of the Hebrews, the individual's share in religion was as a member of the group. With the enlarged conception of Yahweh as an ethical force in the regulation of the life of the group, the sense of individual responsibility begins to assert itself.

We observe this new relationship of the individual to Yahweh for the first time in the days of Jeremiah and Ezekiel; that is, at the time of the extinction of the political independence of the ancient Hebrews. When the final catastrophe came, in 586 B.C., the people, drawing the lesson from the teachings of the earlier prophets, concluded that the punishment sent upon them was because of the sins of their forefathers which the prophets for a century and a half had denounced. Yahweh was primarily the god of the people as a national unit. The merits of individuals counted for little as against the disloyalty to

THE BOOK OF JOB

the national protector. But the sins of the past were now atoned for by the national misfortune that had overtaken the Hebrews, and hence Jeremiah announces the institution of a new covenant between Yahweh and the "House of Israel" which was to be marked by individual responsibility.

"In those days they shall no more say:
> The fathers have eaten sour grapes
> And the children's teeth are set on edge,

but everyone shall die for his own iniquity; every man that eats sour grapes *his* teeth shall be set on edge." (31, 29-30.)

Ezekiel, writing during the exilic period, is even more explicit and takes the proverbial saying quoted by Jeremiah, as the text for a sermon (chapter 18) on this new doctrine of the individual relationship to Yahweh. No longer will the people be able to lay the flattering unction to their souls, should misfortunes again come, that they are making atonement for the wrongs committed by a former generation. Not only will each generation be punished or rewarded according to its record, but each individual will be judged on his own merits. Correspondingly, the merits of the fathers will not benefit the children. "The soul that sins, it shall die," [118] irrespective of whether the father is righteous or wicked; nor will the righteous son of a wicked father suffer for the transgressions of his parent. This doctrine, passes far beyond the pre-exilic teaching of a "jealous" Yahweh who "visits the iniquity of the fathers upon the children of the third and fourth

---
[118] Ezekiel 18, 20.

THE BOOK OF JOB

generation," [119] as it also discards the correlative of a Yahweh showing mercy to those who are faithful even to the thousandth generation. To emphasize the new doctrine Ezekiel introduces Noah, Daniel and Job as models of piety,[120] and declares that the merits of these men will deliver only their own souls.

The new doctrine not only found room for the inclusion of individual requests to be brought before Yahweh, but placed these requests on the same plane as appeals on behalf of the group. The witness of Yahweh's providence was no longer confined to success in arms or to the blessings of the field which affected the whole people, but in His response to the needs of individuals. Correspondingly, Divine anger directed its blows at the guilty alone, but the new relationship thus evolved, which became the very foundation stone of post-exilic Judaism, led to the problem which is the central theme in the Book of Job. If what the prophets taught was correct then indeed the question became pressing—why should the innocent man suffer? The new doctrine grew in strength as the national Yahweh shades over into the universal Jehovah, who guides the destinies of individuals as well as nations. The thought of making the experiences of a single man the acid test for the prevailing theory on which religion rested is, therefore, to be taken as indicative of an age in which the realization of religion as not only the affair of the group but the concern of the individual as well is almost complete—almost, for it required the final

---
[119] Exodus 20, 5; Deuteronomy 5, 9.
[120] See above, p. 45.

extinction of Israel's hopes as a political unit, which did not take place until the days of Roman control over Palestine, to bring about the final separation from the older view of religion interpreted in the terms of group solidarity.

In further illustration of the stress on individualism in the religious attitude as unfolded in the original Book of Job, it should be pointed out that for the author of the Book of Job, God is shorn of all nationalistic limitations. He does not write as a nationalistic Jew, as little as does Koheleth. There is nothing indeed throughout the Symposium to suggest a Jewish atmosphere, except the fact that the writers are protesting against the current conception, peculiar to Judaism. They avoid, as we have seen, the specific Hebraic name Yahweh for the Deity and prefer general designations like Elohim or El. The Book of Job is thus from its conception, as Carlyle called it, an "all man's book"—and not a specifically Jewish one. The writers were probably not particularly interested in Judaism, just as Koheleth is indifferent to the religion of his forefathers. They are absorbed by the problem with which they deal—independent thinkers, approaching their theories from an intellectually and broadly humanitarian point of view.

IV
THE DEFECTS IN JOB'S PHILOSOPHY

But the original Book of Job in thus demonstrating the difficulties involved in explaining things as they are in this world on the basis of conventional

THE BOOK OF JOB

beliefs also reveals the weakness of the book, for Job protests without furnishing a substitute for the faith which he declares that he is unable to accept as his own. He who questions should feel the obligation to answer the question that he raises; and if he stops short at merely showing the insufficiency of the current answers to the question—what to do with one's life—he must be prepared to find others taking up the task at the point where he left it. Only occasionally—notably at the close of the nineteenth chapter—is the faint hope held out that there is a way out of the darkness, but this goes no further than to suggest that in the distant future some one will arise who will do justice to the innocent sufferer. But how? Merely by showing that Job was right in his protestation of his innocence, and that the friends were wrong in trying to force the confession from his lips that he had sinned and invited his punishment. This hope does not suffice to dispel the darkness in which man is condemned to pass through life, unable to discover the guidance of a just and merciful Providence.

While in thus interpreting the philosophy of Job, it is no part of our task to refute it, yet it is not difficult to discover the weakness of Job's position. In the first place, the writers do not give the friends who are supposed to represent the orthodox contention the opportunity to enlarge upon the factor of faith—strong faith in the justice and mercy of God despite appearances to the contrary. That faith constitutes the support of the psalmist, when tempted to yield to despair. It gives the psalmist the courage

THE BOOK OF JOB

to make his appeal even with the enemies encompassing him with no apparent chance of escape:

"Keep me as the apple of the eye;
Hide me in the shadow of Thy wings." (17, 8.)

There is little of this in the speeches of the friends—an occasional allusion here and there. Eliphaz in his first speech touches upon the theme, but only superficially:

"Out of six dangers He will deliver thee;
And at the seventh will not permit evil to harm thee." (5, 19.)

Bildad urges the appeal to God, because

"Forsooth, God will not reject the upright;
Nor does He strengthen the hand of evildoers." (8, 20.)

And Zophar echoes this assurance (11, 13-18), though always coupled with the assumption that Job is guilty and needs Divine forgiveness. The argument that faith enables one to endure in patience is illustrated in the folktale of Job, but it is not pressed home in the speeches of the friends. The reason is obvious. Consciously—or possibly unconsciously—the writers in Job lay the sole emphasis on the incompatibility of the position assumed by the friends with the facts of experience. They wish to prove by the example of Job that there *is* evil in a world supposed to be created by a Power of Good. The whole book is directed towards this aim. It is difficult for those thus bent on pressing a single point of view to see the other side as strongly and as clearly as they do their own. In other words, the Symposium reveals throughout a *Tendenz*, to use the expressive German term. It begins with a theory and ends with a *quod erat demonstrandum.* Secondly, this same one-sidedness prevents the writers from bringing forward in the arguments of the friends the theory of punishment as a test. Again, we note that while the folktale hinges around this point of view which is a strong weapon that can be wielded with effect in supporting the contention that God is just, even though there be innocent suffering, in the Symposium there is only one clear reference to such a theory, when Eliphaz is made to exclaim:

"Happy the man whom God reproves;
The chastisement of Shaddai one must not reject." (5, 17.)

Neither Bildad nor Zophar bring it forward. Furthermore, the central theme is not dealt with exhaustively in the Symposium, but solely with the object of showing the insufficiency of the conventional view of the relationship of God to man. There is, therefore, a genuine justification for the two appendices that were added to the book, even though this was done in the interest of orthodoxy, which to be sure likewise started with a theory. The argument *was* defective, and it was natural in an age which did not have the sense of unit composition in literary work, that others should arise to try their hand at finding a solution for the problem that the Symposium had left in so unsatisfactory a condition.

V

THE ATTITUDE TOWARDS THE PROBLEM OF EVIL IN THE SPEECHES OF ELIHU

If we have satisfactorily shown that by the application of the critical method we can penetrate into the philosophy of the original book as it grew

THE BOOK OF JOB

under the hands of writers who all emanated from the circle of independent inquiry among the Jews of post-exilic days, and can determine its relationship to the social and political conditions prevailing in Palestine during the close of the fifth century and in the fourth century B. C. when it took shape, we should now be able to put the method to a further test by finding in the two large appendices to the book, namely, the four speeches of Elihu and the collection of eight nature poems, the corrective proposed for the unorthodox teachings of the original book.

That is indeed the case, and since we have already had occasion to touch on the contrast between the original book and the two appendices, we can content ourselves with a brief summary of the manner in which the attempt is made to reach a definite solution of the problem which continued to arouse the interest of both orthodox and unorthodox circles. A main contribution is made in the first speech of Elihu (chapter 33) in which the new thought is put forward that trials and sufferings are warnings sent to man, of the same order as revelations in night visions. Man, even though not conscious of wrongdoing, is in danger of yielding to a sense of self-satisfaction. The virtuous man may develop a pride that is itself sinful. He may not actually have entered upon the path of wrongdoing, but he is always in danger of swerving from the right road, perhaps by an overweening sense of his moral strength; and so sickness and other sorrows are sent to him to recall him to himself before it is too late. Such a man, if he recognizes the warning, will pass safely through tribulations and come out stronger in spirit than before. He will, when properly chastened by suffering, make his appeal and his confession, and again be found worthy of God's grace:

"Behold all this God does,
 Twice and thrice with a man;
 To keep his soul from the pit,
 To enjoy light in the land of the living." (33, 29-30.)

Thus the new thought is summed up, perhaps by a later commentator,[121] and to which there is no further contribution in the second speech (chapter 34). Indeed, this second discourse is in reality a relapse into the method followed by the friends in the Symposium. It is on a decidedly lower plane than the first.

In the third speech we are introduced to a new thought. Since man's deeds—good or bad—affect him alone, and God is neither benefited by the virtues of the good, nor injured by the sins of the wicked, man and not God should be held responsible for the ills that befall one. It is proper to appeal to God for help, but not with the thought that the misfortune has come from God. God's deeds are to be seen in the marvels of nature and in his fundamental care for the beasts of the earth and the birds of heaven. Such manifestations should give us the assurance that when sufferings come for which we cannot assign a cause, it is for some good reason if God does not hearken to one's cry for help. A strange thought—that God is not concerned with the transgressions of men and that misfortunes are not to be attributed to Him but due to human actions, either our own or those of others. The retort

---

[121] See the note to the passage.

THE BOOK OF JOB

is obvious, why does God *permit* men to inflict injuries and tortures on those who have done no wrong? Why does He not interfere to prevent innocent suffering? What satisfaction is there to be told that the blame for human sufferings is not to be ascribed to God, because sufferings come through the deeds of man? For all that, the thought is interesting, both because of its novelty and its subtlety. It anticipates in a way the solution suggested by the nature poems that we must direct our gaze to the large and comprehensive manifestations of Divine government rather than concentrate on man's needs and longings. We must look at the world through the large end of the glass, not through the small one. Man is only a part of the great universe, and an infinitesimal part at that. Why should man suppose that his happiness is the controlling motive in the Divine scheme?

"Shall for thy sake the earth be forsaken,
  And [its] Guardian be removed from His place?" (18, 4.)

asks Bildad in the same spirit which prompts Elihu to emphasize that one must refrain from asking "Where is God" (35, 10) when men commit deeds that bring suffering and misery to their fellows. Elihu recognizes that much of the suffering to which men are subject is due to human wickedness and tyranny. It *should* not be so, but one must seek the true cause, and not attribute it to God's will or His direct interference in the course of events. The argument is a protest against a too literal interpretation of the prophet's view of God as a Power making for righteousness, and which involves us in the dilemma out of which Job cannot extricate himself. The argument of Elihu would fit in better with religions of the older type in which the gods are represented as concerned with the group, whereas post-exilic Judaism clearly stresses the relation of the individual to the Deity by the side of His concern for the national weal. It is interesting, however, to see this thought brought forward by the defenders of orthodoxy; and from various points of view its force is apparent. To be sure, the argument loses sight of the fact that Job's case is a particularly flagrant one because he is portrayed in the folktale as quite the exceptional man. Elihu, however, who is concerned with the general problem can afford to ignore exceptional circumstances. He is bent upon showing that God who is supremely just cannot be the author of wrong and injustice. In order to press this truth home, he calls upon believers to concentrate on the general course of events in this world which reveal a guiding hand.

The fourth speech (chapter 36) again follows along the lines of the first and is in fact almost a replica of it, beginning by the repeated assurance that

"God does not permit the wicked to flourish,
And He judges the cause of the afflicted." (36, 6.)

and that if sorrows and sufferings come apparently unmerited, it is in order to warn men against haughtiness and to keep them from evil ways:

"He opens their ear to discipline,
And tells [them] to return from iniquity." (36, 10.)

The only additional thought in the chapter, following as a corollary from the general position taken in regard to suffering viewed as a warning and discipline, is that those who do not note the warning assume that God is arbitrary and hostile to man, as Job does in the Symposium. They are the impious ones, but even when such men are afflicted it is done in the hope that their ears will be opened and that they will recognize the iniquity of their charges against God.

The speeches of Elihu thus constitute a series of further answers to the problem with which Job wrestles and which the original book leaves in suspense. While from the literary point of view this appendix is inferior to the Symposium, the introductions being prolix and the language far less poetical, though fine passages are interspersed here and there, the speeches serve the purpose for which they were added, to present the case for the current beliefs in a stronger light. With no Job to answer Elihu, the very repetition of the main argument that suffering and sorrows are God's method of disciplining man to virtue and of warning him against dangers to his better nature could not fail to make a deep impression—certainly an impression strong enough to weaken that left by the Symposium.

VI

THE SOLUTION OF THE PROBLEM IN THE NATURE POEMS

We have seen that in one of the speeches of Elihu there is an anticipation of the main argument advanced through the nature poems which form the second appendix, that we are to seek God in nature rather than in the changing fortunes of men. It is

THE BOOK OF JOB

this thought that leads to the insertion of a poem,[122] descriptive of God's majesty as seen in a storm. For beauty and force the poem has few equals in the world's literature. The poet pictures the impression made upon him by the downpour of rain, by the roll of the thunder and the flashes of lightning.

"At this my heart indeed trembles,
And is moved out of its place." (37, 1.)

The animals seeking refuge and men ceasing their activities during the storm and cold blasts from the North are pictured in most eloquent language, and equally beautiful is the passing of the storm and the return of the sunshine as the clouds recede.

The poem forms the transition to a fragment on the wonders of creation (37, 14-20) and to the collection of nature poems in which a magnificent panorama of God's creation of the world, of His regulation of the movements in the heavens and the variety and character of animal life is unrolled before us. The little anthology teaches its own lesson—that in the face of these witnesses to God's power and forethought, man is forced to silent adoration. With this evidence before us of a great Force present in nature, how can there be any further doubts of a directing helm also in the lives of men? And if this assurance is not sufficient, what hope is there that the tiny human intellect can by mere discussion penetrate into a mind of such infinite magnitude?

The four chapters containing the nature poems furnish the final answer of orthodox circles to Job's questionings. Man should desist from the effort of

---
[122] 36, 24–37, 12. See above p. 79, and the translation, placed after Chapter 36.

THE BOOK OF JOB

trying to understand God's mysterious ways. Job's confession in the second epilogue:

"What I did not understand, I uttered;
Things far beyond me of which I had no knowledge." (42, 3ᵇ.)

is put forward as the appropriate attitude in the contemplation of God in nature. What can man know of God? He can merely see the workings of the Infinite and must rest content with a faith aroused in him by such witnesses. The confession forms the corollary to the ecstasy of the psalmist when he asks:

"When I behold Thy heaven, the work of Thy fingers,
The moon and the stars which Thou hast established;
What is man that Thou art mindful of him
And the son of man that Thou thinkest of him?" (Ps. 8, 4-5.)

What arrogance, then, for puny man to measure his intellect with the Infinite mind?

It is not too much to say that the nature poems rise superior by the nobility of their diction and by the force of the descriptions even to the Symposium itself. They are a tribute to the grasp which the conception of God, as developed under the ethical teachings of the prophets, had obtained on the religious minds of post-exilic days. A religious fervor that could produce a group of poets capable of such flights as we encounter in the closing chapters of the book bears eloquent testimony to the complete success of the movement inaugurated by Amos, Hosea, Micah and Isaiah in the eight century, which led to such a striking advance in religious thought. These chapters, besides their value in furnishing the only satisfactory answer to Job's problem that can give some comfort to souls troubled because they feel so

THE BOOK OF JOB

keenly the tragedy of human suffering, also furnish the explanation for the persistence of the religious faith of which they are an exponent. They account for the further products of that faith in giving rise to other great religious systems—Christianity and Islam based on the same spiritualized conception of Divine government of the universe. The critical method thus leads us to an estimate of the Book of Job which, while it discards the traditional interpretation in frankly recognizing the original book as a skeptical production, yet in another sense reinforces tradition by showing that through the second and the third strata the book was actually changed into as strong a bulwark of religious faith as was possible in an age which had not yet evolved the doctrine of retribution in a future world as a compensation for the sufferings in this one. That doctrine when it arose was destined to strengthen man's faith in what cannot be solved by the processes of reasoning and in which faith man, driven by the questioning spirit into an unceasing search, must ultimately rest content.

VII

THE NEW DOCTRINE OF RETRIBUTION IN A FUTURE WORLD

One wonders if the original Book of Job had been written several centuries later, say about 100 B. C., what the attitude of the circle of free inquiry would have been towards the new doctrine of life after death which by that time had taken a firm hold on pious minds, particularly in Pharisaic circles, and according

THE BOOK OF JOB

to which there was a distinction between the ultimate fate of the virtuous and the wicked. A blessed hereafter was in store for the righteous who had followed in the path mapped out by post-exilic Judaism, which had developed a high system of ethics for guidance by the side of an ever-increasing regard for ceremonial niceties in the ritual and in private devotions. Instead of a common gathering place for the dead in which all without distinction were huddled together, conscious but doomed to perpetual inactivity in the cheerless Sheol where one could not even praise Yahweh, a distinction was made between the abode of the righteous and of those who had led wicked lives. [123] As a corollary, the belief in a resurrection of the dead had also begun to take definite shape. It is foreshadowed in the last chapter of the Book of Daniel which dates from the middle of the second century B. C. and in which the awakening of the dead from their sleep "some to everlasting life and some to shame and everlasting abhorrence" (12, 3) is predicted, though the passage may be a somewhat later interpolation. Closely entwined with this new hope held out for the pious members of the community was the dream of a resurrection for Israel, the nation, in a blessed future when the Messianic kingdom would be established. The picture of a heavenly Jerusalem by the side of the earthly one as the center of this kingdom leads to the further step of an eternal abode of the righteous in a heavenly Paradise, while Sheol becomes the "Valley of Abomi-

---

[123] See the elaborate description in the so-called Ethiopic Book of Enoch dating from about 170 B.C. of which Charles, *Eschatology; Hebrew Jewish and Christian* (London, 1899); pp. 184 *et seq.* gives a synopsis.

THE BOOK OF JOB

nation"—the Gehenna [124]—as a place of punishment for the wicked.

It is significant that even in the two appendices attached to the Book of Job there is not the slightest suggestion of a solution of the problem of evil and innocent suffering by holding up a future world of bliss and perfection as a compensation for the sufferings and injustices prevailing in this one. The new doctrine, replacing the older view common to all Semites of one general gathering place, was slow in making its way. There are hints of a more cheerful and more spiritualistic outlook on death in some late Psalms,[125] but even a pious writer of the first quarter of the second century B. C., Jesus Ben Sira, still clings to the older view. This is shown by the numerous references to death in his collection of sayings, all marked by the absence of any thought of retribution beyond the grave.[126] Sheol is for him still the general gathering place where there is no "Thanksgiving," where the dead are plunged in an eternal sleep, and deprived of all delights.

The rise of a higher conception of life after death, while following as a logical corollary from the teachings of the post-exilic Hebrew prophets, since a Power of universal scope, enthroned in justice, could not be supposed to limit His rule to the living, may also be viewed as resulting from the triumph of the

---

[124] Originally *Gê Hinnom* "Valley of Hinnom" outside of Jerusalem, associated in Hebrew traditions with objectionable religious rites.

[125] Psalms 49, 14–15; 73, 24. See the full discussion of the subject by Cheyne, *Origin and Religious Content of the Psalter*, pp. 381–409, who is inclined to stress the influence of Zoroastrianism in bringing about the appearance of the new doctrine.

[126] See, *e.g.*, Ecclesiasticus 14, 16; 17, 8; 22, 11.

THE BOOK OF JOB

skeptical trend in the original Book of Job. Postexilic Judaism, confronted with the disappointment of national hopes and facing the evidence of innocent suffering and prevalent evil in this world, was forced to confess that the circle from which the original Book of Job emanated was justified in its position that the problem was incapable of a satisfactory solution by processes of reasoning. Job was indeed "justified," as was said at the close of the Symposium (32, 1). The faith preached by the nature poems needed a more convincing witness than the majesty of nature and the evidence of extraordinary strength in the animal world. A compensation in a future of perfect bliss and justice to comfort one for the sufferings and injustice in this one offered a much stronger support for faith than the mere contemplation of God's power in nature. The power of God and even His foresight did not suffice to strengthen one's faith. Mercy, justice and love were required; and these were furnished by the new doctrine of a retribution in a future world that would be free from the imperfections of the present one. Hence the attempt of the pious commentators, acting under the influence of the new doctrine, to change a crucial passage like Job 19, 25-27 [127] into conformity with the assurance of a blissful reward of the virtuous and innocent for hardships endured in this life, and of eternal punishment of the wicked who had escaped it while alive. By applying the *goël* as the "vindicator" to God himself, and by giving a different turn to certain phrases, though at the expense of grammatical

---
[127] Above, p. 124 *seq.*

consistency, Job was made to anticipate by several centuries the belief in a future retribution to which he would be a witness "in his own flesh."

"I know that my Redeemer liveth"

became the motto of the philosophical poem in its *traditional* interpretation, and in the face of the many contradictory utterances put into the mouth of Job by the members of the circle of free inquiry that produced the original book.

While one may question whether the successors of this circle in the first century B. C. would have accepted the new doctrine (as the Sadducees refused to accept it), it must be admitted that the philosophy of the Book of Job would have been considerably strengthened by either its acceptance or by its rejection on good grounds. It is perhaps the most serious weakness of the skeptical trend of the original Book of Job that it thus fails—because produced at too early a date—to take into account a solution which when it did arise was strong enough to overcome doubt among Jews, Christians and Mohammedans alike. The doctrine of future retribution was further developed until it became as integral a part of these religious systems as the belief in a spiritual Power of universal rule.

VIII

THE LITERARY FORM OF JOB—A SYMPOSIUM NOT A DRAMA

With the Book of Job thus consisting of three distinct strata, each representing a composite growth, the unity given to the book by the final group of editors

THE BOOK OF JOB

is purely on the surface. These editors welded the three strata together and embodied the hundreds of comments, glosses, additional lines, popular maxims, and reflections of pious commentators into the text as though forming genuine ingredients; but even by accepting the many intentional changes to tone down the sharpness of Job's utterances and the confusing arrangement of speeches in order to put orthodox sentiments into the mouth of Job, no genuine unity could be obtained. There is no inherent unity in the completed Book of Job if we accept the results of a critical analysis, any more than there is such a unity in the Pentateuch, composed of several documents enclosed in a framework of laws of gradual growth with all kinds of comments, additions and illustrative instances.

The question, therefore, that is often raised whether Job is a drama is almost irrelevant, since a drama implies an inherent unity in its composition. The situation in the folktale of Job is, to be sure, dramatic, but the same applies to the romantic story of Joseph in Genesis and to many incidents in the historical books of the Bible, as *e. g.*, Saul's visit to the Witch of Endor, to David's encounters with Saul or Nathan's appearance before Solomon. The story of Ruth is dramatic as is the tale of Esther, but neither is for that reason a drama; they belong in the category of the romantic novel written as political and religious propaganda, not unlike the modern novel "with a purpose." The story of Job has dramatic possibilities, as have dozens of tales woven into Biblical narratives. Job can be made into a drama but the circumstance that the story, as we have seen, is to be separated from the original Symposium, and this again from the two appendices precludes the possibility of interpreting even the apparent unity given to the book in its final form as a dramatic composition. The drama is foreign to the ancient Hebrew spirit. Nor is it encountered in the old civilizations of the East. The drama is the outcome of individual authorship, whereas, as we have seen, the methods of literary composition in the ancient Orient tend to place the author in the background. Where we find the drama in the Orient as among the Hindus, it is late and may be due to outside influences. [128] At all events, it is not accidental that the Greeks among whom we first encounter individual authorship are also the ones who gave to the world the drama in the real sense of the term, as a distinct subdivision of literature.

The unity of the Book of Job even in its final form does not go further than the attempt to connect the three strata by editorial headings attached to the chapters, and by occasional editorial comments and by additions to gloss over discrepancies in the various strata of which the book consists. The main concern of the final editors, indeed their *only* concern, was to present the book as a support for the current orthodoxy. The thought of regarding the completed book as a progressive and systematically constructed dramatic composition could not have entered the

---

[128] Some Indologists like Weber and Windisch were inclined to ascribe the Sanskrit drama, which does not make its appearance till the first century of our era, to contact with the Greeks, but this view has now been abandoned. See Macdonnell, *Sanskrit Literature*, p. 416.

THE BOOK OF JOB

mind of the final editors, for the sufficient reason that as Orientals they were under the sway of the oriental method of composition as a gradual growth. If we wish to specify the literary character of the book more precisely than by designating it as a composite philosophical poem, we may call it a composite Symposium, but never a drama.

All efforts to present the Book of Job as a drama rest on the assumption now shown to be erroneous that the book is a literary unit. This applies to the two recent attempts by Prof. R. G. Moulton [129] and by Dr. H. M. Kallen, [130] as it does to all earlier ones. Prof. Moulton does not go so far as to divide the book into acts and scenes as did Theodor Beza as far back as 1587, but he does assume *dramatis personae* and introduces "asides" and other stage directions in his division of the book into fifty continuous sections instead of into chapters. Now all this is as foreign to the whole character of the book as possible. Quite apart from the total lack of evidence that the Jews of post-exilic days, even after they had come under Greek influence, ever developed the drama as a species of literary composition, we fail to penetrate into the spirit of Job by regarding it as a composition, logically and progressively unfolding a theme as is demanded by the canons of dramatic composition. The point is that the Book of Job consists of a foundation on which a number of independent super-structures have been erected. There is no logical development of a theme, but merely a series of discussions of

---
[129] *The Book of Job* in the "Modern Reader's Bible" (New York, 1896).
[130] *The Book of Job as a Greek Tragedy* (New York, 1918).

one and the same theme from various angles. All attempts, therefore, to distinguish in the book a progressive series of solutions for the mystery of suffering,[131] corresponding in a measure to the successive acts of a drama, are doomed to failure. Even in the original Book of Job there is no such progressive evolution to be noted as a dramatic composition assumes. The speeches are not in the nature of logical replies, answering point for point and opposing argument by counter argument. There are only four distinct points brought forward by the three friends [132] and these are emphasized by all, irrespective of Job's replies. Nor is there any progress in the setting forth of the problem as we proceed from one series of speeches to the next. In fact, it would be nearer to the truth to call one series of speeches an imitation of the other, the three series representing so many endeavors to present the same thoughts and the same arguments in different fashion. This applies also to the ten speeches of Job. In all of them he complains of his sufferings, in all he protests his innocence and in all he hurls back the rebukes which the three friends introduce in their speeches with counter accusations of lack of sympathy and with ironical or bitter retorts. Job in his replies does not specifically take into account what Eliphaz, Bildad or Zophar has said. One could take any of his speeches and transfer it to another place in the Symposium without affecting the argument. Similarly, the reply to Eliphaz's first speech would fit in just as well

---

[131] Prof. Moulton in his Introduction assumes five solutions successively brought forward.
[132] Above p. 72.

THE BOOK OF JOB

as a reply to a speech of Bildad or Zophar; and so with the other replies.

In view of all this, it is needless to enlarge upon Dr. Kallen's theory that the Book of Job as we have it, is actually based on the model of a Greek tragedy, and that the thought of writing a Jewish drama was suggested to a Jewish writer by having witnessed a production of a play of Euripides in some Greek city. Prof. Moulton does not go quite so far and contents himself with describing Job as "Wisdom Literature Dramatized," whereas Dr. Kallen regards the book as it stands written as a drama, not only with acts and scenes of action—although there is no action in any proper sense—but with a chorus and semi-chorus and a *Deus ex machina* introduced towards the close, just as in a drama of Euripides. But in order to get a "drama" out of Job, Kallen takes portions of speeches of Job and arbitrarily assigns them to a purely hypothetical chorus and semi-chorus. Yahweh speaking out of the whirlwind corresponds, according to Dr. Kallen, to the appearance of the Deity in a Greek play.[133] to pronounce a final verdict or to unravel the problem of the play. All this is ingenious but entirely beside the mark. The theory misconceives the entire spirit of the book both in its original and in its enlarged form. Job as a drama is devoid of meaning. Job as a series of discussions of a vital religious problem grad-

---

[133] In order to carry out his theory, Dr. Kallen is obliged to offer a translation for a verb in the epilogue 42, 6 for which there is no warrant; and other liberties are taken by Dr. Kallen in a reconstruction which is not based on a *critical* study of the text. Dr. Kallen follows the conventional Authorized Version without apparently realizing that hundreds of passages are now differently rendered by modern scholars on the basis of critical researches.

THE BOOK OF JOB

ually taking shape under many hands with the problem viewed from various angles—unorthodox and orthodox—is full of significance. Such a composite production is precisely what we should expect to find issuing out of the intellectual and religious atmosphere prevailing in Palestine from the close of the fifth century B. C. and continuing to the threshold of the Christian era.

If there is any influence of Greek literary models to be sought in Job it lies in the Greek Symposium as a medium for the discussion of philosophic theories—always involving religious beliefs—which becomes through Plato such a characteristic division of Greek literature. But even this hypothesis is entirely unnecessary, since we can account for the book without it. At the same time, if we could bring down the date of the original Book of Job to as late a period as the close of the fourth century B. C. when Greek influence even of a literary character could be assumed to have penetrated into Palestine, there would be nothing inherently improbable in the conjecture that the Symposium in Job was suggested by the Greek dialogue.[134] We have seen, however, that we need not go further down than the end of the fifth century to account for the rise of an independent group of thinkers among the Jews, free enough from conventional views to seek an answer for the mystery of innocent suffering in a world created by a Power conceived of as just and merciful.

---

[134] It should be remembered, however, that we have the dialogue in ancient Babylonian Literature. See a specimen in a German translation by Ebbeling (*Mitteilungen Der Deutsch Orientgesellschaft*, No. 58, pp. 35–38.)

THE BOOK OF JOB

If we could discover traces of Greek philosophical thought and speculation in any part of Job, one could more readily admit Greek influence, but though some scholars incline to see in the skeptical trend of the original book the reaction of the freedom of the Greek mind in boldly investigating in a rationalistic spirit the phenomena of nature and of human experiences, it must be confessed that the evidence is not satisfactory. It is certainly not decisive, just as the endeavor to see in the philosophy of Koheleth the influence of the Stoic attitude or of Epicurean thought is futile. [135] Perhaps in a very general way one may conjecture that a wave of rationalism spread over the ancient Orient in the fifth and succeeding centuries which would account for the rise of such a remarkable religious system as Zoroastrianism. [136] Intellectual currents having their rise in Greece may possibly have flowed eastwards even before the Greek armies of Alexander brought about a free interchange between Orient and Occident that was destined to be fraught with such significant results. In this way we may help to account for the strength which free thought, untrammelled by piety or tradition, must have acquired in Palestine before circles could have arisen bold enough to challenge generally accepted beliefs.

IX

ZOROASTRIANISM AND THE BOOK OF JOB

The mention of the new religious system which arose in Persia in the sixth century and became the

---

[135] See *A Gentle Cynic*, p. 147 *seq.*
[136] Or more correctly Zarathushtrianism, since the founder's name is Zarathushtra, of which Zoroaster is a corrupt form.

THE BOOK OF JOB

official religion during the reign of Darius I (522-486 B. C.) suggests a brief inquiry as to the possible influence of the main doctrine of Zoroastrianism, resting on a dualistic division of government of the universe on the attitude towards evil in the original Book of Job. The suggestion has frequently been made [137] that the figure of Satan in the prologue has some affinities with Ahriman of Zoroastrianism who is held responsible for the existence of evil in this world created by Ahuramazda, a beneficent Power, possessed of all attributes except that of omnipotence, which is limited by his lack of control over Ahriman, the independent power of evil. Ahuramazda is all-good, all-wise, all-just and all-merciful, but he is engaged in a constant struggle with Ahriman, and not till he overcomes the evil power, which will be after the lapse of aeons, will Ahuramazda also become the all-powerful.

It is indeed conceivable that this interesting and suggestive doctrine which thus proposed to solve the problem of how evil came into the world should have been a contributing factor in bringing the central theme in the Book of Job to the front. The Jews came into close contact with Zoroastrianism during the Persian control of the East which stretched from the Euphrates to the Nile; and it is widely held by scholars that the emphasis in one of the orations included in the miscellaneous collection grouped under the name of Isaiah and dating from various periods between 720

---

[137] See Stave, *Einfluss des Parsismus auf das Judenthum* (Haarlem, 1898); also Cheyne *Origin and Religious Contents of the Psalter*. (London, 1891), pp. 394–409 for other aspects of the influence of Zoroastrianism on later Jewish doctrines, as found in certain Psalms and in other late Biblical writings. See also, above p. 55.

THE BOOK OF JOB

B. C. to circa 300 B. C., on Yahweh as the "creator of light *and* darkness" (Isaiah 45, 7) reflects the position of the strict monotheist against any division in the Divine control of the universe. Ahuramazda is the god of light in the Persian system, and Ahriman is the power of darkness. The contrast between Judaism and Zoroastrianism was thus forced upon the attention of the Jews in the fifth and succeeding centuries. The dualism of Zoroastrianism must be looked upon as the Persian attempt to find a way out of a dilemma which necessarily arises when ethical traits become the significant attributes of a Power of universal scope, just as the doctrine of the "suffering servant," explaining that injustice must be endured by Israel as a vicarious punishment for the sins of the nations, represents a Jewish solution. This point of view, though not as yet brought forward in the Book of Job, leads in its further unfolding to the Pauline doctrine of salvation for the individual—and eventually for the entire world—through the acceptance of Christ, the only and beloved Son of God, whose death on the cross was a vicarious sacrifice to redeem the world from sin, inherited from the first parents of the human race.

Beyond, however, the assumption that the spread of Zoroastrianism helped to focus the dilemma, and led to the further development of Satan from a semi-independent being in the Book of Job and in the prophecies of Zechariah into a wilful opponent of God as he appears in the full-fledged doctrine of an independent tempter, and as the cause of bringing sin into the world, we are hardly justified in going. It was

THE BOOK OF JOB

natural and, as we have seen, inevitable that the problem discussed in the Book of Job with such freedom from traditional and pietistic restraint should arise among the Jews; and it is significant that this problem of evil is one which is fundamental to all the great religious systems of the ancient world. We encounter it in as fully intensified a form in the distant East, where it leads to Buddhism which rests on the assumption that the source of all evil is the desire of life and that, therefore, the only hope of overcoming sorrow, suffering and wickedness is to free oneself from this desire. Nirvana involving, with the complete suppression of all desires, the extinction of consciousness is the logical outcome of the view taken of the cause of evil in Buddhism, as the doctrine of retribution in another world for the evils and sufferings of this one represents a logical expression of a faith which looks upon life as a bounty and a gift of Divine grace.

For the circle from which emanated the original Book of Job, the problem was, however, insoluble, since it could neither ascribe the existence of suffering and evil to any other Power except Yahweh, nor bring itself to the point of regarding life itself as an evil. Those in misery and despair should be released. (3,20.) Job longs for death merely because he suffers, but nowhere does he express the view that life itself is an evil.[138] The original book begins and ends with the question "Why." Its philosophy stops short with a cry of despair,

"Why do the wicked flourish?
Grow old and even wax mighty?" (21, 7.)

---

[138] Cf. the beautiful passage 10, 8–12 (above p. 150), descriptive of God's grace in creating man.

THE BOOK OF JOB

X

JOB AND PROMETHEUS

The spirit of the discussions in Job is genuinely Hebraic. To account for its philosophy we need not go outside of Palestine. The attitude of the circle whose views and outlook on life are reflected in the original book is an outgrowth of religious conditions peculiar to Palestine in the post-exilic period. Even the skepticism is distinctively Jewish, as can best be seen by a comparison that naturally suggests itself between Job and the Prometheus Bound of Aeschylus. [139] Prometheus like Job is a great questioner. He betrays the same rebellious spirit as Job, but the Greek dramatist approaches the subject in an entirely different manner. Prometheus defies the gods. Greek rationalism led to the view that the gods are hostile to human progress, because of the fear that intellectual advance may lead man to become independent of the gods. ' Knowledge gives man the strength to break the shackles with which man by the overpowering forces of nature is bound. Both Job and Prometheus typify the suffering to which human flesh is heir, but according to the Greek view suffering is due to man's defiance of the gods. The conception of the gods is still that of early antiquity that they represent strong but arbitrary forces. Such forces demand not only blind obedience from man, but that he should willingly submit to their tyrannous con-

---

[139] The comparison has often been instituted, *e.g.*, by Addis, *Job* (Temple Bible), p. xiv. See also for a larger treatment of the theme, Owen, *The Five Great Skeptical Dramas of History* (London, 1896) chapter II.

trol. Prometheus is the benefactor of man, but he is also a rebel toward the gods. He leads man on the road to progress, but this leadership involves an opposition to the gods. Fire, the symbol of progress, is stolen by him from heaven and against the will of the gods. Hence the tortures that follow which typify the martyrdom of man in his struggle to rise above nature.

There is a trace of this spirit among the Hebrews in the third chapter of Genesis (v. 22) where God is portrayed as begrudging man the knowledge of good and evil and expressing a fear that man may discover the tree of life and become immortal, like God Himself. The strange phrase,

"Behold man is become as one of us." (Genesis 3, 22.)

suggests a fear of advancing man on the part of the Deity, which is not unlike the jealous mood ascribed in the philosophy of Aeschylus to the gods who wish to keep man under their control. There is nothing of this spirit, however, in Job. The conflict is here between the conventional conception of a just and merciful Providence and the sad reality of innocent suffering and of all manner of injustice in this world. The setting of the problem is peculiarly Hebraic in Job, as it is characteristically Greek in the drama of Aeschylus. The skepticism in Job presupposes the development of the god idea along ethical lines. It arises from the struggle of a religious soul to reconcile his faith with the facts of experience. The writers in Job while rebellious in spirit never pass beyond the limits of faith. They merely protest that the prob-

THE BOOK OF JOB

lem with which Job wrestles cannot be solved by the conventional arguments that suffering comes as the result of wrongdoing and that those who merit punishment receive it. The last word of the popular religion of the Greeks is that the gods are strong. Their will prevails. Man must submit. Hence the inevitable conflict between religion and philosophy in Greece, which leads eventually to the overthrow of the Greek religion. The god idea of the Hebrews triumphs, despite the mental conflict and anguish to which it gives rise. Faith in a just Deity overcomes philosophic doubt, not indeed by finding a solution for the mysteries of human experience, but by a confession that man is not strong enough to penetrate the ways of gods.

This answer, to be sure, is not given by Job. It is suggested in the speech of the friends, by Eliphaz when he asks:

"Hast thou overheard the secret of God?
And hast thou monopolized wisdom?" (15, 8.)

It is hinted at by Bildad when he points out:

"For we have no knowledge of yesterday,
Since our days are a shadow upon earth." (8, 9.)

It is more directly put forward by Zophar:

"Canst thou penetrate to the essence of God?
Attain the bounds of Shaddai?" (11, 7.)

but the full force of the argument is brought to bear upon the problem by the nature poems, added for the express purpose of showing that in the presence of the evidence of God's supreme Power in nature and in the animal world, so far beyond comprehension and too mysterious to be fathomed by men, an attitude of humiliation is becoming; and this consciousness of man's puniness will lead him to take to faith as his last refuge.

This solution, in full accord with the orthodoxy defended in the two appendices, stamps the Book of Job in its final form as distinctively Hebraic, even more so than the book was in its earlier stage.

XI

THE MESSAGE OF JOB TO THE PRESENT AGE

It is not surprising, that by the verdict of poets, thinkers and critics of all lands and of every age, the Book of Job has been accorded a place quite by itself. Though misunderstood and subject to misinterpretation by the traditional view that grew up around the book, its impressiveness is independent of the view that we take of its origin and growth. Even without penetrating to its deeper meaning, the mere beauty of its diction throughout all three strata and the dignity of its stanzas, whether correctly grasped or distorted by an erroneous exegesis, suffice to make a universal appeal. Job belongs to those choice productions—few in number—that take their place outside of the environment in which they arise and become the possession of humanity at large. Like the dramas of Euripides and Aeschylus and the poems of Horace, the immortal productions of Dante and Milton, like Shakespeare's Hamlet and Goethe's Faust, the Book of Job belongs to all the ages.

As one of the earliest of attempts to deal with the most perplexing of religious problems, it has exer-

THE BOOK OF JOB

cised a profound influence on the literature of Western nations. [140] One can trace that influence in all the great poems and dramas of the Western world that deal with the tragedy of human suffering and of human wrongs, whether we turn to Dante's Divina Commedia or to Milton's Paradise Lost and Regained, to Shakespeare's Hamlet or to Goethe's Faust. The philosophy of Job has colored the thought of the greatest thinkers from Spinoza and the English Deists down to Schopenhauer and Nietzsche. Optimists and pessimists alike have made their appeal to Job and have found in the book a confirmation of their views or a support for their outlook on life. Above all it has been a source of consolation to troubled souls, bowed down by grief and sorrow, though—one must sadly confess—the solace has generally been based on passages that have been misunderstood and in some cases wilfully distorted by an uncritical tradition. Can it still render that service when read and interpreted in the light of modern criticism, or must we limit ourselves to an appreciation of Job as a literary masterpiece?

The answer depends upon the mood in which we approach it. If we are willing to regard the Symposium as a portrayal of an inner struggle which all must face who experience grief and disappointment, we can, while recognizing that the original book offers no solution for the problem which forms the central theme, derive a strengthening of our faith in the ul-

---

[140] See, *e.g.*, the many indications of this influence in English writers from Langland and Chaucer to Browning and Longfellow given by W. E. Addis in his edition of Job in the *Temple Bible*, pp. 143–152.

THE BOOK OF JOB

timate triumph of right and justice from the evidence furnished in the nature poems that there *is* design in this world, even though man cannot fathom the mystery of his own life—which involves suffering without apparent justification, as well as guilt which goes unpunished. We may accept the implication of the original book that the problem is insoluble, and yet conquer our skepticism by a realization that human life is no more mysterious than the mystery in the regular order of the phenomena of the heavens. The writers of the nature poems have an inkling of the struggle for existence which is a part of the natural law. They suggest that, since the struggle leads to the preservation of life and to the development of strength, our gaze should be directed towards the *outcome* of the struggle as a proof of higher design, rather than on the struggle itself.

The late Prof. Genung many years ago called the Book of Job "An Epic of the Inner Life."[141] If we make allowance for his futile attempt to find a *progressive* treatment of the central theme in Job in dramatic form, due to his still being under the sway of the supposed literary unity of the composition, the designation may be accepted as a particularly happy one. The sympathetic portrayal of the inner struggle of a troubled soul makes its appeal as strongly today as it did when it received its definite shape over 2,000 years ago. That is the human side of the book. In the same way, the overcoming of this struggle by a su-

---
[141] The title of his translation of Job, published in 1891, to which he prefixes an introductory essay of great charm and of sympathetic insight into the spirit of the Book of Job, even though much in the book is now antiquated and his general conception of Job is untenable.

preme effort of faith to rise superior to it through the concentration of our thought on the larger manifestations of mysterious forces at work in the universe can still find a response even in our days, dominated by a scientific spirit which seeks for law in nature and in the life of man, rather than for the expression of a Divine will. That is the spiritual side of the book, which comes to remind us that the discovery of law does not solve the mystery involved in the existence of the law.

The Symposium, with its abandonment of the problem as one incapable of solution through the processes of reasoning, and the nature poems with their insistence upon humble faith in a Divine will (of which nature furnishes the evidence) as the only solution of the problem—both have their message for us of the present day. The arguments of the three friends, as the two new thoughts contributed by Elihu, have merely a transitory value. They are attempts to solve the problem which have no more force than the many other endeavors that have since been made in philosophical systems and in theological discussions, to pierce a mystery that is genuinely beyond human comprehension, but which, despite his failures, man is impelled by a hidden spring in his nature to persist in attacking.

Ruskin [142] with remarkable insight recognized that the principal lesson to be taught by the Book of Job is "the holy and humbling influence of natural science on the human heart." He clearly had in

---

[142] In his *Stones of Venice*, Chapter II, § 32.

THE BOOK OF JOB

mind the great nature poems at the close of the book when he gave this striking verdict.

If a great scientist of our time—the late DuBois-Reymond—could utter as the final word of a life devoted to the quest of truth, "Ignoramus, Ignorabimus," [143] what is that except expressing in different language the final word in the immortal Book of Job that faith in the presence of unfathomable mystery is the only secure foundation on which we can build our lives?

Such faith rises superior to argument and speculation, because it realizes that the highest truth accessible to man is never a solid that can be grasped, but an atmosphere to be breathed.

---

[143] *Ueber die Grenzen des Naturerkennens.* (Sixth edition. Leipzig, 1884). p. 46.

PART II

*THE BOOK OF JOB
A NEW TRANSLATION*

EXPLANATORY NOTE:—In order to avoid the cumbersome use of more than two figures in the consecutive enumeration of the notes to the translation, it has seemed preferable to group them in separate series, each series running from 1 to 99.

In referring to the notes it will, therefore, be necessary to indicate the page with the number of the note.

Verses that represent later amplifications of the text are placed in brackets; and such verses or lines or parts of lines that are clearly interpolated, interrupting the context, or that represent variants or comments to the text are given in connection with the notes. In some cases where there is a doubt as to the exact character of the addition to the text, preference has been given to placing the addition within the text, but enclosed in brackets.

All words or parts of lines, to be recognized as "superfluous" by the principles laid down in the study of the book (chapters III and IV) are likewise relegated to the notes.

To facilitate comparison with the original text and with other translations of the Book of Job, every fifth verse is noted on the margin; and in case of the omission of an entire verse or verses, the number of the verse preceding and that following the omission is likewise noted on the margin.

Words added in the translation and that are not in the original are placed in brackets. All deviations from the original in the revised text on which my translation is based are indicated in the notes.

The abbreviation AV means the authorized (or King James) version of the Bible (1611); RV is the revised version of 1885. Special attention is called to the divergence in the enumeration of the verses in Chapters 40 and 41 in the AV and RV, (as well as in other English translations dependent upon these) from the enumeration in the Hebrew text. The first poem on the crocodile is in the Hebrew Text 40, 25–41, 4, whereas in the AV and RV the enumeration is 41, 1–12; in the second poem 41, 5–13 of the Hebrew Text = 41, 13–21 of AV and RV; and in the third poem 41, 14–26 = 41, 22–34 of AV and RV.

I

THE STORY OF JOB

(Chapters 1 and 2)

There was a man in the land of Uz [1] whose name 1, 1 was Job; and that man was pious and upright,[2] God-fearing and removed from evil;[3] and seven sons and three daughters were born unto him. His possessions were seven thousand sheep and three thousand camels, and five hundred yoke of oxen, and five hundred she-asses and a very great household;[4] so that the man was greater than any of the sons of the East.[5]

---

[1] There can be no doubt that the author places the home of Job in northern Arabia, however we are to explain the name Uz. From the three occurrences of the name in genealogical lists Gen. 10, 23 (P. document); 22, 21 (J. document) 36, 28 (P. document) as well as from Lamentations 4, 21 where "dweller of the land of Uz" appears in parallelism to "daughter of Edom," we may further specify that Uz is a district or section of Edom.

[2] Literally "perfect and straight," but the "perfection" intended, as the following synonymous expressions show, had reference to Job's piety and the upright life that he had led.

[3] "God-fearing," used of Abraham (Gen. 22, 12 J. Document) and frequently in Psalms and Proverbs. "Removed from evil" is found in Proverbs 14, 16.

[4] More literally "retinue," occurring also Gen. 26, 14, hardly "work animals" as Ehrlich, *Randglossen zur Hebräischen Bibel* 6 p. 180, proposes.

[5] "Sons of the East" here used as a general designation of those dwelling to the East of Palestine proper. "Greater" (or greatest) means the wealthiest and, therefore, the most renowned and influential.

THE BOOK OF JOB

And His sons were in the habit of arranging a feast, each one upon his day; [6] and they would invite their three sisters to eat and drink with them.[7] And the feast days would make their round, and Job would direct all of them [8] to bring burnt offerings at sunrise [9] according to their number, for Job was wont to say, "It may be that my sons have sinned, and cursed [10] God in their mind." [11] Thus Job acted at all times.

Now it fell on a certain day, when the Sons of God [12] came to gather around Yahweh,[13] that Satan [14]

---

[6] Text has a superfluous "in the house," a gloss to indicate that the feast took place in the house of each one of the sons in turn during an annual holyday week.

[7] But not at the same table with them. Men and women did not sit together in the ancient Orient.

[8] The ordinary translation "sanctify" misses the point. The verb implies giving directions to prepare for the holy sacrifice.

[9] Literally "he arose early in the morning and offered burnt-offerings"—a trace of the custom of greeting the rising sun by ceremonial observances.

[10] Text here as well as 2, 5 and 9 "bless," euphemistically substituted for "curse" by some pious editor. The Greek translation retains the original reading, though curiously enough elsewhere, as for example, I Kings 21, 10, it is the Greek translation which euphemistically substitutes "bless" for the Hebrew "curse."

[11] Literally "in their heart," but here, as throughout the Old Testament, the "heart" is the seat of the intellect. To illustrate the extreme to which Job's piety went, he is represented as cleansing his sons from possible sins through the sacrificial rites, for fear that they may have had sinful thoughts, while celebrating the festival week.

[12] The "Sons of God," as its occurrence Gen. 6, 2 shows, is an expression introduced to veil an early polytheistic conception of Divine government. The "Sons of God" are originally the gods who control the universe, and who with the rise of monotheism became inferior divine beings, acting as messengers and courtiers who stand around the throne, ready to do the bidding of their Divine Master. They shade over into the angels (*angelos* =

THE BOOK OF JOB

also came with them, and Yahweh said to Satan: "Whence comest thou?" And Satan answered Yahweh: "From roaming over the earth in all directions." [15] And Yahweh said to Satan: "Hast thou observed my servant Job, that there is none like him in the earth, a pious and upright man, God-

---

messenger) of Jewish and Christian theology. See further above, p. 56 *seq.*

[13] This specific name—originally the national deity of the Hebrews—as against general designations for Deity, El, Eloah, Elohim and also Shaddai which are used in the Symposium and in the speeches of Elihu, occurs in the dialogue between God and Satan in the Prologue (chapters 1 and 2), and in Job's pious utterance (1, 21). This appears to be a quotation, perhaps inserted at a later date, since 2, 10 Job uses Elohim, as does also Job's wife (2, 9). Elohim is thus used 11 times in the Prologue. In the dialogue with Satan, however, the specific name appears to be intentionally introduced to correspond to the specification of the tempter by a personal name. For the same reason Yahweh is introduced in the editorial headings and links of chaps. 38–41, and in the prose epilogues 42, 7–17 to emphasize the *personal* phase of the conception of Divine intervention, through speech and action. The single occurrence of Yahweh in the philosophical poem proper (12, 9) is either a slip, or to be accounted for because the line in question is a later gloss. See the note to the passage. On the use of El, Eloah, Elohim and Shaddai, see the note to 5, 17. (p. 215)

[14] Literally "adversary" and used in historical books (*e.g.*, I Samuel 29, 4; II Samuel 19, 23; I Kings 5, 18; 11, 14), to designate an ordinary human adversary. It is not till we reach late post-exilic days that Satan becomes the designation of a semi-divine being—an "angel" or "messenger" whose special function it is to act as an accuser and a tempter. So in Zachariah, chap. 3, 1 *seq.* and I Chronicles 21, 1 where Satan as the tempter replaces Yahweh himself in the earlier parallel, II Samuel 24, 1. See further on the figure of Satan, above, p. 52 *seq.*

[15] Satan, while in the service of Yahweh, is free to go where he pleases; he is not on the same plane as the other messengers of gods, though he appears with them.

THE BOOK OF JOB

fearing and removed from evil?" And Satan answered Yahweh; "Is Job God-fearing for nought? 10 Hast Thou not protected him and his house and all that he has? His handiwork Thou hast blessed, and his possessions have increased in the land. But now put forth Thy hand and strike all that he has [and see] whether he will not forthwith [16] curse Thee." And Yahweh said to Satan: "Behold, all that he has is in thy hands—only against himself do not put forth thy hand." And Satan left the presence of Yahweh.

Now it fell on a certain day, when the sons [of Job] [17] and his daughters were eating and drinking in the house of their eldest brother,[18] that a messenger came to Job and said: "While the oxen were ploughing, and the she-asses grazing at their side, Sabeans [19] 15 made a raid and took them away. They slew the servants,[20] and I barely escaped to tell thee." While this one was still speaking, another came and said: "Lightning [21] fell from heaven, and burned the flock and consumed the servants and I alone escaped to tell thee." While this one was still speaking, another came and said: "Chaldaeans [22] in three divisions [23]

---

[16] Literally, "to thy face" which, however, has the force of "at once, forthwith." Text again "bless." See above, note 10.
[17] So read, following the Greek text.
[18] The first day, therefore, of the festival week.
[19] Here used in the general sense of marauders.
[20] Literally "young men" which the Greek text interprets as "shepherds," though the term includes also other servants.
[21] Literally, "fire of God."
[22] Likewise intended here as a general term for plunderers.
[23] The division into three appears to have been the common method of attack. So, e.g., Judges 7, 16 (Gideon); Judges 9, 43 (Abimelech); I Samuel 11, 11 (Saul).

THE BOOK OF JOB

made a raid upon the camels, took them and slew the servants and I barely escaped to tell thee." While this one was still speaking, another came and said: "Thy sons and daughters were eating and drinking in the house of their eldest brother, when a great storm came from the wilderness and struck the four corners of the house, so that it fell on the servants who were killed, and I barely escaped to tell thee." [24]

---

[24] One is inclined to suspect that in an older form of the story, this was the single misfortune brought about by Satan to test Job's piety, since v. 18 clearly harks back to v. 13. It would be natural for the story as it passed from mouth to mouth to become overweighted with further incidents and details. The single misfortune of the destruction of the house in which Job's children were feasting would be a sufficient calamity to bring Job to the extreme of grief. While the dramatic effect is heightened by having one piece of bad news follow on the heels of another, there is an inherent weakness in the situation in having the "servants" slain four times. It looks as though the four calamities were variants, combined in consequence of the natural tendency of stories to grow by accretions, and for the purpose of heightening the impression of Job's patience. If this view be correct, verses 18–19, joining on to v. 13, would originally have read as follows: "And a messenger came to Job and said 'Thy sons and daughters were eating and drinking in the house of their eldest brother, when a great storm came from the wilderness, struck the four corners of the house which fell so that they (*i.e.*, the sons and daughters) were killed.'" A trace of this original reading appears in the Greek text which reads "And the house fell." The words "on the servants" are clearly out of place—introduced merely by way of analogy, after the four incidents, originally variants of one another, had been combined. Note further that of the four incidents the first and third are occasioned through human agencies; the second and fourth through divine intervention. This division likewise points to two series of variant traditions that were combined in the final form.

THE BOOK OF JOB

20 Then Job arose and tore his upper garment,[25] and cut off his hair [26] and prostrated himself,[27] saying:

"Naked came I forth from my mother's womb,
And naked shall I return thither.[28]
Yahweh has given, and Yahweh has taken;
Blessed be the name of Yahweh." [29]

For all this, Job did not sin and uttered no reproach [30] against God.

2, 1 Now it fell on a certain day when again the Sons of God came to gather around Yahweh, that Satan also came with them.[31] And Yahweh said to Satan; "Whence comest thou?" and Satan answered Yahweh; "From roaming over the earth in all directions"; and Yahweh said to Satan: "Hast thou observed

---

[25] The tearing off of the upper garment, *i.e.*, stripping oneself to the waist is still a mourning custom among the Jews of Persia.

[26] Another ancient mourning custom, consisting originally of tearing out of the hair, as depicted on Egyptian monuments. In Babylonian literature we also come across descriptions of violent grief, manifested by rending of one's garments, and tearing one's flesh.

[27] An attitude of prayer.

[28] "Thither," a veiled expression for Sheol or the nether world.

[29] The stanza of four lines is poetic in form—a snatch of a lamentation hymn or of a prayer. The first two lines appear to be quoted in Ecclesiastes 5, 14.

[30] The word rendered "reproach" occurs only here and Jer. 23, 13, for in Job 24, 12 a different vocalization, giving us the word for "prayer," is required by the context. See the note to the passage. The meaning of the word must be gathered from the context and from the synonymous expression at the close of 2, 10.

[31] The text adds tautologically "to gather around Yahweh," which is omitted in the original Greek version.

THE BOOK OF JOB

my servant Job, that there is none like him in the earth, a pious and upright man, God-fearing and removed from evil, and still steadfast in his piety, although thou didst challenge me to destroy him without cause?" And Satan said to Yahweh: "There is a skin beneath the skin;[32] and a man will give all that he has for his life. But now put forth 5 Thy hand and strike his own bone and his flesh [and see] whether he will not forthwith curse[33] Thee." And Yahweh said to Satan: "Behold, he is in thy hand; only spare his life."[34]

And Satan left the presence of Yahweh, and smote Job with malignant boils from the sole of his feet to his crown. And he took a potsherd to scrape himself, and, as he sat among the ashes,[35] his wife said to him: "Art thou still steadfast in thy piety? Curse God and die."[36] And he said to her: "Thou 10 speakest as one of the worthless women. Should we indeed receive the good from God, but the evil we

---

[32] *i.e.*, only the surface has been scratched. Scratch deeper and you will see what Job will do. So far Job himself has not been afflicted.

[33] Text again euphemistically "curse thee," as above 1, 11.

[34] Strike him with sickness, but do not kill him—a somewhat superfluous restriction, for the test would naturally have come to an end with Job's death.

[35] *i.e.*, outside of the city, as the Greek text adds. Job is treated as the "leper" in Leviticus 14, 2 who dwells "outside of the camp." Ash heaps, used as dumps, are still to be seen in the outskirts of Palestinian villages.

[36] Commit suicide! Text again has euphemistically "bless." The blasphemer is stricken with death. In the Greek text Job's wife indulges in a long speech, which is an interesting illustration of the tendency to amplify a popular tale.

THE BOOK OF JOB

should not receive?" For all this, Job did not sin with his lips.[37]

Now three of Job's friends heard of all the evil that had come upon him; and they came, each from his home, Eliphaz, the Temanite,[38] and Bildad, the Shuhite, and Zophar, the Naamathite;[39] and they made an appointment together to come to sympathize with him and to comfort him. And when they saw him at some distance, they did not recognize him. And they wept aloud and tore their upper garments[40] and sprinkled dust over their heads.[41]

---

[37] *i.e.*, he never even uttered a complaint. Cf. Psalms, 39, 2 where "sinning with the tongue" is similarly used.

[38] Eliphaz is mentioned, Genesis 36, 4 and 10 as the first-born of Edom (or Esau). Tema is in northern Arabia and may have been reckoned as part of Edom.

[39] The home of Bildad and of Zophar must also be sought in the region of northern Arabia. Gen. 36, 11 and I Chronicles 1, 36, Teman, Omar and Zepho are registered as sons of Eliphaz; and since the Greek text has in the former passage Zophar instead of Zepho, it is tempting to correct the Hebrew text of Job (2, 11) accordingly. An interchange between *r* and the final *waw* of Zepho would be quite simple, being merely the difference of a small stroke. The Greek text speaks of the three friends as "kings"—an interesting additional touch of the legendary tale, and showing again the variations that the story received in the course of its wanderings.

[40] As above 1, 20 a sign of mourning. The friends show their grief by mourning over Job as though he were already dead, just as in the Babylonian poem (see above p. 37), the suffering king says of himself that his family had already lamented over him as over one who was dead. (Jastrow in *Journal of Biblical Literature*, Vol. 25, p. 173.)

"Though not yet dead, the lamentation was recited;
The people of my land had already said 'Alas' over me."

[41] Text adds "towards heaven"—omitted in the Greek text, and evidently a gloss to indicate that the dust was thrown

Then they sat down with him on the ground for seven days and seven nights,[42] without speaking a word to him, for they saw how very great was [his] pain.

---

upwards over the head. The old custom no longer understood by the glossator, was to take the dust from the grave and as a sign of grief to rub it over the head and the face (Jastrow, *Earth, Dust and Ashes*, in the *Journal of the American Oriental Society*, Vol. 20, pp. 150–173). Acts 22, 23 is reminiscent of our passage.

[42] The conventional period of deepest mourning (Cf. Gen. 50, 10; I Samuel 31, 13), still observed by Orthodox Jews during which time the mourners sit on the ground. The period is popularly known as "Shivah" which means "seven." Sitting in silence on the ground instead of on divans is a sign of mourning. Cf. Lamentations 2, 10.

II

THE SYMPOSIUM BETWEEN JOB AND HIS FRIENDS

(Chapters 3-21)

<small>3, 1</small> After this Job opened his mouth and cursed his fate:[43]

<small>3–10
Job curses
his fate.</small> Perish the day on which I was born,
And the night when a male was conceived![44]
May God not seek it out on high,[45]
That light may not shine upon it.
<small>5</small> Darkness and deep shadows claim it;

---

[43] Literally, "his day," which does not necessarily mean the day of his birth. The chapter has an additional introductory clause, (not found in the older Greek versions), "And Job began to speak," or more literally, "in answer spoke," evidently not in place here and inserted to bring about an analogy with the conventional opening of the chapters (4, 1; 6, 1; 8, 1; 9, 1; etc., etc.). A striking parallel to chap. 3, 1–12 is found in Jeremiah 20, 14–18—a section evidently not in place there and which reads like a bit of the Book of Job that has, through some curious chance of circumstance, wandered from its context.

[44] The line is too long by one beat. The word "it was said" appears to be an explanatory comment, and is omitted in one of the Greek versions.

[45] The line is again too long. It is clear that "God" has been added to explain "on high." Moreover, since the general construction of the poem consists of stanzas of four lines, (see above p. 105), we are justified in removing redundant hemistichs as glosses or variants. So, the beginning of v. 4, "That day be darkness" is a comment to "night," to indicate that a dark night is meant.

THE BOOK OF JOB

And denseness cover it![46]
Among the days of the year be it not reckoned;[47]
Nor enter into the number of the months.
May that night be barren;[48]
No song penetrate it.
May those that rouse up the sea[49] ban it,
Those who are ready to stir up the dragon.[50]
May its twilight stars remain dark;[51]
May it not see the eyelids of dawn;[52]

---

[46] The two words at the close of the verse explained by a gloss as "clouds rest upon it," are to be combined into one *kamririm* in the sense of "denseness."

[47] The beginning of this verse, "That night—may density (*ōphēl*) take hold of it" is a comment to the first hemistich of v. 7 or perhaps to v. 5. In King John III, 1, 12–20 we have a conscious imitation of our passage in Job. See Furness, *Variorum Edition of King John*, p. 180, note 16.

[48] The word "behold" at the beginning of the verse is to be omitted. The term translated 'barren" (*galmud*) is a rare word, which the Greek text renders "sorrowful." If the gloss referred to in the preceding note is a comment to this hemistich, the meaning of *galmud* is to be taken as "gloom."

[49] An obscure stanza. Instead of "cursers of the day," I read with Gunkel (*Schöpfung und Chaos*, p. 95) followed by Ehrlich (*Randglossen* 6, p. 190) by a slight correction, "cursers of the sea," the reference being to diviners who invoke the spirits of the deep.

[50] Text "Leviathan"—the term for dragon as the personification of the deep, so frequently referred to in the Old Testament, *e.g.*, Isaiah 27, 1; Psalms 74, 14; 104, 26, etc. See Jastrow, *Hebrew and Babylonian Traditions*, pp. 107–115.

[51] *i. e.*, may the faint stars announcing the approach of morning remain faint. A gloss adds "hoping for light which comes not."

[52] The "eyelids of dawn" suggests the Greek personification of Dawn as a lovely maiden whose eyelids are lightbeams that stream from the opening clouds. See Strahan, *Job*, p. 53.

THE BOOK OF JOB

10   Because it [53] closed not the doors of my [mother's] lap,[54]
And hid trouble from my eyes.

11-26
Longing for death.
Why did I not die at the womb,
Come forth from the lap and perish?
Why did knees receive me?[55]
And why were there breasts to give me suck?
For now I would quietly be in repose;
There would be sleep and rest for me;
With the kings and counsellors of the earth,
Who build themselves mausoleums;[56]

15   Or with the merchant princes,[57]
Who fill their houses with silver;
Or like a buried fœtus,[58] I would never have been;
Like babes that have never seen the light.
There where the toilers cease from care;
And the workers are at rest.[59]

---

[53] *i. e.*, that night in which I was born. Ehrlich (*Randglossen* 6, 190,) by a slight textual change reads:
"For oh that he had closed my mother's lap,
And had hidden trouble from my eyes."

[54] Literally, "belly."

[55] Referring to the custom of the father legitimizing his new-born child by receiving it on his knees.

[56] A sarcastic reference to the vanity of kings in building huge mausoleums—literally "deserted places"—for themselves as the Egyptian Pharaohs who spent years in building the pyramids that were to receive their bodies. To refer the term to the rebuilding of cities, as a favorite ambition of kings, seems somewhat far-fetched.

[57] Literally "princes of gold" meaning the nabobs.

[58] More literally "hidden untimely birth."

[59] I confess to a feeling of pain in proposing a change for the famous and impressive rendering;
"There, the wicked cease from troubling;
And there the weary are at rest."

THE BOOK OF JOB

Where the imprisoned are gathered in quiet;
Not hearing the voice of the overseer,
Where small and great are [gathered];
And the servant is free from his master.
Why should light be given to the unhappy, 20
And life to those in despair?
[To the man whose way is hidden [from God],
Whom God has hedged about? [60]]
Who long for death, which cometh not;
Who dig for it more than for treasure;
Who rejoice at the [thought of the] mound,[61]
Are jubilant upon finding the grave?
For as my food, are my sighs;[62]
My groans are poured out like water.[63]

---

but neither "wicked" and "weary" on the one hand nor "troubling" and "at rest" on the other form either a contrast or a parallelism; and one of the two is demanded by the canons of Hebrew poetry. The Hebrew phrase usually rendered "exhausted of strength" or "weary" can only mean "overpowered," *i.e.*, the submerged masses or the workers, forced to servitude by those of superior power. Instead of "wicked," we must read by a slight change a term which refers to the proletariat toilers. It is not they who cause "trouble," but who must endure it. In Sheol, however, they are free from all worry.

[60] This is verse 23 in the text, but appears to be misplaced. It may have been added on the margin of a manuscript, and then inserted at a wrong place by a later copyist.

[61] Instead of *gil*, read by a slight change *gal*, the funeral mound, marked by a stone.

[62] The word "comes" which makes the line too long is an explanatory addition. It is omitted in two codices.

[63] Compare the refrain in Babylonian lamentation hymns:

"Instead of food, I eat bitter tears;
Instead of wine, I drink waters of misery."
(Jastrow, *Religion of Babylonia and Assyria*, p. 222.)

THE BOOK OF JOB

25 For the terror I dreaded has overwhelmed me;
What I feared has come to me,
I have no peace and no quiet,
No rest, since trouble has come.

4, 1

1–9
Only the
guilty are
punished.

Then Eliphaz in answer said:
May one venture a word with thee, [64]
And yet how can one restrain speech? [65]
In truth, thou hast supported [66] many,
Strengthened weak hands.
Thy words have sustained the tottering,
Lending support to feeble knees.

---

[64] An explanatory comment adds "wilt thou be annoyed?" The addition gives the line four beats, instead of three.

[65] Eliphaz, who introduces his first discourse with an apology for hurting Job's feelings, reminds him that offering advice while useful is not always agreeable to the one to whom it is offered. Job himself, he adds, has indulged in this practice; and to smooth matters over, Eliphaz emphasizes how valuable Job has been to the weak and the faltering by his wise counsel. He ought to be willing to take some of the medicine that he has so frequently poured down the throats of others. There is a human touch in Eliphaz's suggestion that Job relied upon his piety as a guarantee against misfortune; and now that it has come to him, he does not relish the possibility of his being reproved and lectured to, as he was in the habit of doing to others. Eliphaz feels, or pretends to feel, the call to tell Job the truth and so rather cleverly, if somewhat unctuously, claims that one can not restrain one's words when one hears such blasphemous complaints as Job has just uttered. Even at the risk of hurting Job, Eliphaz *must* speak out; and he begins by bluntly and tactlessly suggesting that since no innocent person has ever been punished, Job must be an awful sinner.

[66] So read by a slight change (supported by the Greek and Aramaic versions) instead of "rebuked," or "instructed." Verses 3–4, are quoted in the Epistle to the Hebrews 12, 12.

THE BOOK OF JOB

But now it comes to thee; [67] 5
It touches thee and thou art aghast.
Was not thy fear [of God] thy hope,
And thy pious ways thy trust?
Recall now, an innocent who has perished? [68]
And where are the upright who have been cut off?
As I have seen, those who have ploughed iniquity
And sowed trouble, have reaped it [69]
Through God's wrath [70] they have perished, 9
And have been consumed through His anger.[71]

Now, a word came stealthily to me,   12–21
And my ear heard a whisper; [72]   *Man cannot be pure in*
In the play of thoughts during night visions,   *the sight of God.*
When deep sleep falls on men;
Terror and trembling came over me,
And fear shook my bones.

---

[67] The same commentator as in verse 2, adds: "thou art annoyed."
[68] The line has a superfluous particle that makes it too long.
[69] Eliphaz may be quoting the saying Prov. 22, 8.
[70] Literally, "through the breath of God."
[71] At this point some later editor or pious commentator has inserted (v. 10–11) some popular saws in the style of the Proverbs, in illustration of the conventional view that guilt is punished and that vice versa there is no punishment without guilt:

> "The lion may roar and the fierce one howl,
> But the teeth of the young lions are broken.
> The old lion perishes for lack of prey,
> And the whelps of the lioness are scattered."

[72] The word used *shemes* occurs only here and Job 26, 14, and is equivalent to our "inkling." There is an overhanging "of it" at the end of the line, which needs to be removed to reduce the line to three beats.

THE BOOK OF JOB

15 A breath passed before my face,
 That made the hair of my flesh stand up.[73]
 A form that I knew not stood there,[74]
 And I heard a small voice:
 "Can man be more righteous than God?
 Can a man be purer than his Maker?"[75]
 Since He does not put trust in His servants,
 And finds error in His messengers;
 How much more in those who live in clay houses,[76]
 Crushed like the empty nest.[77]
20 Shattered from morning till evening;
 Perishing without help.[78]

---

[73] *i.e.*, made me shiver.

[74] "An image was before my eyes" is added as an explanatory gloss.

[75] Eliphaz is placed in the rather ridiculous position of suggesting that what he is about to say is a divine intuition. Hence the writer makes Eliphaz use the phraseology of a theophany (1) "night visions" as in the case of the Elohist document of the Pentateuch, *e.g.*, Gen. 15, 12 *seq* (Abraham); 28, 11 *seq*. (Jacob), etc. The analogy is further carried out by the use of the term "deep sleep" as Gen. 15, 12 "deep sleep fell on Abraham;" (2) a spirit passing before one's face as happened to Moses (Exodus 34, 6); (3) "the still small voice" as in the case of the revelation to Elijah (I Kings, 19, 12). After this elaborate introduction, comes the message which is quite banal—to wit, that man is not perfect.

[76] Comment "whose foundation is in the dust," *i.e.*, clay houses without solid foundation that may be blown away by a gust of wind. The "clay houses" do not refer to human bodies, but are to be taken literally as mud huts—the primitive dwellings of men, to illustrate the transitory character of human fortunes.

[77] So Ehrlich's explanation (*Randglossen* 6, p. 194) which I accept.

[78] Gloss, "forever," which needs to be removed to reduce the line to three beats.

THE BOOK OF JOB

When their tent-cord is plucked up,[79]
They die through lack of foresight.[80]

Call now [to judgment] whether any one will 5, 1
  respond to thee? [81]
Which of the divine beings [82] wilt thou accuse?
Fretting kills the foolish,   1–7
And envy brings about the death of the silly one.[83] *The triumph of the wicked is short.*
I have seen the foolish take root,[84]
But his habitation of a sudden is swept away; [85]
His sons far from salvation,
And crushed,[86] with none to save [them].
What they gather, the hungry eat; [87]   5

---

[79] The metaphor is changed to that of a tent which falls to pieces when the tent pin is pulled out. The body is compared to a tent, of which the soul or vital essence is the pin.

[80] Literally: "without wisdom."

[81] The "call" and "response" represent legal phraseology, which is used by Job throughout chapter 9, and frequently in later speeches.

[82] Literally: "the holy ones" used here, as also 15, 15 (in a speech of the same Eliphaz), for a lower order of divine beings, the ministers or angels of God. Eliphaz asks Job what he is going to do about it, seeing that he cannot claim to be free from sin. To whom can he appeal? Some scholars, as for example, Siegfried, regard this first verse as a later interpolation, but there seems to be no necessity for this.

[83] Eliphaz is quoting a popular saying. Cf. Prov. 19, 3.

[84] Or possibly "uprooted" by a different vocalization. The line has a superfluous "I" at the beginning.

[85] Some such meaning is demanded by the context and is favored by the Greek text.

[86] Text adds "in the gate"—a misplaced gloss, belonging to the preceding stanza after the words "take root."

[87] So the Greek translation. The text adds as a gloss "gathering it into the granaries." I follow Ehrlich's reading and interpretation of the somewhat obscure, because corrupt, text.

THE BOOK OF JOB

8
8–27
Those who seek God will find salvation.
10

And the thirsty (?) drain their substance.[88]
However, I [89] would seek out God,[90]
And unto God commit my cause;
Who does great things beyond searching,
And marvels without number;
Who gives rain upon the earth,
And sends water over the highways.[91]
Raises the lowly on high,
And by salvation exalts those bent down.
Who frustrates the devices of the crafty,
That their hands fail of success.[92]
Who overpowers the crafty in their deceit,
So that the plan of the wily is defeated.
By day they grope in darkness,
And as though it were night they stumble at high noon.

---

[88] Verses 6–7 are again proverbial sayings, added by some pious commentator but which interrupt the sequence:

> "Yet iniquity comes not from the dust;
> Nor does trouble spring out of the ground;
> But man produces trouble,
> As sparks fly upwards."

The last line is obscure. Taking the text as it stands, the thought seems to be that man is the source of his trouble, by the same law which makes the sparks fly upwards.

[89] *i.e.*, in thy place. The line has a superfluous "I," which makes it too long.

[90] Job's only course is to appeal to God's mercy, but he must not accuse God of injustice.

[91] Cf. Jeremiah 10, 13. In each line there is a superfluous "the face," which is omitted in the Greek version.

[92] Literally: "insight" but in the sense of failure through the lack of "insight."

THE BOOK OF JOB

He saves [the poor (?)] [93] from their mouth,[94]   15
And the needy from their strong hand.
So that hope springs up for the poor,
As iniquity closes her mouth.[95]
Happy [96] the man whom God reproves;
The chastisement of Shaddai [97] one must not reject.[98]
For He strikes, and [also] binds up;
His hands wound but [also] heal.
Out of six dangers he will deliver thee;
And at the seventh will not permit evil to harm thee.[99]

---

[93] A word needs to be supplied. The parallelism suggests *oni* "poor." Budde (*Hiob*, p. 24) proposes "orphan."

[94] A comment or variant: "from the sword."

[95] *i.e.*, when the tricksters and crooks are crushed into silence.

[96] The text has a superfluous word "behold" (not in the Greek version), which needs to be removed, to reduce the line to three beats. Cf. Prov. 3, 11.

[97] Occurring 24 times in the Symposium and Supplements, 6 times in the speeches of Elihu and once in the poetical epilogue, by the side of *El* 35 times in the Symposium, 19 times in the speeches of Elihu and 3 times in the poetical epilogue; *Eloah* 34 times in the Symposium, 5 times in the speeches of Elihu and twice in the poetical epilogue, and *Elohim* 3 times in the Symposium and twice in the speeches of Elihu and once in the nature poems—all generic designation for God. *Shaddai* conveying the idea of "strength" is rendered "Almighty" in the English versions, but as a specific name, older than Yahweh (Exodus 6, 2), it is preferable to retain the Hebrew form. See above, p. 199, note 13.

[98] A saying in the style of the Proverbs (cf. Prov. 3, 11)—perhaps a quotation from a collection. A further extension of the thought leads to the view set forth in the famous passage in the Epistles to the Hebrews, 12, 5–11.

[99] Another saying in the style of Proverbs (cf. Prov. 6, 16).

THE BOOK OF JOB

20 In want He will redeem thee from death;
And in war from the power of the sword.
Against the leaping flame [1] thou shalt be secure;
And thou shalt not be afraid of misfortune.[2]

22 At misfortune and famine thou wilt laugh;
And not be afraid of the beasts of the earth.[3]

24 And thou shalt know thy tent to be safe;
Thou shalt muster thy estate and nothing shall be missing.[4]

26 Thou shalt come to the grave in fullness,
Like a shock of corn in its season.
Behold, this we have ascertained;[5]
We have heard it [6]—and do thou bear it in mind!

6, 1–12 Job justifies his complaint.

And Job in answer said:
If my trouble could only be weighed,
With my calamity together in scales,[7]

---

[1] Text "tongue" for "tongue of fire." So Ehrlich.

[2] The text has an addition "when it comes"—clearly an explanatory comment.

[3] The following verse, the first half of which (v. 23) is omitted in the Greek version, strikes one as an addition—taken perhaps from some collection of sayings, and suggested by the reference to the "beasts of the earth;"
"For with the stones of the field is thy pact;
And the beasts of the field furnish security for thee."

[4] Somewhat like Proverbs 3, 9–10—plenty as the reward of piety. Verse 25 appears to be a later addition—perhaps quoted from some collection:
"And thou shalt know that thy seed shall be great;
And thy offspring as the grass of the earth."

[5] A glossator adds: "So it is," which makes the line too long.

[6] So the Greek translation.

[7] A superfluous word "laid" makes the line too long. It is clearly an amplifying gloss.

THE BOOK OF JOB

It would indeed be heavier than the sand; [8]
—Therefore, my flow of words.
The arrows of Shaddai are within me,[9]
The terrors of God are arrayed against me.
Does the wild ass bray over grass? [10]   5
Does the ox low over his fodder?
Can what is tasteless be eaten without salt?
Or is there any taste in halamuth-juice? [11]
My soul refuses to touch [them];
They are the spoilers of my food.
Oh that my request were granted,
That God would accede to my wish! [12]
That it might please God to crush me;
To let loose His hand, and cut me off!

---

[8] Similarly, in this line "of the seas" after "sand" is a comment, which needs to be removed to reduce the line to three beats.

[9] A commentator adds a superfluous line (in prose form): "Whose poison drains my spirit."

[10] He brays when he is hungry or in distress—*i.e.*, for some good cause.

[11] Halamuth has been commonly rendered "white of egg" because of the Talmudic term *halman* which has this meaning, but it is more likely the name of a plant, the equivalent of the Syriac Halmetha-Anchusa (Alkanna tinctoria) the name given to a genus of boraginaceous herbs, the roots of which are used medicinally. The reference is to a juice which is not fit to eat, and that cannot serve as food. There are certain things, says Job, which cannot be endured. One does not want to eat something that has no taste. Such things spoil one's pleasure; they deprive one of joy in life. The comparison does not appeal to our modern point of view, but the implication is clear that life has become unendurable for Job, and that he has good reason for his disgust with existence.

[12] So by a slight change in the text.

THE BOOK OF JOB

<small>13–30
Faithless
and deceptive
friends.</small>

10   Then there would still be a comfort to me;
And I would exult despite relentless pain.[13]
What endurance have I [left] to sustain hope?
And what goal have I that I should drag on my life?[14]
Have I the strength of stones?
Is my flesh of brass?
Behold,[15] there is no help in me;
And salvation[16] is denied to me.
From his friends the one in despair deserves kindness,
Even though he forsakes the fear of Shaddai.
15   My brethren have proved false like a brook,[17]
Like overflowing river beds,
Running black by reason of the ice,
Mixed (?) with the snow;
But which when the heat comes are dry;[18]

---

[13] A pious commentator, in order to give a more reverent tone to the cry of anguish, adds a superfluous line: "that I had not denied the words of the Holy One." Job is hardly in a mood for such a thought. Moreover, the line is in prose form.

[14] There is a limit even to Job's strength, and moreover why should he continue to suffer, seeing that the only end to his sufferings must be death.

[15] So by a slight change.

[16] So read by a slight change, supported by the Greek version. The Hebrew text has "insight" which is not a good parallel to "help."

[17] The metaphor, found also in Jer. 15, 18, is suggested by the many little river beds in Palestine, known as *wadis*, which during the rainy season are filled with the water coming from the hills and often indeed become rushing torrents, but which when the summer sun comes are entirely dry.

[18] *i.e.*, the water in the river bed evaporates and the brooks disappear.

THE BOOK OF JOB

Through the heat disappear from their place.
Their courses are changed;[19]
They rise as vapor and are lost.
The caravans of Tema depended upon [them];[20]
The companies of Sheba hoped for [them].
They are confused because of [their][21] trust;   20
They come to the spot, and are put to shame.
So you have now become to me;[22]
You look at the terror,[23] and are shocked.
Did I ask you to give me?
And through your strength to intercede for me?[24]
To deliver me from the hand of the adversary?[25]
Or to ransom me from the hand of oppressors?
Teach me,[26] and I will keep silent;
Make clear to me wherein I have erred.
Why do you deny the force of proper words?[27]   25
What does your rebuke prove?
Do you consider your mere assertions a proof,

---

[19] So by a necessary emendation of the text.

[20] *i.e.*, upon these river beds where they hoped to find water, but are doomed to disappointment. Tema lay in northern Arabia; Sheba (*i.e.*, Sabaea) in South Arabia.

[21] A word must be added to get three beats to this line.

[22] The friends of Job are compared to river beds which are empty when one has most need of them. Read "to me," as the Greek and Syriac versions, instead of "for him."

[23] Meaning himself and his terrible condition.

[24] Not only do Job's friends desert him in his trouble, but their advice and reproaches are gratuitous, since Job never asked any help from them.

[25] *i.e.*, God.

[26] Show me my wrong, instead of reproaching me.

[27] So by a slight change of the text. The "proper words" are Job's complaints and charges.

THE BOOK OF JOB

And the utterances of the one in despair mere wind? [28]
Then would you cast [lots] [29] for the orphan,
And bargain away your friend.
Be pleased to turn to me; [30]
And I will not disappoint you [31]
Listen again, let there be no incrimination;
Listen again to my justification!
30 [And see] whether there is any injustice in my tongue?
Or whether my palate is insensible to perversity?

7, 1
1–10
The misery of life and the hopelessness of death.

Is not man's (life) on earth a service? [32]
And are not his days like those of a hireling?
Like [those of] a servant longing for the shadow [of evening]?
As a hireling looking for his wages? [33]

---

[28] Job's friends are inconsistent. They consider their empty words to be a real argument, whereas they pay no attention to Job's profession of his innocence, regarding such utterances as the mere babble of a man in despair.

[29] The word "lot" needs to be added to get three beats for this line. Cf. I Sam. 14, 42.

[30] Job by a sudden turn implores his friends to reconsider his case, and see whether he is not justified in his claim that he has been unjustly punished. He feels assured that if he has really done wrong, he would be capable of recognizing it.

[31] Literally "lie to your face" in the sense, however, of justifying the consideration that Job asks of his friends.

[32] Life is a constant toil imposed upon man by a hard taskmaster. Siegfried, *Book of Job*, p. 4, takes this entire section, 7, 1–10, as an independent parallel composition to the preceding chapter, but there seems to be no warrant for such a view.

[33] One is reminded of the stanza in Cymbeline—

"Thou thy worldly task hast done,
Home art gone and ta'en thy wages." (IV, 2, 337–338.)

220

THE BOOK OF JOB

So I have been allotted [34] months of misery,
And wearisome nights have been appointed to me
When I lie down, when shall I arise? [35]
And I am worn out [and] restless till evening.[36]
My body is clothed with decay;[37]
My skin breaks and suppurates. [38]
My days [fly] swifter than a weaver's shuttle,
And pass away without hope.
Oh, remember that when my breath of life [is gone],
My eyes will never see happiness again.
[The eye of the one who looks for me shall not find me
Thy eyes may be upon me, but I shall not be there.][39]
The cloud dissolves and is gone,
So the one who goes down [40] does not come up.
He shall return no more to his house,

---

[34] Note the bitterness of Job's complaint that in this world of service, his share is to spend his days and nights in suffering. The word "to me" in the text after the rest makes the line too long; it is an amplifying gloss, superinduced by the same word at the close of the following line.

[35] *i.e.*, how long till morning comes? Cf. Deut. 28, 67. A glossator adds "I say," which makes the line too long.

[36] This line has a superfluous "when the night is spent," which gives the line five beats instead of three.

[37] A glossator adds "earth clods," to explain that the "decay" refers to the crusts of the sores with which Job's body is covered, and which he likens to clumps of mud.

[38] So the explanation of the line by Ibn Ezra and other Jewish exegetes.

[39] Verse 8 is not found in the original Greek text and impresses one as a later addition, amplifying the thought in verse 7.

[40] Gloss "to Sheol," the gathering place of the dead.

<small>11-21
Job curses his fate and hurls reproaches at God.</small>

And his place shall know him no more.
Therefore, I will not restrain my mouth;
I will give voice to my despair.[41]
Am I a sea or a sea-monster,
That thou settest a watch over me?[42]
When I think that my bed will comfort me,
That my couch shall ease my plaint,
Thou scarest me with dreams,
And startlest me with visions.

15 So that I prefer[43] strangling of my soul,
Death, rather than my pains.[44]
I refuse to live any longer;[45]
Cease,[46] for my days are vanity.
What is man, that Thou shouldst rear him,[47]
And put Thy mind upon him,
Seek him out every morning,
Try him every moment?
How long before Thou wilt look away from me,

---

[41] A variant adds "I will speak in the anguish of my spirit" and which is missing in the original Greek version. Cf. 10, 1.

[42] The reference is to the ancient myth, representing Yahweh as overcoming and chaining the unruly monsters of the deep, which symbolized the primæval chaos that existed before the creation of the world. See Jastrow, *Hebrew and Babylonian Traditions*, p. 108.

[43] So read by changing a single letter.

[44] By a slight change of the text one obtains the more satisfactory "my pains" in place of "my bones."

[45] Literally "forever," but in the sense of living on.

[46] The text has a superfluous "from me," which makes the line too long.

[47] An embittered turn given to the famous phrase. Psalms 8, 5. "What is man that Thou art mindful of him?" which the writer has in mind.

THE BOOK OF JOB

To let me alone till I swallow my spittle?[48]
What have I done to Thee, Guardian of man?[49] 20
Why hast Thou made me a mark?[50]
And why dost Thou not pardon my transgression
And forgive my iniquity?
For then I could lie down in the dust;[51]
Thou wouldst seek me, but I would not be there.

8, 1
1–12
God is just—is the testimony of the past.

And Bildad, the Shuhite, in answer said:
How long wilt thou babble thus?
Thy words are a mighty wind.[52]
Does God pervert judgment? 3
Does Shaddai pervert right?[53]
If thou wouldst seek out God 5

---

[48] *i.e.*, grant a respite long enough to swallow the spittle which is choking Job.

[49] In bitter irony Job calls God a "Guardian" who watches man closely. The words "I have sinned" make the line too long and appear to be an amplification by some pious commentator to tone down the bitterness by having Job at least confess that he has sinned. The alternative would be to regard the three words "Guardian of man" as added.

[50] The text adds "for thee," followed by an amplifying gloss "so that I have become a burden to Thee." Read "for Thee" (so the Greek text) instead of "for myself." Both Ibn Ezra and Rashi (following the Jewish tradition) recognize that the sense here requires "for Thee." The change was intentionally made after the gloss had crept into the text in order to soften the bitter taunt. The glossator interpreted "mark" in the sense of "burden."

[51] *i.e.*, death as a release would be a sign of God's grace. The utterance harks back to 6, 8–10.

[52] *i.e.*, "full of sound and fury, signifying nothing."

[53] A commentator has added, v. 4 (in prose form). "If thy children had sinned against Him, He would give them up because of their transgression."

THE BOOK OF JOB

    And implore Shaddai;[54]
    [He would bear witness for thee,[55]
    And would in equity restore thy position.[56]
    Thy former state would appear small,
    And thy later one be very great.][57]
    For inquire of the former generation,
    And turn to what the fathers have searched out.[58]
    For we have no knowledge of yesterday,
    Since our days are a shadow upon earth.
10. Surely they will teach thee and tell thee
    And reveal the thoughts in their mind:[59]

    Does papyrus[60] grow without marsh?
    Does Nile reed[61] flourish without water?
    While still in its blossom, before it is ripe,
    It would wither quicker than grass.

---

[54] Verses 6–7 which are only partially reproduced in the Greek text may represent a later addition. Various expressions betray a later period than the body of the text. In any case (6ª) "Provided thou wert pure and upright" is an amplifying comment, added by some pious glossator. See below note 70.

[55] So by a slight change in the text.

[56] I follow Ehrlich's restoration of the text.

[57] In comparison to thy future greatness as a reward for obtaining the forgiveness of God, thy former condition, prosperous as it was, would appear insignificant. See note to verses 21–22.

[58] *i.e.*, the wisdom of the ancients.

[59] The following two lines (verse 11) embody some saying to illustrate that without a proper foundation things will not prosper in this world.

[60] Passages like Exodus 2, 3 and Isaiah 18, 2, furnishing an Egyptian environment and in which the same word is used as in our passage, show that the papyrus stalk is meant.

[61] The Egyptian word for Nile reed is here used by the author.

THE BOOK OF JOB

Such is the end [62] of all that forget God.
The hope of the impious will perish;
Whose confidence is a gossamer thread,
And whose trust a spider's web.
[He shall lean upon his house, but it shall not stand;[63]
He shall take hold of it, but it shall not endure.][64]
Green in spite of the sun,
Its shoot spreads over its roof.[65]
About a stone heap its roots are entwined;
It clutches rocky soil.[66]
If one plucks it from its place
[That place] will deny it "I never saw thee." [67]
Behold, such is the joy [68] of its course,
And out of the dust something else will sprout.
Forsooth, God will not reject the upright; [69]
Nor does He strengthen the hand of evildoers.

13–22
The doom of the impious.

15

20

---

[62] So to be read, as in the Greek text, by a slight change in the text.

[63] So read by a slight change of the text. The meaning is that his substance will perish, and that the structure which he rears will fall to pieces.

[64] Verse 15 appears to be another proverbial saying, introduced here as appropriate.

[65] *i.e.*, the roof of the house. The picture is that of a shoot of some kind that grows upon roofs, but which has no roots in deep soil. Such a shoot never ripens; it remains green.

[66] The author introduces another illustration of a shoot coming up out of a rocky soil which, like the one that grows on a roof, will not last.

[67] The shoot makes no lasting impress. It disappears and even the place in which it temporarily thrived knows nothing of it. So the wicked perish without a trace.

[68] Sarcastically used. The Greek text reads: "This is the end of the godless."

[69] The same word as the one used (1, 1) to describe Job.

THE BOOK OF JOB

[Thy mind will yet be filled with laughter,
And thy life with joy.
Thy haters shall be clothed with shame;
And the tent of the wicked shall be no more.] [70]

9, 1   Then Job in answer said:

1-7 One cannot bring a suit against God who is mighty but also unapproachable.

I know full well that this is so;
But how can a man win a suit [71] against God?
If one should undertake to summon [72] Him,
There is not a chance in a thousand that He
would respond. [73]
Wise and strong as one may be,
Who could venture against Him and come out
whole? [74]

5   Who removes mountains and they know it not,
When in His anger [75] He overturns them.
Who shakes the earth out of her place,
That her foundations quake. [76]

---

[70] These last two verses (21 and 22) appear to be misplaced. They fit in after verse 5. They have been put here so as to make Bildad's speech end with a consolation, instead of with a denunciation. If verses 6 and 7 are later additions as has, above note 54, been suggested, then these misplaced verses 21–22 may represent the original reading after verse 5.

[71] The term used—literally "to be right"—is a legal one to indicate the one who is justified by the outcome of a suit.

[72] Again a legal term to designate the summoning of the opponent to appear in Court.

[73] The point that Job makes is that since his complaint is against God, there is no use in pressing it, since God is not an adversary with whom one can be brought face to face to thresh the matter out.

[74] The translation "prosper" (AV and RV) misses the point completely.

[75] Geological upheavals pictured as signs of God's terrible anger.

THE BOOK OF JOB

    Who commands the sun not to shine,[77]   7
    And seals up the stars.[78]
    He goes by me, without my seeing Him;   11
    He passes on, without my knowing.   11–24
    If he passes by,[79] who can hinder Him?   *God is callous and*
    [And] can say unto Him—What doest Thou? [80] *strikes the just and*
    God would not withdraw His anger,   *unjust alike.*

[76] Earthquakes.

[77] Eclipses.

[78] The invisibility of the planets at stated periods, likewise regarded as symptoms of Divine displeasure and giving rise among ancient nations to mythical tales of the capture and imprisonment of the sun, moon or planets as the case may be. Verses 8 to 10 giving an entirely different turn to Job's thought, as though he were merely intent upon describing the marvels (see p. 214) of nature as Eliphaz does (5, 9–10) are to be regarded as additions to the text by a pious commentator. The 10th verse (again quoted 36, 6), is directly taken over from the speech of Eliphaz (5, 9), and thus is revealed as a later insertion. Job's contention (verses 5–7) is that it is of no use to argue with a Being whose wrath is shown by violent interruptions of the course of nature, whose powerful will is merely the expression of His morose disposition, who does what He pleases. Verses 8–10, on the other hand, carry us into an entirely different area of thought. They describe God's supreme control and guidance of nature.

    8.   "Who, by Himself, stretches out the heavens,
            And treads their heights.

(so read instead of "heights of sea.")

    9.   Who makes the Aldebaran [and] Orion;
            The Pleiades and the constellations of the South.

(Verse 9, which does not read very smoothly, may be an amplification of v. 8 in prose form.)

    10.   Who does great things past finding out,
            And wonders without number."

[79] So by a slight change in the text.

[80] You cannot get at God. No one can see Him, no one can follow God's course. He cannot be controlled; he cannot be questioned.

THE BOOK OF JOB

Though the companions of Rahab stoop.[81]
How then could I answer Him,
Choose my words with Him? [82]
15 Even if I were in the right, I could not plead, [83]
[And] make my appeal to my judge.[84]
[If I were to summon, and He were to respond to me,
I could not be certain that He would give ear to me] [85]
He who crushes[86] me for a trifle,[87]
And increases my wounds without cause;
Does not permit me to take breath,
But satiates me with bitterness.[88]

---

[81] The text has a superfluous "under him." The allusion is (as in 7, 12) to the myth of Yahweh's conflict with monsters, symbolizing the primæval chaos and who are subdued by Yahweh. Rahab is one of the names of the monster who as the leader of an army proceeds to fight with Yahweh, but is forced to yield. See above the notes to 3, 8 and 7, 12. Yahweh in his wrath crushes the monsters who appeal in vain to His mercy. What then can man expect of such a Being?

[82] The picture of the lawsuit is continued. "Answering" refers to the plea before a court. So also the Greek text takes it.

[83] Literally "answer," but again in the legal sense of pleading ones case.

[84] Again the dilemma, arising out of the circumstance that the accusation is against the judge.

[85] Even if God were to accept the summons to the suit, it would be of little use, since one could not be sure that He would pay heed to one's presentation of one's case. This 16th verse may be a later amplification of the thought implied in the preceding verse.

[86] Same verb as in Genesis 3, 15, "crush under foot."
[87] Literally, "for a hair"—following Ehrlich's reading.
[88] In the sense of "woe." The same phrase is found Lam. 3, 15, just as Lam. 3, 14 suggests Job 30, 1 and 9. If there is

THE BOOK OF JOB

If it is a test of strength, He is surely superior!
But if it is a [question] of justice, who can arraign Him?[89]
If I were in the right, His mouth would condemn me;[90] [20]
If I were entirely right,[91] He would twist the verdict.
I am guiltless—[92] I care not;[93]
[Aye][94] I loathe my life!

---

any question of dependency involved, the chapter in Lamentations presupposes the Book of Job.

[89] Read "Him" instead of "me" and see for such intentional changes above p. 109 *seq.* and below note to 9, 35. Note again the use of legal terms "justice" (or "judgment") and "arraign." Job becomes increasingly bold and refuses to mince matters. He admits that if the contest is one of strength, he has been worsted by God, but if it is a question to be judged on its merits by a court, who can bring a charge against God, though God knows, as is admitted in the popular tale, that Job is "pious" and "upright" (1, 1 and 8 and 2, 3)?

[90] By asserting his innocence Job would merely bring about his conviction. The original reading was clearly "His mouth," but this was regarded by the editor as *too* objectionable, since the sense would be that God by His decision deliberately condemns innocence. He, therefore, changed it to "my."

[91] The same word (*tam*) used of Job in 1, 1 and 8 and 2, 3.

[92] The "patient" Job is here revealed as throwing down the challenge to God, though he knows that he may be instantly killed for such blasphemous conduct. The Greek version tries to tone down the blasphemous implication by a deliberate change of text. Instead of "I am guiltless" etc., it renders: "If I were guilty, I would know nothing except that my life would be taken."

[93] Literally: "I know not my soul" in the sense of "I set my life as nought."

[94] Some such word must be added to complete the line to three beats—perhaps *amnam* "indeed," which occurs frequently in Job.

THE BOOK OF JOB

It's all one—therefore I say:
The guiltless and the wicked He destroys.
If a scourge should suddenly strike one,
He would [merely] laugh at the death [95] of the innocent.
The earth is given into the hand of the wicked;[96]
The faces of her judges are covered.[97]
[If it is not so, how is it?][98]

25
25-35
God is
arbitrary.

Now my days pass swifter than a runner;[99]
[And] they flee without seeing joy.[1]
They flit past as the reed boats;[2]

---

[95] So read by a slight change.
[96] A veiled allusion that God himself is wicked.
[97] i.e., the judges are blind. There is no justice in a world, created by a supposedly just God.
[98] The line, as it stands, has no parallel to go with it. Either a line has dropped out, or the question is introduced by some commentator, sympathizing with Job, and who intended to quote 24, 25 in full. The translation, "How is it?" is preferable to "Who is it?" The poem here reaches its climax in showing that a man innocently punished as Job was would be driven to despair and to blasphemies. He would boldly declare that there can be no justice in a world in which such things are permitted. The alternative, which is here broached, is that blind cruel fate rules the world, which assertion would cut at the root of the prophet's conception of Yahweh as the just and merciful Ruler and thus remove the very basis on which post-exilic Judaism rests.
[99] Note again the psychological finesse of a return to the plaint of the sufferer, as a reaction from the mental strain which has led Job to utter charges against God. Verses 25-26 are similar to 7, 6 seq.
[1] Literally "Seeing good" in the sense of enjoyment for which Ecclesiastes uses the less classical construction to "look upon good." See Jastrow, *A Gentle Cynic*, p. 205, note 18.
[2] i.e., the rafts that sweep down the stream.

THE BOOK OF JOB

As an eagle swooping on the prey,
If I say "I will forget my trouble,
Change my expression and be of good cheer,"
I shudder at all my pains;   28
I know that Thou wilt not release me.[3]
If I were to wash myself white as snow,[4]   30
And to cleanse my hands with lye,
Thou wouldst nevertheless sink me into the mire,[5]
And my clothes would abhor me.[6]
For He is not a man as I am, that I could answer Him;[7]
Come, let us go to court together.
There is no arbiter[8] betwixt us,
To lay his hands on both of us.

---

[3] Again a legal term to indicate a verdict of not guilty. Verse 29 reading:

"I am judged guilty, why then this vain effort?"

is a comment to 28[b], revealed as such by its prosaic form.

[4] So read by a slight change.

[5] The text has "into the pit," one of the names of the nether world, but the reading of the Greek version "into the mire" fits the context better.

[6] By a slight change we can obtain this reading in Hebrew. With his naked body sunk in the mud, Job could say that his soiled clothes would abhor the thought of their being placed on him.

[7] Again, in the legal sense of answering a summons. See in this connection an interesting study on "The Summons" by Prof. D. W. Amram in the University of Pennsylvania Law Review for November, 1919.

[8] Literally, "the one who reproves," *i.e.*, the umpire who stands between the contending parties and reproves the one who is in the wrong.

THE BOOK OF JOB

If he would only remove His[9] rod from me,
And not let His terror startle me,
35 Then I would declare without fear of Him,[10]
That He is not fair to me.[11]

10, 1 I am weary of my life;
1–7 I will give free course to my complaint.[12]
No escape I will say unto God: Thou canst not declare me
from God's   guilty.
wrath. Let me know what Thy charge is against me.[13]
Is it pleasing to Thee to distort [justice],[14]
To despise the work of Thy hands?[15]
[Hast Thou eyes of flesh,
Or seest Thou with man's eyes?
5 Are Thy days as the days of man?
Thy years as the years of mortal?
That Thou probest my transgression;
And searchest my sin?

---

[9] *i.e.*, God's rod, for which the parallel passage (13, 21) uses "hand."

[10] Job dares not speak while God's rod is over him and he is startled by the fear of God.

[11] So Ehrlich's happy and ingenious interpretation of the closing phrase which has puzzled all commentators. In the text "I" is used for "Him" as elsewhere in Job to remove a reference to God that seemed particularly distasteful to pious commentators.

[12] An extra line suggested by the variant to 7, 11 reads:
    "I will speak in the bitterness of my soul."

[13] Note again the legal terms in continuation of the picture of a lawsuit.

[14] So Ehrlich's reading by a transposition of two letters.

[15] A superfluous line,
    "Thou dost shine upon the counsel of the wicked"
is an amplifying gloss to explain the first part of the verse.

THE BOOK OF JOB

Since Thou knowest that I am not to be saved,[16]
That there is no escape from Thy hands.][17]
Thy hands [first] moulded and fashioned me,   8–17
And *then* Thou decidest [18] to altogether destroy *God the creator is*
me.   *also the destroyer.*
Remember that like clay Thou didst mould me,
And unto dust wilt bring me again.[19]
Didst Thou not pour me out as milk,   10
And like cheese didst curdle me;[20]
Clothed me with skin and flesh,
And knitted me together with bones and sinews?
Grace[21] Thou didst grant me;

---

[16] So by a slight change in the text, which as it stands,
"I shall not be condemned,"
says just the contrary of what Job has in mind.

[17] Verses 4–7 interrupt the context, though they are in line with Job's indictment of God as betraying a cruelty which one might expect of a vicious and malicious human persecutor, bent upon searching for a guilt which does not exist. The verses may represent the amplification of the indictment by some one who wished to further emphasize the callousness of God to innocent suffering.

[18] I follow the reading of the Greek text—"then" (or, "afterwards") instead of "together." The Hebrew text has a superfluous "on all sides"—an erroneous comment to the reading "together." Job here (verses 8–15) brings a new charge—and one of a still bolder character.

[19] The reference is to the creation of man in the Yahwist narrative (Genesis 2, 7) out of the dust of the ground as a potter moulds his clay, but only to be returned to the dust (Genesis 3, 19). The Book of Job thus assumes the existence of the Genesis tale in its present form.

[20] The whitish color of the *semen* is compared to milk and cheese.

[21] A glossator added "life," which was erroneously embodied into the text. It makes the line too long by one beat.

THE BOOK OF JOB

And Thy providence watched over my spirit?
And yet such things [22] Thou didst hide in Thy mind!
I *know* that this is Thy way;
[That] if I sinned even while Thou kept watch over me,
Thou wouldst not acquit me of my iniquity.[23]

15 If I *am* guilty—woe is me;
But [even] if I were guiltless, I could not lift my head.[24]
Wilt Thou [25] hunt me down as a lion,
And thus unceasingly manifest Thy superiority?
Constantly renewing Thy attack upon me,
With ever-increasing anger towards me?[26]

18-22
*Would that
I had not
been born.*

Why didst Thou bring me forth from the womb?

---

[22] *i.e.*, misery and suffering during life which not only come from God, but which God intended should come.

[23] Job argues that if there is such a thing as Divine providence watching over men, then since sin comes despite this care, God should consistently not hold man to account.

[24] Again a return to the thought, that even if one were innocent it would make no difference, since one bowed down with shame and misery cannot raise his head as the virtuous and innocent man has a right to do (11, 15; 22, 26). A glossator added as a superfluous line, "filled with disgrace and satiated with misery and trouble." By a slight change in this gloss one obtains "satiated" instead of "look upon" which gives no sense; and the strange word at the beginning of the following verse is a corruption for the term for "trouble" (*yagôn*). So Ehrlich, (*Randglossen*, 6 p. 222) whom I follow.

[25] In bitter irony Job asks whether in this way by hunting a helpless innocent man like a lion God's marvelous power is to be displayed?

[26] A gloss to the first half of the verse adds: "with changes of warfare towards me."

THE BOOK OF JOB

Why did I [not][27] expire, and no eye would have seen me?
As though I had never been, would I now be;
Carried directly from the womb to the grave.[28]
Are not the days of my life [29] few?   20
Cease [30] and grant me some cheer,
Before I go, without return, to the land of darkness,
The land of dense gloom, and without change.[31]

Thereupon Zophar, the Naamathite, in answer said: 11, 1
Should one full of words remain unanswered?
Should a babbler be acquitted?   1–12
Thy foolish talk may silence dullards,   *God is just and sees*
Prattling as though there were none to refute thee.   *what is hidden from*
Now thou sayest "my argument[32] is clear;"   *man.*

---

[27] Add "not," following the Greek text.

[28] Harking back to 3, 11–13. Verses 18–22 represent another independent attempt to express the same thought, which dominates chapter 3.

[29] So according to the Greek text, which gives us a more complete line than the Hebrew text.

[30] A variant or comment adds: "Let (me) alone."

[31] More literally: "without any order," *i.e.*, without any fixed succession of light after darkness. The nether world whither the dead go is perpetually dark.
There are two glosses to this verse—a gloss and a supergloss
  (a) "it lights up like dense darkness" (*ōphēl*)
to explain the force of the first part of the verse, which contains an obscure word (*ēphāthā*).
  (b) "like *ōphēl*" = *salmaweth* ("dense gloom"),
explaining the strange word *ōphēl* in the gloss by a more familiar one, which is erroneously inserted also at the end of v. 21.

[32] This seems to be the force of the term usually rendered "doctrine."

THE BOOK OF JOB

And thou art pure in thine eyes.[33]
5 But oh if God might speak,
And open His lips against thee.
He would reveal to thee what is hidden;[34]
And that God holds thee to account.[35]
Canst thou penetrate to the essence of God?[36]
Attain the bounds of Shaddai?
8 [Look at] the high heavens—what canst thou do?
Of that which is deeper than Sheol—what canst thou know?[37]
11 For He knows false men,

---

[33] Read "thou art" instead of "I am." The change was probably intentionally made. The Greek text to further tone down Job's audacity renders "do not say: I am blameless before Him."

[34] *i.e.*, "wisdom" as a commentator adds to suggest that Divine wisdom is something different from human insight. Another commentator adds "for there are two sides to insight," *i.e.*, an outward or superficial side accessible to man, and an inner and hidden one, known to God alone.

[35] Text adds by way of explanation: "of thy iniquity." I follow Ehrlich's emendation and interpretation of this difficult line.

[36] More literally: "source." The word occurs again 38, 16.

[37] An amplifier adds, v. 9;

"Longer than the earth is its measure (*i.e.*, of Sheol)
Broader than the sea"

Another commentator harking back to Job's complaint (9, 11–12) that no one can follow God's course and no one can restrain Him, gives a pious turn to the thought of Job by placing in Zophar's mouth (v. 10):

"If He seizes and imprisons or calls to the tribunal,
Who can hinder Him?"

"Imprison" refers to punishment through disease; "calling to the tribunal" may mean gathering to the dead—and to judgment.

THE BOOK OF JOB

And sees iniquity which they do not discern.[38]
But a brainless man will get understanding,
[Only] when a wild ass is born as a man.[39]
If thou wouldst set thy mind aright,[40]
And stretch out thy hand towards Him,—
Removing thy guilt far from thee,
And not permitting wrong to dwell with thee,
Then thou couldst lift up thy face;[41]
And stand firmly rooted, without fear.
Then thou wouldst forget trouble;
Recall it merely as days [42] gone by.
Deep darkness[43] would become as morning;
And denseness [44] brighter than high noon,[45]
And thou wouldst be secure for there would be
 hope;[46]

13–20
The appeal of the penitent to God will find response.

15

---

[38] God knows how corrupt mortals are, and that many sins are committed which are never recognized as such, except by God.

[39] A bitter taunt to suggest that Job is hopelessly stupid in not recognizing how useless it is to pretend to any *real* knowledge, which is reserved for God. Zophar may be quoting a popular saying.

[40] Like Psalm 51, 12, "a clean mind."

[41] The text has a superfluous word "without blemish," which is probably a corruption (by a slight change) for "on high"—a comment to "lift up."

[42] So read by a slight change instead of "waters." Trouble would be merely a faint memory.

[43] So by a slight change of the text, suggested by Ehrlich.

[44] Meaning "sorrow" that would no longer weigh one down.

[45] In contrast to Sheol (10, 22) where there is perpetual darkness without hope of any light. I follow the Greek text in changing the order of the lines, so as to place "morning" before "high noon."

[46] Followed by a variant line:
"Thou wilt feel assured to lie down in safety."

THE BOOK OF JOB

19ᵃ Thou wouldst lie down, with none to make thee afraid.
    Many will seek thy favor,
20   While the eyes of the wicked grow dim.
    Their refuge shall fail them,
    And their hope become a disappointment.[47]

12, 1 Then Job in answer said:
1–6   No doubt but you are the people,
Job a laughing-stock and a butt.   And with you wisdom will die.[48]
    But I have a mind as well as you;[49]
    And who does not know [all] these things?[50]
    A laughing-stock to his neighbor has he become,[51]
    Who calls upon God to answer him;[52]
5   A worthless torch to those free from care (?);
    A target for their blows.[53]

---

[47] Cf. 31, 39, where a similar phrase occurs. Some codices of the Greek translation, as for example, the Alexandrinus, add the words "for with Him is wisdom and power." The addition must have been in the Hebrew text on which the Alexandrine codex is based, and furnishes an illustration and proof of the amplification to which the Book of Job must have been subject before the present text was finally evolved. The addition, however, is clearly out of place. It belongs perhaps earlier in the chapter, and becomes intelligible as a pious comment (taken over from 12, 13) to verse 5 or 6.

[48] Uttered in bitter sarcasm.

[49] A comment or variant, missing in the Greek version, adds: "I am not inferior to you," taken over from 13 : 2.

[50] *i.e.*, your obvious platitudes.

[51] So read, as the Greek text does, instead of the first person.

[52] Cf. Jer. 20, 7. A sympathetic glossator adds: "a laughing stock—the perfect righteous man." Cf. Gen. 6, 1, where Noah is thus described. See also Ps. 15, 2.

[53] The entire 5th verse, which has occasioned much difficulty to commentators, is almost hopelessly corrupt—especially

THE BOOK OF JOB

While the tents of the robbers prosper,
And there is security for those who provoke
   God.[54]
But ask now of the beasts;[55]
And the bird of heaven to tell thee;
What crawls[56] on the earth to teach thee;
And the fish of the sea to tell thee.
[Who does not know all these things
That the hand of Yahweh does this?][57]
Cannot the ear test words,
And the palate taste for itself?[58]

7-15
God builds up but also tears down.

9

11

---

the second half. I follow Ehrlich's restoration as the most probable solution, though not altogether satisfactory. The first half contains a superfluous word "the one of ease," which is a comment to the strange and perhaps corrupt word that precedes.

[54] A pious annotator adds "whom God holds in His power."

[55] A comment, which makes the line too long, adds: "to teach thee."

[56] So read by a slight change of the text, suggested many years ago by Hitzig (*Hiob*, p. 91). The line is missing in the original Greek version.

[57] A pious commentator adds (verse 10) in prose form, though in elevated diction:
"In whose hand is the soul of every living being and the breath of all mankind."

The insertion is inartistic, because it interrupts the sequence of the thought. Moreover, it is banal to dwell upon what is obvious, particularly when in verses 13 *seq.* the argument of Zophar that God's will and power are alike supreme, is summarized in an impressive and poetic manner. The introduction of the name Yahweh in 9ª, not used by the author of the philosophical poem (except in 28, 28—an added chapter which has no connection with the Book of Job), suggests that the 9th verse may likewise be a later addition. It is missing in the earlier Greek versions.

[58] *i.e.*, everybody can find this out for himself. It is as simple as hearing and tasting. The verse is a popular saying which is quoted again 34, 3. It is missing in some Hebrew codices.

THE BOOK OF JOB

14		If He tears down, it is not rebuilt; If He shuts a man in, he is not released.[59]
15		If He withholds the waters, they remain in their place;[60] If He sends them out, they engulf the earth.
16–24 *Overthrow* *of leaders.*		With Him is strength and insight; Under Him is the error and its cause.[61]
20		He takes away speech from the trustworthy,[62]

Verses 12–13 are maxims added by some commentator in view of v. 16.

"[Not] with greybeards is wisdom,
Nor understanding with the aged.
With Him is wisdom and might;
With Him is counsel and intelligence."

The addition of "not" seems to be required by the context and is favored by the parallel 32, 9.

[59] The Targum refers this line to the grave.

[60] So read instead of "dry up," as a better parallel to "engulf."

[61] Literally "what causes error." A fine though bold thought that the sinner acts under God's control, that there can be no sin, therefore, unless God wills it.

[62] *i.e.*, deprives them of their reason. The "trustworthy ones" are the elders, whose wisdom is their distinguishing mark. Verses 17–19 represent expansions of the thought expressed in verses 20–21. These additions, while furnishing further illustrations of how God lowers those who once occupied high positions, also are intended to give a different turn to Job's thought. See the following note:

(17) "He strips counsellors of authority
And makes judges fools."

is an amplification of verse 20, with 19 as a variant:

"He strips priests of authority,
And overthrows those who were [regarded as] permanent."

"Counsellors" and the "permanent ones" are taken as synonyms of the "trustworthy"; "priests" and "judges," as the equivalents to "elders." Verse 18 is the expansion of v. 21.

THE BOOK OF JOB

And deprives elders of understanding.
He pours contempt upon the nobles,   21
And loosens the belt of the rulers.[63]
He takes away the reason of the chiefs,[64]   24
And leads them astray into a trackless chaos.[65]

---

[63] Nobles and rulers are synonymous. "Loosening the belt" is the metaphor for loss of authority. The amplifier introduces as an expansion of this thought v. 18.:

> "He loosens the girdle [*i.e.*, their strength or authority] of kings"

and then by way of contrast, adds:

> "And binds their loins with a (common) girdle"

i.e., reduces their rank to that of the ordinary man. The line is missing in all the earlier Greek versions, as also v. 21[a]. Note, however, that the main thought of verses 20, 21 and 24 is to show how God lowers those of high estate [the "trustworthy," "elders," "nobles," "rulers" and "chiefs"] and not how the lowly are raised to high positions, which has no bearing on the argument. For this reason, v. 23, which emphasizes the vicissitudes in the fortunes of peoples from high to low and *vice versa* is likewise to be regarded as an insertion, apart from the fact that in passing from the fate of individuals controlled by God to peoples, a further nuance is introduced which is foreign to the main argument. The 23rd verse reads:

> "He exalts nations, and destroys them;
> He spreads peoples, and overthrows them."

Also v. 22:

> "He reveals hidden things out of darkness;
> He brings what is dark to the light."

is evidently a saying introduced here by some amplifier, but entirely out of the context.

[64] The line has a superfluous word "people," which makes it too long.

[65] The line together with 21[a] is found again Psalms 107, 40. A pious amplifier adds (v. 25) by way of comment:

> "So that they grope in darkness without light,
> And He makes them stagger like a drunken man."

THE BOOK OF JOB

13, 1 All this my eye has seen;[66]
My ear has heard and understood.
As much as you know, I know;
I am not inferior to you.

3-12
Job denounces his friends as falsifiers of the truth.
But I wish to address myself to Shaddai;[67]
My desire is to argue with God.
You are merely plasterers of lies;[68]
Quacks,[69] all of you.

5 If you would only hold your peace,
It would be wisdom on your part. [70]
Listen now to my argument, [71]
And hearken to my pleading!
Will you undertake to defend God by a falsehood?

---

[66] While this entire section 12, 7-25 is thus shown to contain many insertions and amplifications, there is no reason to follow Siegfried, who takes the whole section as a later interpolation in the interest of orthodoxy. If one reads the section in the correct spirit, it will be found that Job is merely anxious to show that he knows that changes in fortunes are due to God. The later additions, however, *are* due to orthodox amplifiers of the original book. See above to 12, 3.

[67] Job returns to his point that he has a charge to bring against God. He does not deny that all that happens is due to God and that He brings about the fall of those of high estate. The point is that God does this without giving those who are to be severely dealt with a chance to plead their cause. God acts wilfully and not like a fair judge who decides after hearing testimony. Throughout this chapter as in chapter 10, legal terminology is freely introduced.

[68] You coat your utterances with lies.

[69] Literally: "worthless healers." There is a superfluous "But" or "However" at the beginning of this line, repeated by error from the preceeding verse.

[70] Cf. Proverbs 17, 28.

[71] So the Greek text.

THE BOOK OF JOB

To make a deceitful plea for Him?[72]
[Do you propose to show favor to Him,[73]
Or to plead on behalf of God?[74]]
Would it be well if He should examine you? 9
Or do you think to deceive Him as one deceives
    a man?[75]
Does His majesty not terrify you, 11
And fear of Him not overwhelm you?
Your sayings [76] are without point;[77]
Your arguments are mere clay.[78]
Hold your peace [79] that I may speak,
Whatever may come to me.[80]
I will bite[81] my flesh with my teeth,

*13–22
Job defies
God in the
assurance
of his
innocence.*

---

[72] Job charges his friends with pleading God's case by forging lies and by utterances which they know to be deceitful.

[73] *i.e.*, to twist facts so as to show God to be in the right.

[74] *i.e.*, to plead His cause, as though God needed you to act as His defendants? The verse contains only two beats in each line. It may be a later insertion by someone who tried his hand at expressing the same thought as in v. 7.

[75] Verse 10, in prose form, appears to be an explanatory addition to v. 7. It reads: "He would surely rebuke you, if you secretly showed favor."

[76] Literally, "reminders."

[77] Literally, "ash proverbs," *i.e.*, without vitality.

[78] I follow Ehrlich's happy interpretation of this line. Literally "your hints are clay lumps" in the sense of worthless arguments, as easily crushed as bits of clay.

[79] Hebrew text has "before me" which is superfluous and is not found in the Greek version.

[80] Literally, "what upon what" in the sense of "whatsoever."

[81] So read by a slight change in the text. To bite one's own flesh is a picturesque metaphor to indicate that one will take the responsibility for injury on oneself. The word "wherefore" at the beginning of this verse in the ordinary English translations is part of the idiomatic phrase at the close of the preceding verse. See the preceding note.

THE BOOK OF JOB

And put my life in my hand.
15 Aye, though He slay me, I tremble not;[82]
For all that, I will maintain His[83] course to His face.[84]
17 Listen, therefore, to my speech,
That I may declare it to your ears!
Behold, I have prepared my case,[85]
I know that I am innocent.
Who is there that can contend with me,[86]

---

[82] The traditional translation "though he slay me, yet will I trust in Him," has long been abandoned by modern scholars. Even the RV admits as a marginal reading, "I have no hope." The translation of the American Jewish Publication Society is alone in retaining the traditional rendering, which is just the contrary of what Job in his anguish declares. This traditional rendering rests upon an intentional change on the part of the Jewish theologians—the Massoretes—of the word "not" to "in him." In Hebrew the two words sound alike. The text has correctly "not" while the marginal reading proposes "to him." The verb following is to be read *ahîl*, "I tremble," as Ehrlich has recognized. The Massoretes inverted two letters to get a different meaning. See above p. 121 *seq.*

[83] Read "His course" instead of "my course" by a slight change. This change was likewise made with intent to tone down the blasphemous audacity of Job in throwing down the challenge to God.

[84] *i.e.*, I will continue to charge God with injustice towards me. The phraseology is legal. The conciliatory glossator to take off the sharp edge of Job's severe indictment of God adds in prose form (v. 16):

"Aye, this will be my salvation, that the impious will not come before Him."

That is precisely what Job in his present mood did *not* and could not say.

[85] Again legal phraseology. Cf. 23, 4.

[86] *i.e.*, answer me in court.

THE BOOK OF JOB

That I should now hold my peace and die?[87]
Only two things do not [88] unto me,   20
Then I will not hide myself from Thee.[89]
Only remove Thy hand [90] from me;
And let Thy terror not startle me.
Then call [to judgment]; and I will answer the
    summons;[91]
Or let me speak [92] and Thou answer me.
How many are my iniquities and sins?   *23–28*
Let me know my transgression and sin!   *God is*
Why dost Thou hide Thy face from me,   *cruel to Job.*
And regardest me as Thy enemy?
Harassing a driven leaf,   25
And pursuing dry stubble.
For Thou inscribest against me past deeds,[93]
And chargest me with the iniquities of my
    youth.
Thou puttest my feet in stocks,[94]
Which press against my ankles;[95]

---

[87] The line is missing in the earlier Greek version.
[88] The Greek text omits "not," which does not, however, affect the meaning of the verse.
[89] *i.e.*, not be afraid of God, as Job confesses he is, because of God's terrible and unjustifiable anger. The line is missing in the original Greek version.
[90] Literally: "palm" in the sense of control or grasp. Cf. above 9, 34.
[91] To defend myself. Note again the legal phraseology.
[92] *i.e.*, bring the charge against God.
[93] So Ehrlich's interpretation.
[94] A superfluous line reading:

    "And Thou keepest guard over all my ways"

is inserted from 33, 11.
[95] The joints or ankles—not the soles—are meant.

THE BOOK OF JOB

So that I [96] am like a decaying substance,
Like a moth-eaten garment.

<small>14, 1
1-22
Death without further hope as the end of man's short and troublesome existence.
3
5</small>

Man is born of woman,
Few of days and full of trouble.
He comes forth like a flower and withers;
Fleeing as a disappearing shadow.
Hast Thou indeed considered this, [97]
In bringing him [98] to judgment? [99]
Since his days are determined,
And his months numbered with Thee,[1]
Look away from him and desist,
Until he accomplishes his day [2] as a hireling.
For there is hope for a tree if cut down,[3]
That its tendril will not cease.
Though its root wax old in the earth,
And its stock die in the ground;

---

[96] So read instead of "he." Here the translation of the American Jewish Publication Society makes the change, but without indicating that it is deviating from the Massoretic text, the inviolability of which it usually maintains with the rigidity of a dogma. The same metaphor is found Is. 50, 9, though in a different connection.

[97] This is the force of the phrase "hast Thou opened Thy eyes in regard to this?"

[98] So read as in the Greek and Syriac versions, instead of "me."

[99] Text has an additional "with Thee" which makes the line too long. A pious glossator adds verse 4: "Can one bring clean out of unclean? Not one." *i.e.*, every man is by nature unclean,—full of sin. Similarly, Psalm 14, 3[b].

[1] An explanatory gloss, forming a superfluous line, adds, "Thou hast appointed his limit, which is not to be passed."

[2] *i.e.*, satisfies the master by completing the day's work.

[3] A gloss adds "that it will sprout again," which makes the line too long by one beat.

THE BOOK OF JOB

Through the scent of water [4] it will bud,
And put forth boughs like a shoot.
But man dies and passes away;   10
He expires, and how is it with him?[5]
Man when he lies down will not rise;[6]   12
Till the heavens be no more, they shall not awake.[7]
Oh that Thou wouldst hide me in Sheol,
Conceal me till Thy anger is past![8]
[Appoint a time for me and [then] remember me,
If [forsooth] a man who dies can revive.][9]

---

[4] Not the "odor of water" for, as Ehrlich properly says, water ordinarily has no odor.

[5] Not "where is he" which is banal. Verse 11 reading:
> "Waters drain the sea,
> And the stream dries up."

interrupts the context, and is an inserted quotation from Isaiah 19, 5.

[6] The tree is revived though the proximity of water, but man cannot be resuscitated though all the water in the world be poured over him.

[7] A commentator adds a superfluous line:
> "They shall not be roused out of their sleep"

The words are missing in the original Greek version and in Jerome's translation.

[8] Job longs for death, but with a human touch only as a temporary state.

[9] To take this line, as is usually done, as though Job were asking a question, would be in place if the question were asked by some commentator, but this presupposes that Job voices his belief in a revival of the dead. That surely cannot be the case in view of what he has just said (verses 10–12). We have therefore the alternative of regarding the line,
> "Appoint a time for me and remember me"

(a) as a variant or explanation to v. 13^b and then take 14^a as

THE BOOK OF JOB

All the days of my service[10] would I wait,
Until my charged estate should come.
15 Thou wouldst call, and I would answer Thee;
Eager for Thy act of grace.[11]
In that case Thou wouldst guide [12] my steps,
And not keep track of my sin.[13]
My transgression would be sealed in a bag,
And thou wouldst cover [14] up my iniquity.
But instead,[15]—[as] the falling mountain crumbles,
And the rock is torn from its place;
And water wears the stones;
And the shower washes away the soil;[16]
20 Thou art wroth with him, and he passes away;[17]

---

an interpolated question, or (b) if 13ᶜ and 14ᵃ are to form a hemistich, then we must take the words as indicated in the translation—expressing the *doubt* as to the realization of the wish expressed.

[10] *i.e.*, whatever period Thou wouldst assign to me as my term in Sheol.

[11] Literally: "The work of Thy hands," but in the sense of what "Thou wouldst do to me," *viz.*, restore me to life after divine anger is past.

[12] Literally: "count" as a loving father follows the first efforts of the child at walking. The common translation of v. 16 is entirely astray.

[13] As God is doing now. See above 13, 27ᵇ (gloss).

[14] Literally, "plaster."

[15] Job realizes that there is no hope of man coming back to life again after death has come.

[16] A commentator adds a superfluous line, "So thou destroyest man's hope." The verse is missing in the older Greek versions and in Jerome's translation.

[17] Text adds "forever," which is in place, but makes the line too long.

THE BOOK OF JOB

In anger,[18] Thou dismissest him.
His sons may come to honor, but he does not know it;
They may be brought low, but he does not perceive it.
Only his own flesh pains him,
And he grieves for himself alone [19]

Then Eliphaz the Temanite in answer said: 15, 1
Should a wise man answer wind,[20]
And fill his belly with east wind?
Reasoning without purpose,   1–16
And with words that are of no avail?   *Eliphaz taunts Job*
Just as little canst thou argue away fear of God,[21]   *with his iniquity and*
And diminish respect before God.   *his vaunted*
When thy iniquity instructs thy mouth,[22]   *superiority.*
And thou choosest the manner of sophists,[23]   5
Thy mouth convicts thee—not He;[24]

---

[18] Literally: "changing his countenance," for which we have a parallel phrase in Assyrian, used in the sense of "being distressed or angry" like "fallen countenance" (Genesis 4, 5). Since the phrase refers to God, we should perhaps read "changing Thy countenance."

[19] In Sheol man is only conscious of his own hopeless state.

[20] Text adds "knowledge" before "wind," *i.e.*, knowledge that is mere wind, without substance. This is clearly a comment and makes the line too long. Cf. 8, 1 and 16, 3.

[21] *i.e.*, to answer thee is as futile as thy attempt to diminish reverence by thy blasphemous charges against God.

[22] *i.e.*, when thy wickedness puts thy words into thy mouth.

[23] Literally: "the tongue of the crafty," *i.e.*, word twisters.

[24] Text "I," an intentional change to avoid an objectionable reference to God, as above, 9, 20 and 13, 15 and elsewhere.

THE BOOK OF JOB

Thy lips testify against thee.[25]
Wast thou born at the beginning?[26]
Brought forth before the hills?
Hast thou overheard the secret of God?
And hast thou monopolized wisdom?
What dost thou know that we do not know?
And what understanding hast thou which is not with us?
10 [Elder and greybeard are among us—
More than old enough to be thy father[27]]
Are consolations [28] too small for thee,
And the word that deals gently with thee?
What has taken hold of thy mind?
And why are thy eyes haughty?[29]
[And] thou desirest to give thy spirit back to God,[30]

---

[25] Again legal phraseology.

[26] An allusion to Proverbs 8, 22 where wisdom says, "The Lord made me as the beginning of His way." Eliphaz asks Job whether he regards himself as older and, therefore, superior to wisdom? The sarcastic insertion 38, 21 harks back to our verse.

[27] Not to be taken literally, as though Job's father were still alive. Eliphaz is here quoting a popular saying, as Elihu does, 32, 9, or somebody has inserted the maxim at this point as appropriate. The verse is missing in the older Greek versions and in Jerome's translation.

[28] Such as the three friends have offered. A commentator adds "God" after consolations, which misses the point and makes the line too long by one beat. The Greek versions omit the word.

[29] So the Greek text, as in Proverbs 30, 13.

[30] *i.e.*, that thou wishest to die. So Ehrlich's happy interpretation with a reference, perhaps to the addition to Ecclesiastes 12, 7.

THE BOOK OF JOB

And givest utterance to [foolish] talk?[31]
What is man that he should think himself pure?
And the one born of woman that he should be
    innocent?
Even his holy ones [32] he does not trust—   15
And the heavens are not pure in his sight;[33]
How much less one that is of low estate and im-
    pure,
Man who drinks iniquity like water?[34]

Listen to what I will tell thee;   17–35
And what I have seen I will declare unto   *The bitter fate of the wicked.*
    thee—
What wise men have told,
And what their fathers have not concealed from
    them;[35]
[To whom the land belonged
With no stranger in their midst].[36]
All his days the wicked is in terror,   20

---

[31] Eliphaz knows that Job does not mean what he says when he longs for death. That is idle chatter.

[32] *i.e.*, his angels or ministers. Cf. 4, 18, which is here repeated.

[33] The Alexandrine Codex of the Greek version has an additional phrase; "and the stars are not pure."

[34] *i.e.*, commits sin, as readily as one drinks water. A similar phrase, perhaps quoted from our passage, occurs 34, 7 in a speech of Elihu, who applies it to Job.

[35] So by a slight change, supported by the Greek text.

[36] An obscure verse—usually explained as a reference to the great age of the traditional wisdom which Eliphaz is revealing, going back to the days when the population was not yet mixed through the advent of strangers. The verse may represent a later addition. It is only partially preserved in the original Greek version. The word "alone" in the first half is clearly superfluous.

THE BOOK OF JOB

And the number of [his] years are limited.[37]
A sound of terror is in his ears;
Even when secure, he [imagines] a destroyer to be coming against him.[38]

22 He has no hope to escape from darkness;
[Believes himself] destined for the sword.[39]

24 Distress and anguish startle him,
Overpower him as fated (?) for destruction [40] (?)

25 Because he stretched out his hand against God,
And showed himself insolent against Shaddai;
[Who rushes upon him as against a foe;[41]
Shatters (?) .... his shield.[42]
Though he has covered his face with his fatness,
And added to the fat on his loins;]
He will inhabit ruined cities,

---

[37] The text adds: "for the oppressor," which makes the line too long.

[38] The wicked is haunted by fear, even when he is perfectly safe.

[39] *i.e.*, to be murdered. Verse 23 consists of a series of glosses, erroneously united together (a) "he wanders about for bread"—a gloss to 24ª (b) "where is it"—perhaps a supergloss, (c) he knows that it is ready at hand"—a gloss to "destined for the sword," (d) "day of darkness," either an explanation of "darkness" (v. 22) or a variant.

[40] The line is obscure, because of the corruptness of the text. The word "king," for which the Greek version has "general" is clearly a gloss—perhaps at a wrong place. The last word, usually rendered "battle" is entirely obscure. The general sense is all that one can gather.

[41] So the reading proposed by Ehrlich instead of "neck" which gives no sense.

[42] Text again corrupt. The context demands a reference to God's shattering the shield of the wicked. Verses 26–27 are missing in the older Greek versions.

THE BOOK OF JOB

Houses that are deserted of man.[43]
His riches[44] and substance shall not endure,
And his possession (?)[45] shall not cling (?) to the ground.
The hot flame shall dry up his branch,   30
And his fruit [46] shall pass away.[47]
Before its time his palm branch [48] shall wither;[49] 32
And his leafage shall not remain green.
He shall shake off as a vine his unripe grape;
And he shall cast off as an olive tree his blossom.
For the company of the impious shall be desolate,
And fire shall consume the tents of bribery.
Conceiving mischief and iniquity,[50]   35
Their belly will bring forth deception.[51]

Then Job in answer said: 16, 1
I have heard many such things;

---

[43] A glossator adds "destined for mound heaps," as the explanation to the first half of the verse.

[44] More literally: "He shall not remain rich."

[45] The Hebrew text is corrupt, but the parallelism suggests a synonym for substance. Verse 30ª "He shall not escape from the darkness" is a misplaced gloss to v. 22ª.

[46] So by a slight change in the text, favored by the Greek version.

[47] Verse 31 (in prose form):
"Let him not trust in deceptive vanity, for it will be vanity,"
represents a pious reflection by some commentator.

[48] So by a different vocalization of the word wrongly attached to the preceding verse.

[49] So by a textual change.

[50] The same phrase Is. 59:4. The line appears to have four beats, instead of the usual three. Perhaps "breeding" is to be omitted.

[51] *i.e.*, though the evil doers plan mischief—the result will be disappointment to them. They will be cheated of their aim.

THE BOOK OF JOB

*1–17
A cry of despair without hope.*

Sorry comforters [52] that you are.
Is there any end to windy words? [53]
Or what do you suffer [54] when answering?
I also could speak like you,
If you were in my stead.
I could overwhelm you [55] with words,
And shake my head at you.
5 But I would strengthen you by my speech;
And the sympathy of my lips [56] would give ease. [57]
Though now if I do speak, my pain is not assuaged;
And if I forbear, what do I gain by it? [58]
For Thou [59] hast worsted me;
Thou hast confused all my arguments.
[Thou has shrivelled me up to become a witness; [60]
And my leanness rises up against me. [61]]

---

[52] The comfort that Job's friends offer is to prove in long and tedious discourses that he must be an awful sinner. What purpose does that serve? says Job.

[53] *i.e.*, one could go on forever talking nonsensically.

[54] It is easy enough to speak when one is not in pain.

[55] A verbal form is used, indicative of stringing words together in a somewhat contemptuous sense.

[56] Literally, "movement of my lips."

[57] *i.e.*, in your place, I would speak words that would give comfort and that would ease the pain of a suffering fellow-man.

[58] Speaking or keeping silent—it is all the same.

[59] So read instead of "now," and change the verb to the second person.

[60] This eighth verse is not found in the original Greek version and may well be a later insertion. The sense seems to be that Job's body, emaciated through disease, is a witness to God's anger at him, though for no justifiable cause.

[61] A commentator by way of explanation adds "answers against him."

[He [62] has shown his contempt [63] and humiliated me;
He has gnashed his teeth upon me.][64]
They gape upon me with their mouth;[65]
They smite my cheeks scornfully. [66]
God delivers me unto the evildoers;
Into the hands of the wicked He casts me.

I was at ease and He crushed me;
He seized hold of my neck and dashed me to pieces;
He set me up as His target,[67]
With many [68] encompassing me;
He split my reins mercilessly,
And poured out my gall [69] upon the ground.

---

[62] *i.e.*, my human adversary.

[63] Literally: "He has turned up his nose." So Ehrlich's explanation.

[64] A glossator adds as a variant, "My adversary fixes his eyes upon me." Because of the change from the singular (v. 9) to the plural (v. 10) one of the two verses may be a later insertion. By omitting verse 9 as a later addition, we avoid the strange transitions from the address to God (v. 7) to a human adversary (v. 9) and then (v. 10) again to enemies in general.

[65] Cf. Psalm 22, 14, from which our line may be a quotation. The original Greek version omits the entire verse, and all the Greek versions omit the first half.

[66] Gloss, "Altogether they combine against me"—to suggest that each of his opponents helps the other in further humiliating and persecuting him remorselessly—one by turning up his nose, another by showing his teeth, a third by gaping at him and a fourth smiting him.

[67] Cf. Lam. 3, 12–13.

[68] So read, following Ehrlich and others.

[69] The "gall" stands for the "liver" which, with the "reins," is synonymous with the seat of life.

Breach upon breach [70] He opened against me;
Running against me like a giant.[71]
15 A sackcloth I have sewed on my skin,[72]
And I have rolled my strength [73] in the dust.
My face burns with weeping,
And deep darkness is on my eyelids.[74]
Although there is no violence in my hands,[75]
And my prayer is pure.
18 18–22 *Vain appeal for justice.* O Earth, do not cover up my blood,[76]
That there be no occasion for my outcry!
20 On high[77] my thoughts [78] are my intercessors;
To God my eye makes the appeal;
That mortal may secure justice from God,

---

[70] The text has a superfluous "face" before the second "breach."

[71] Literally: "Mighty man."

[72] A fine metaphor to suggest that Job is a perpetual mourner; his mourning garb is sewed to his body, so that it never comes off.

[73] Literally: "horn," used to describe one's beauty and vigor.

[74] His eyes are so filled with tears that he cannot see.

[75] Cf. Isaiah 53, 9.

[76] The covering up of the blood means that the wrong done is concealed. The uncovered blood cries for vengeance, as in the famous passage, Genesis 4, 10. A pious commentator, intent upon giving an orthodox turn to Job's despair, seized upon this opportunity to give expression to his own faith in God, which is in direct contradiction to the whole tenor of Job's bitter complaint (v. 19), "Even now my witness is in heaven" to which we have a more usual word for "witness" as a variant or comment. The last word of this verse "on high" belongs to the following stanza. See above, p. 116.

[77] To be taken over from the close of the inserted verse.

[78] So correctly on the basis of Psalm 139, 17, the translation of the Jewish Publication Society.

THE BOOK OF JOB

As between[79] a man and his fellow.[80]
For a few years will pass,
And I shall go the way of no return,[81]

My spirit is broken within me;[82]
The grave is ready (?)[83] for me.
Surely, mockers (?) are with me;
And I must endure their provocation.[84]
Be Thou my pledge which is already with Thee![85]
Who else can be surety for me?
Since Thou hast closed their mind against reason,[86]

17, 1
1–10
Job, the man of sorrows, abandoned by God and man alike.

4

---

[79] So by a slight change.

[80] The line is missing in the earlier Greek versions; and the entire stanza in the original Greek version.

[81] *i.e.*, there is no hope of securing justice during life. One must not read into this verse any thought of retribution after death, of which there is no trace either in the original or in the amplified Book of Job.

[82] So read by a slight change.

[83] Some such meaning for the strange verb used is demanded by the context. The text has the plural "graves" which in poetical usage has the force of the "deep grave," as in Ps. 137, 1, "rivers" stands for "great river," *i.e.*, the Euphrates.

[84] The line is missing in the Greek version.

[85] Job appeals to God to be his pledge—since God has already taken all that he has from him.

[86] Verse 5 seems to be a popular saying:

> "Among friends one divides one's fortune,
> While one's own sons languish,"

and either out of place, or introduced here by some pedantically inclined commentator to explain by a popular saying the thought of v. 4, which (as well as 5ᵃ) is missing in the original Greek version. If God were to favor the friends of Job at the cost of condemning the innocent sufferer, it would be like dividing one's property among one's neighbors, and leaving one's children unprovided for.

THE BOOK OF JOB

Thou canst not let them be victorious.[87]
6 He has made me a by-word of the people;
An abhorrence[88] have I become for children.[89]
My eye is dimmed through vexation,
And my form reduced to a shadow.
8 The upright must rejoice[90] at this,
And the innocent be aroused against the impious.[91]
10 But now all of you[92] come back;[93]
And I shall not find a wise man among you.

11
11–16
The grave as the only hope.

My days have passed [forever (?)][94]
The plans of my mind are broken.[95]

---

[87] So by a different vocalization of the text. The verse is missing in the earlier Greek versions.

[88] Topheth—the place in the valley of Hinnom where children were offered to Moloch. See Hastings, *Dictionary of the Bible*, s.v. Topheth is, therefore, a synonym for "horror" or "abhorrence."

[89] So read by a slight change of the text.

[90] So read by the insertion of a letter. For the same combination of the two verbs, "rejoice," and "aroused," see Job 31, 29. Job is speaking in bitter irony.

[91] Meaning himself. A pious commentator offended at this bitter exclamation and wishing to tone down the irony, adds (v. 9):
> "The righteous clings to his way,
> And the clean of hand increases in strength,"—

perhaps a proverbial saying.

[92] So read by the insertion of a letter.

[93] The repetition of the invitation 6, 29, but in a spirit of increased bitterness. The text has a superfluous "come now," which makes the line too long.

[94] Some word like "forever" is to be expected here to make up the three beats. Its place is taken by the comment "my thoughts," for which see the following note.

[95] A commentator in order to explain the unusual word (perhaps corrupt) adds "My thoughts." Verse 12, which is

THE BOOK OF JOB

If I could make [96] Sheol my house;   13
In the darkness spread my couch;
Could call the pit, "My father," [97]
And the worm, "My mother and sister."
Where, indeed, is my hope?   15
And who can track out my longing?[98]
Will they [99] go down to Sheol with me?[1]
Shall we lie down [2] in the dust together?

Then Bildad in answer said: 18, 1
How long will you indulge in pricks?[3]   1–21
Be sensible and then we will speak.   *The Doom of the Wicked.*
Why should we be counted as beasts,
Be looked upon [as cattle][4] in thy eyes?[5]

---

missing in the original Greek version, interrupts the context and can best be explained as a combination of two glosses to 18, 6. See below note 8.

[96] So by a slight change in the text—demanded by the parallelism.

[97] The text has a superfluous "thou," which makes the line too long.

[98] The repetition of "My hope" in the Hebrew text is probably an error. The parallelism demands a word like "longing."

[99] *i.e.*, "my hope and my longing, will they be entombed with me?"

[1] So the Greek text.

[2] So the sense of the Greek text. Siegfried is again too radical, and quite unnecessarily so, in regarding the six closing verses of the chapter (11–16) as interpolations. A correct principle, wrongfully applied, is equivalent to a wrong principle.

[3] A commentator adds: "as words," *i.e.*, as arguments.

[4] The parallelism, as well as the completion of the line to three beats, demands the addition of this word.

[5] So according to the Greek text. At the beginning of v. 4 there is an obscure apostrophe to Job "O raging and violent one," which is either to be regarded as misplaced or we must assume that a line has dropped out.

THE BOOK OF JOB

Shall for thy sake the earth be forsaken?
And [its] Guardian[6] be removed from His place?
Surely, the light of the wicked is put out;[7]
And the spark of his fire shall not shine.
Light becomes darkness in his tent,
And his lamp is put out for him.[8]
His once mighty steps shall be straitened;
His own counsel shall bring about his fall.
Headlong [9] he is cast into a net;
And he walks upon a trap.
[A gin shall catch his heel,
And a snare (?) hold him fast.
A noose for him is hid in the ground,
And a trap for him on the highway.][10]
Terrors startle him on all sides,
And clog his steps.[11]

---

[6] Literally, "rock," but here used as elsewhere in the Old Testament as a designation of God.

[7] Quoted from Prov. 24, 20?

[8] To this verse, 17, 12 appears to be a gloss as above suggested:

(a) "Night they change to day"

to indicate that the wicked also ply their trade at night. To this interpretation some one who erroneously took the two words ôr hoshekh together as "light of darkness" apparently objected and added by way of explanation ôr ("light") is preferable to hoshekh ("darkness"). The comment was suggested by a certain ambiguity in the use of the Hebrew word ôr (as well as the Aramaic form uryâ) for both "light" and "darkness," for which see Jastrow *Talmudic Dictionary* sub ôr.

[9] Literally, "by his feet."

[10] Verses 9–10 are missing in the earlier Greek versions; they are probably later amplifications of v. 8.

[11] This is the sense of a phrase that appears to be an idiomatic expression, the exact construction of which escapes us.

THE BOOK OF JOB

His offspring shall endure hunger,   12
And calamity is in store for his mate.[12]
Deadly disease[13] shall consume his limbs;[14]   13b
His hope [15] shall be plucked out of his tent.   14a
Terror [16] shall dwell in his tent;[17]   15
And brimstone be scattered on his habitation.[18]
Below its roots shall dry up;
And above its branch shall wither.
His remembrance shall perish from the earth;
And nowhere will there be a memorial of him.
They shall drive him from light into darkness;
And out of the earth they shall chase him.
Without son or grandson among his people,
And without any survivor in his place of sojourn.
Those from the West shall stand aghast,[19]   20

  [12] Literally, his "rib," *i.e.*, his wife in view of Genesis 2, 21, where the wife of the first man is formed of his rib. So the interpretation in the Targum to Job, embodying no doubt a traditional explanation.

  [13] Literally, "first-born of death"—a picturesque phrase for a fatal disease, perhaps of a specific character. The Greek text has simply "death."

  [14] The phrase "consuming his limbs" (so read) is repeated and explained as "his skin." At the close of v. 14 there is an obscure gloss, usually rendered "and thou bringest him to the King." The word "terrors" that follows is to be taken to the following verse.

  [15] Meaning his children, as the hope of the future. He and his children will perish.

  [16] This word to be taken over from the preceding verse as the subject of "dwell."

  [17] A comment adds, "that is not his," to further emphasize the punishment, but which makes the line too long.

  [18] A picture of desolation with an allusion to the fate of Sodom and Gomorrah (Gen. 19, 24).

  [19] There is an unintelligible gloss "at his day" at the beginning of this verse—either a misplaced comment, or a textual

THE BOOK OF JOB

And fright shall seize hold of those from the East.[20]
Such indeed is the fate [21] of the wicked;
Such the destiny [22] of him that knows not God.

19, 1
1–12
God is responsible for Job's misery.

Then Job in answer said:
How long will you vex my soul,
And attempt to crush me with words?
Ten [23] times have you tried to refute me;
And you are not ashamed to return to the attack.[24]
Is it indeed true that I have erred,
And that my error remains with me?[25]

5 Or have you indeed prevailed over me,
And have proved my downfall [26] to me?
Know that it is God who has overthrown me,
And His net has caught me.
If I cry "violence," I am not answered;[27]
I cry for help, but there is no justice.

---

error for "on his right" as a comment to "those from the West" or "those from behind." The West is that which is behind; the East, what is in front.

[20] So Dillman's explanation in his commentary on Job.

[21] Literally "dwellings," but here used, as Ehrlich has pointed out, to designate the fate that overwhelms the dwellings.

[22] Literally "place," meaning again the fate in store for the place in which the wicked dwell.

[23] Ten is used as a large round number, by the side of seven—in earlier times.

[24] So Ehrlich's interpretation by a different vocalization of the verb.

[25] *i.e.*, am I still steeped in error and sin by my declining to admit my guilt?

[26] Literally "my disgrace."

[27] Cf. Jer. 20 : 8—God does not answer my charge, though I am treated with violence.

THE ·BOOK OF JOB

He has fenced up my way against passing;[28]
He has set darkness on my paths.
My glory, He has stripped off me,
And has taken the crown from my head.
He has shattered me so that I am undone;   10
And He has plucked up my hope like a tree.
He has kindled His wrath against me,
And has accounted me among His adversaries.
His troops [29] come in a body towards me,   13–20
And block the way against me.[30]   *Forsaken by*
He has removed my brothers from me,   *friends and kin.*
And my acquaintances have become estranged from me.
My relatives and intimates have fallen away,
[And] the inmates of my house have forgotten me.
My maids count me for a stranger;   15
I have become an alien in their eyes.
I call to my servant, but he does not answer;
Though with my mouth I implore him.
My wife stands in horror of me,
And I have become loathsome to my offspring.[31]
Urchins [32] show their contempt for me;

---

[28] Lam. 3, 7–9 is closely parallel to Job 19, 7–8.
[29] Meaning the false friends.
[30] A commentator adds by way of explanation of the somewhat obscure phrase, "they encamp around my tent."
[31] Literally, "the sons of my womb" for "the sons of the womb of my wife." Note the gradual rise to the climax in verses 12–17 (a) brothers and acquaintances, *i.e.*, his friends; (b) relatives and the inmates of his house, *i.e.*, those who live with him; (c) maids and servants; (d) wife and children.
[32] *i.e.*, ragamuffins.

THE BOOK OF JOB

<small>20</small>

<small>21–29
Job's vain
appeal for
sympathy as
one smitten
by God.

23ª
24ᵇ</small>

When I appear they speak against me.
Those closest to me abhor me,
And those whom I loved have turned against me.[33]
My bone cleaves to my flesh [34]
And I am left with the skin of my teeth.[35]
Pity me, pity me, O [36] my friends;
For the hand of God has touched me.
Why do you pursue me like a stag,[37]
Since you cannot be satiated with my flesh? [38]
Oh that my words could be inscribed,[39]
Graven for all times in the rock.

---

[33] A general summary.
[34] A gloss adds "to my skin." The same phrase occurs, Psalm 102, 6.
[35] A picturesque phrase to indicate that only his gums remain.
[36] The text has an overhanging "you," which makes the line too long.
[37] So read by a slight change of the text.
[38] I am so emaciated that I would not furnish a satisfactory meal.
[39] The line has a superfluous "somewhere." Two glosses have also been inserted:
(a) "Oh that they might be inscribed in a book" to 23ª and
(b) "With an iron stylus and lead" (missing in the original Greek version) to 24ᵇ.

The second gloss is proper, but not the first, for Job is not thinking of a writing on papyrus or skin which is perishable; he wants his complaints of his sufferings and his charges against God to be hewn permanently into an imperishable substance, following the example of Assyrian and Persian rulers, so that in distant days some one will read them and rise up as his defender. The first gloss has been added with intent in order to give a different turn to Job's thought.

THE BOOK OF JOB

Then I would know that my defender[40] will arise,[41] 25
Even though he arise in the distant future.[42]
Only under *my* skin is this indited,[43] 26
And within *my* flesh do I see these [44] [words].

[40] Or "vindicator." The Hebrew term *goël* means originally the nearest of kin who, according to ancient Semitic custom, was called upon to avenge a wrong done to his kinsman. Here the term is used in the general sense of "defender," which it naturally acquired. It cannot possibly refer to God, as the Jewish translator of the O.T. into Arabic, Saadia, recognized as far back as the ninth century of our era. The RV properly adds in a marginal note that the sense is "vindicator" and not "redeemer" in the religious sense. For all that, the new translation of the Jewish Publication Society retains "Redeemer" with a capital letter. See further on the famous verse above, p. 124 *seq.*

[41] Literally, "is alive," but clearly in the sense that he will be alive in the future.

[42] Literally, "as the last," to indicate the remote future. Job's point is that if his complaints and charges could only be given a permanent form, he would feel confident that some day he will be justified by a defender who will "live," *i.e.*, be born at some time, though perhaps not till the very remote future.

[43] The record of his case instead of being hewn into the rock is only written in his own person. There can be little doubt that this verse has been interfered with by pious exegetes who tried to twist it into a suggestion of a future life, of which, however, Job is not thinking. The passage has been intentionally distorted in the interest of Jewish orthodoxy.

[44] Read by a slight change "these" instead of "God." By "these" Job means the record which he would like to see hewn into the rock. He complains that instead, he alone sees the record written in his person and in his flesh. Verse 27 is an explanatory amplification to v. 26,

"I alone can see it for myself;
Mine eyes see it, but not another's."

At the end of v. 27 is a gloss, "My reins are consumed within me" added as an explanation to v. 26b, before the verse was manipulated by pious commentators.

THE BOOK OF JOB

28 When, therefore, you say, how we shall pursue him![45]
29ᵃ Tremble before the sword![46]

20, 1 Then Zophar, the Naamathite, in answer said:

*1–29
Again the
doom of the
wicked.*

Because of this [47] my thoughts urge me on;
Because of the agitation within me,
That I must listen to rebuke in return for my argument,[48]
And to idle words [49] in answer to my logic.[50]
Surely thou knowest this of old;
That since man was placed upon earth,

---

[45] Harking back to v. 22. A gloss, "the root of the thing is found in me" (not found in the original Greek text) is an attempted explanation by some commentator to 26ᵃ "under my skin is this indited," likewise before the verse was intentionally distorted.

[46] The balance of this verse (29) is unintelligible. The last words can be translated, "That ye may know that there is a judge," which I am inclined to take as an explanatory gloss to 25ᵃ, "I know that my defender lives" (*i.e.*, "will arise"), based on the traditional explanation that the *goël* is God who will arise as "judge." The remaining words "for wrath are the iniquities of the sword" give no sense whatsoever. The word "bringeth" in AV and RV is not in the text, which the translators of the Jewish Publication Society *fail* to indicate. It may be that the phrase "iniquities of the sword" constitutes an explanation of "sword" and that the words "for wrath" or "because of wrath" are an independent gloss to the verb "tremble," but this is a pure guess. It is better to confess the hopelessness of making anything out of these words, beyond the conjecture that as glosses they do not belong to the original text.

[47] *i.e.*, because of the sentiments expressed by Job at the close of the previous chapter.

[48] So the sense required by the parallelism and which can be obtained by a textual change in the second word of the verse.

[49] Literally, "wind" (as 15, 2) or as we would say, colloquially "gas."

[50] More literally, "my intelligence."

THE BOOK OF JOB

The joy of the wicked is short; 5
And the joy of the impious for a moment.
Though his ambition mount up to heaven,
And his head reach unto the cloud,
By the measure of his greatness [51] he shall perish forever;
Those who saw him will say "Where is he?"
Like a dream, he shall fly away, and none shall find him;
Chased away as a vision of the night.
[The eye which saw him shall see him no more;
His place [52] shall no longer behold him].[53]
His sons must recompense [54] the poor; 10
And his own hands must hand over his offspring.[55]
[His bones may be full of marrow,
But with him they [56] shall lie down in the dust.
Though wickedness be sweet in his mouth,
Retaining it under his tongue:[57]
Sparing, and unwilling to let it go, [58]

---

[51] So Ehrlich by a slight change of the text, instead of an absurd reading "like his dung."

[52] *i.e.*, his city, or the place where he dwells.

[53] This 9th verse, reminiscent of 7, 8–10, is omitted by the Greek text. It may be a later amplification.

[54] More literally: "placate." The verb used occurs in Leviticus 26, 34, in the sense of satisfying or requiting the poor who have been robbed by the wicked, but to whom, by way of compensation, the children of the wicked are handed over as slaves.

[55] So the sense of this word as in Job 18, 12. See above p. 261.

[56] *i.e.*, his bones.

[57] Like a tidbit.

[58] The text appears to have a superfluous word, which makes the line too long.

THE BOOK OF JOB

And keeping it within his mouth;][59]
His food [60] shall be turned in his bowels,
[As] gall of asps within him.
15 The wealth that he has swallowed he must vomit;
Out of his belly God shall drive it.[61]
17 He shall not enjoy the flow [62] of his streams;
The brooks of honey and cream.
The gain that he cannot swallow, he must restore,
His profit as the sand,[63]—he shall not enjoy.
Because he has torn down the huts [64] of the poor,
He shall not rebuild the house that he has robbed.
20 Because he knew no ease within him,
And in his avarice suffered naught to escape;
Therefore he shall not enjoy his wealth.[65]

---

[59] Verses 11–13 are missing in the original Greek text and are not required for the context. They may well be subsequent additions.

[60] *i.e.*, his substance as the result of his designs.

[61] Verse 16, which appears to be a popular saying, is added because of the reference to "gall of asps" in v. 14:

"He who sucks the poison of asps,
The tongue of the viper shall kill him."

The first part of the verse is missing in the original Greek verse.

[62] Cf. the meaning of the parallel stem in Assyrian *palāgu* "spread, flow," etc., from which *palgu* "canal" is derived.

[63] So read with Ehrlich, by a slight change in the text.

[64] So the interpretation of Ehrlich (*Randglossen* 6, p. 262), who takes the third word of the verse as a substantive.

[65] At the beginning of v. 21 there is comment reading "There was no survivor to his greed." The original Greek text lacks 20[b] and 21[a] and reads therefore:

"Because he knew no ease within him,
He shall not enjoy his wealth."

THE BOOK OF JOB

In his overflowing abundance, he shall be in straits.[66]
He shall cast upon him His fierce wrath,[67]
And shall cause His terror [68] to rain upon him.
He shall be transfixed [69] by an iron weapon;
A brazen bow shall pierce him.
One unsheaths [the sword,] and it comes out of his back,[70]   25
And the glittering point passes out of his gall.
Every concealed terror [71] is laid up for his protected ones;
It shall go ill with the survivors in his tent.
The heavens shall reveal his iniquity,   27
And the earth shall rise up against him.[72]

---

[66] A superfluous line forming a comment reads: "Every kind of misery shall come upon him."

[67] The words at the beginning of this 23d verse "to be for filling his belly" are another gloss, as is shown by their omission in the original Greek text; they are added to explain 22ᵃ, the second word of which is a rare and difficult term for "abundance."

[68] So by a slight change in the text, to secure a meaning demanded by the parallelism.

[69] The verb is to be vocalized as passive and to be explained according to Ehrlich, *Randglossen* 6, p. 263.

[70] So the Greek text. The sword is unsheathed to be driven through him.

[71] Literally, "darkness," explained by a gloss (placed at the close of the preceding verse), "terror upon him." A second gloss inserted in v. 26, reads:

"A fire not blown [by man] shall consume him,"

which is clearly a gloss to v. 27ᵃ to explain rather pedantically the phrase "The heavens will reveal his iniquity." The first part of v. 26 is missing in the original Greek version.

[72] Verse 28, which weakens the forcible climax of the preceding verse must again be looked upon as a comment.

THE BOOK OF JOB

<small>29</small> Such is the portion of the wicked man from God;
And the disposition of his heritage [73] from God.

<small>21, 1
1–16
*The true
picture of
what happens
to the wicked.*</small>

Thereupon Job in answer said:
Listen now to my speech;
And may it afford you satisfaction.[74]
Suffer me to speak;
And after that you may mock.[75]
Should I allow my complaint to cease?[76]
And why should I not be impatient?

<small>5</small> Mark me and be dumbfounded;
And lay [your] hand upon [your] mouth.[77]
When I think of it, I am dismayed,
And horror takes hold of me.[78]
Why do the wicked flourish,
Grow old and even wax mighty?
Their seed is secure before them;[79]
Their offspring is in their presence.
Their homes are safe from terror;

"The produce of his estate (lit.: "*house*") will flow away,
. . . . on the day of his wrath."

The text as it stands cannot be correct, corrupted probably by later editors who no longer understood that the verse was a comment.

[73] This the meaning of the word, as in Arabic.

[74] Ironically meant in the sense of, "I hope that you will derive comfort from what I shall have to say."

[75] Read the plural.

[76] So read by a change in the text, instead of the meaningless "for man."

[77] Keep silent—you will have no answer to make.

[78] Literally: "my flesh."

[79] *i.e.*, their children flourish—a reply to 15, 34 (Eliphaz), 18, 19 (Bildad) and 20, 10 (Zophar). The text has a superfluous "with them," not found in the original Greek text and which makes the line too long.

THE BOOK OF JOB

The scourge of God is not upon them.
His bull genders without fail;[80]　　　　　　10
His cow calves and does not miscarry.
They bring forth their little ones like a flock,
And their children skip about.[81]
They dance to the timbrel and zither,
And make merry to the sound of the pipe.
They round out their days in happiness,
And peacefully [82] sink down into Sheol.[83]
To God they say, "Away from us;
We desire not the knowledge of Thy ways."[84]
["What is Shaddai that we should serve Him?　　15
And what profit, that we should secure His intercession?"] [85]
How often is the lamp of the wicked put out,[86]　17

---

[80] The seed enters the cow.
[81] Like lambkins.
[82] This is the sense demanded by the context. The reading of the text, "in a moment," appears to be an intentional change to suggest sudden death as a punishment. Job, however, is arguing just the other way.
[83] The common belief was that if one goes down to the nether world in a happy frame of mind, one will continue in that frame. Therefore, Jacob (Gen. 37 : 35) laments that he is going to Sheol in sorrow, which implies that he will be unhappy in the nether world.
[84] The thought is taken up again by Eliphaz, 22, 17.
[85] This verse is not in the earlier Greek versions and may be a variant to v. 14 or an amplifying comment. Some pious reader, shocked at Job's bitter irony, adds (v. 16):

> "Ah, there is no happiness in their hand;
> The course of the wicked be far from me."

The second line is also inserted in a speech of Eliphaz (22, 18ᵇ).
[86] Answer to Bildad (18, 5), "The light of the wicked is put out."

THE BOOK OF JOB

17–26
The wicked is not punished in this world.

Does calamity come upon them?[87]
That they become as stubble before the wind,
And as chaff scattered by the storm?[88]
His punishment is stored up for his sons[89]—
Let Him requite *him* that *he* may know it.[90]
20 Let *his* eyes see his destruction;
Let him drink of the wrath of Shaddai.
21 For what is his concern [91] in his house after him?[92]
When the number of his months is completed?[93]
23 This one dies in his full strength;
Wholly at ease and in peace.[94]
His legs (?) [95] full of fat,

---

[87] A commentator adds: *i.e.*, "Does He apportion sufferings in His anger?"

[88] Cf. Ps. 1, 4.

[89] A commentator adds "God" (omitted in the Greek text) as subject to "store up," but which makes the line too long.

[90] Job says: if you argue that God reserves punishment and will visit it, according to the orthodox belief, on a wicked man's sons what justice is there in this? The one who does wrong should be punished, so that *he* may become conscious of his guilt and directly suffer for it.

[91] A totally wrong impression is conveyed by the translation "pleasure" in the AV and RV.

[92] *i.e.*, after he dies.

[93] A pious reader or commentator, again shocked at Job's audacity in setting forth what God *ought* to do, adds the reflection (v. 22)
> "Shall one presume to teach God,
> Him who judges on high?"

[94] The verse is missing in the original Greek version.

[95] So the rendering in the Greek text. The word in the Hebrew text, designating some part of the body, occurs only in this passage. The exact meaning, therefore, is doubtful, but it is surely not "pails" as the ordinary translations have it.

THE BOOK OF JOB

And the marrow of his bones moistened.
And that one dies in despair,   25
Without having tasted happiness.
They lie down alike [96] in the dust,
And the worm covers them.
Ah, I know your thoughts,   27-34
And the arguments that you twist against me.[97]   *The wicked is spared*
When ye say "Where is the house of the noble?"   *from calamity and is happy*
And where the habitation [98] of the wicked?"[99]   *to the end.*
Ask those who note the course of events,[1]
And you will admit with them:[2]
That up to [his] fatal day,[3] the wicked is spared;[4]   30
To the day that he is carried to the grave.[5]
And whoever tells such a one [6] his way?
And who repays him for what he has done?

---

[96] The fate of all, the wicked and the good, the happy and the miserable, is the same. It is the sentiment which runs throughout the Book of Koheleth. See Jastrow, *A Gentle Cynic*, page 129 *seq.*

[97] The following verse indicates what the argument is.

[98] A gloss adds "tent" as the explanation of the plural "habitations." The original Greek version omits no less than six verses (28-33), *i.e.*, the balance of the chapter except the last verse (34).

[99] The friends argue as follows: Note the difference between the fate of the good and the bad. The good man's house survives, while that of the wicked perishes. Job vehemently denies this, and declares that the facts belie the assumption that there is a reward for virtuous deeds.

[1] So Ehrlich's happy interpretation (*Randglossen* 6, p. 269) of the phrase, "those who pass by the way."

[2] Literally, "Their tokens ye will not fail to recognize."

[3] *i.e.*, to his last hour.

[4] So by a slight change of the text.

[5] So by a slight change.

[6] *i.e.*, to the wicked man.

THE BOOK OF JOB

When he is carried to the grave,
And rests tranquilly [7] on his bier?
The clods of the valley[8] seem sweet to him,
As the whole population draws after him.[9]
How then can you comfort me with vanity,
Since your arguments are a tissue of falsehood?[10]

---

[7] So by a slight change required by the context.

[8] *i.e.*, the earth that is heaped over his coffin.

[9] He has a big funeral with the whole town following in procession behind the coffin. A glossator adds, "And before him without number," *i.e.*, a large concourse also precedes the coffin.

[10] This the general force of the obscure, because apparently idiomatic, phrase with which the chapter closes.

III
A THIRD SERIES OF SPEECHES
(Chapters 22–27)

A
The Third Speech of Eliphaz and Job's Reply

Thereupon, Eliphaz in answer said: 22, 1
Does a man help God,
When he helps [people] out of consideration?[11]
Is it any advantage to Shaddai, if thou art righteous?
Has He any profit if thou perfectest thy ways?
Does He punish thee *because* of thy reverence,[12]
When He brings thee to judgment?
Surely thy wickedness must be great,   5
And there can be no end to thy iniquities.
For thou must have taken pledges of thy brother wrongfully,
And stripped the garments of the naked.[13]
[Or] thou didst not give water to the weary,   7
And didst withhold bread from the hungry.[14]

1–10 Job is punished because of his wickedness.

---
[11] So Ehrlich's explanation.
[12] Ironically meant. Surely God does not punish thee because thou fearest Him, but because of the reverse.
[13] *i.e.*, of the poor who were thus forced to go naked. This reference is to the law in the Code of the Covenant, Exodus 22, 25–26 and in the Deuteronomic Code 24, 12–13.
[14] Verse 8 interrupts the context and is besides obscure.
    "The man of might—to him is the earth,
    And the exalted dwells therein."
The verse is clearly out of place. It has drifted away from Job's

THE BOOK OF JOB

9 [Or] thou dost send widows away empty,
And thy arm [15] didst crush the orphans.

10 Therefore, snares are round about thee,
And sudden terror startles thee.[16]

12 Since God is on high [17]

12–20 Eliphaz warns Job against continuing his evil ways

And thou seest [18] how high the stars are,
Thou sayest: "What does God know?[19]
Can He judge behind the dark cloud?
Since the clouds are a covering to Him, so that He cannot see,
And the heavenly sphere is revolving."[20]

15 Wilt thou continue in the path of old,
Which the wicked have trodden?

16 [Who were snatched away before their time;
Whose foundation was poured out as a stream?][21]

---

speech in chapter 21 where it properly belongs. It impresses one as a popular saying, perhaps added as a gloss to 21, 31 by some commentator.

[15] So read instead of "arms."

[16] Verse 11 consists of two glosses (a) "Or [because of] darkness thou canst not see"—a variant reading or explanation to v. 10b. (b) "A mass (?) of waters covers thee," a variant or explanation to v. 10a.

[17] Text adds "heaven," which makes the line too long.

[18] So read by a slight change and omit the word "head" before "stars" which gives no sense.

[19] *i.e.*, of what is occurring on earth. Verses 13–16 are missing in the original Greek version.

[20] *i.e.*, constantly moving. So Ehrlich's explanation which I adopt, though with some hesitation.

[21] This 16th verse is among those missing in the original Greek version. It strikes one as a later amplification. At this point there is a strange confusion in the text. Verses 17–18 are clearly snatches of a paraphrase or repetition of Job's utterances in 21, 14–15 which perhaps were placed on the margin by a commentator as variants, and then slipped into Eliphaz's speech

THE BOOK OF JOB

[The righteous shall see and rejoice,   19
And the innocent shall laugh them to scorn:
"Surely their substance is cut off   20
And fire has consumed their wealth."][22]
Endeavor to make thy peace with Him;[23]   21–30
And thereby [24] happiness shall come to thee.[25]   *Job should reconcile himself with God.*
Receive instruction [26] from His mouth;
And lay up His words in thy mind.
If thou wilt humbly return to Shaddai,   23

---

through an error. We must separate the verses into three sections as follows:

(a) 17ᵃ "Who say to God; Away from us,
And what can Shaddai do to us"—

a paraphrase or variant to 21, 14 (read "to us," as the Greek version, instead of "to them")

(b) "And He fills their houses with happiness,"

perhaps a variant to 21, 16ᵃ added by some one, who felt that the text as it stands could not be an utterance of Job's

(c) "the counsel of the wicked be far from me"

is repeated from 21, 16ᵇ.

[22] Verse 20 must be taken to represent the exclamation of the righteous innocent over the discomfiture of the wicked, but I cannot help feeling that these two verses (19–20) which strike one as particularly commonplace and superfluous—besides postponing the climax which begins in v. 21,—are likewise later additions. The 20th verse is missing in the original Greek text. The speech in any case is much stronger without 16–20, since verse 21 joins on directly to v. 15.

[23] This is the meaning of a line that is difficult, because of the evident corruption of the text.

[24] So read instead of "by them."

[25] So read by a slight change of the text.

[26] It is interesting to find the term *Torah*—later the technical term for the Pentateuchal Codes—used here in the general sense of "instruction."

THE BOOK OF JOB

      [And] remove unrighteousness from thy tents;[27]
25   Then Shaddai will be thy goldmine,
      And silver in superabundance to thee.
      Then shalt thou have delight in Shaddai[28]
      And shall lift up thy hands to God.[29]
      Thou wilt entreat Him, and He will hearken to thee;
      And thou wilt be able to perform thy vows.[30]
      Thou wilt decree a thing, and it shall be established,
      And light shall shine upon thy ways.
29b   [For] the humble He will save,[31]
30a   And the innocent [32] one He will deliver.[33]

---

[27] Verse 24—omitted in the original Greek version—is an attempt to interpret the metaphor in v. 25 and, as generally happens, when a metaphor is taken literally, the effect is spoiled.

"Gold ore will be regarded as dust (*i.e.*, it will be so abundant),
And Ophir gold (*i.e.*, the purest gold) as the rock of the valleys."

(Read "as" instead of "in.")

[28] The verb suggests "playing" or sporting with God. God will treat you like a spoiled child, and do anything that thou askest of Him. So Ehrlich's interpretation.

[29] So read by a slight change in the text, and which, in view of the following verse, gives a better sense than "raise thy face."

[30] *i. e.*, carry out all thy desires.

[31] At the beginning of v. 29 there is an addition which seems to be a gloss to the sentiment that "God will save the humble." Some commentator added: "If He (*i.e.*, God) lowers one, thou shouldst say "he was haughty." The original Greek version omits verses 29 and 30 altogether.

[32] Read by a slight change "innocent man," instead of "the not innocent," which is clearly out of place.

[33] Again a gloss is added, forming v. 30b in the received text. "He shall save because of the purity of thy hands," which is clearly intended to be an explanation of 30a. By remov-

THE BOOK OF JOB

Then Job in answer said: 23, 1
Even now,[34] I would restrain [35] my complaint;
Suppress [36] my sighs.
If I only knew where to find Him,   1–17
And to come to His seat!   *God is hidden from men.*
I would place [my] case before Him,   *He does what He pleases*
And fill my mouth with arguments.   *and there is*
I would know the words of His answer to me, *no escape* 5
And grasp what He would say unto me.   *from His decision.*
Were He to contend with me in the greatness of His power,
He indeed would not prevail against me.[37]
It would be an upright [38] one who would reason with Him;
And I would be delivered forever from my judges.[39]

---

ing these two glosses (29ª and 30ᵇ) we can combine verses 29 and 30 into one stanza, and avoid the awkward double change from the third to the second person, apart from other ambiguities that result from the endeavor to translate the two verses as they stand. The thought that the humble and innocent will be saved through Job's virtues is entirely foreign to the argument and outside of the horizon of Eliphaz, as he is depicted in the discussion.

[34] Literally, "to-day" and used in contrast to the double "then" in verses 25–26 of Eliphaz's speech.

[35] So read with Ehrlich and as demanded by the context.

[36] This the sense of the phrase "pressing the hand" upon one's sighs.

[37] Referring to a former utterance (9, 19) in which Job admitted that if it is a question of strength he is worsted. He now declares that if he could bring his case before God, even the superior power of the Deity would not prevent his winning out.

[38] Referring to himself (1, 1). God would be forced to recognize Job's innocence.

[39] Meaning his friends who act as his judges and condemn

THE BOOK OF JOB

But, now, I go forward, and He is not there;
And backward but I cannot perceive Him:
[Bending to the left, I cannot take hold [of Him];
Turning to the right, I cannot see [Him].[40]

10   He knows what my way has been;[41]
Were He to test me, I would come out as gold.[42]
My foot has held to His steps;
His way I have kept without swerving.
From the command of His lips I have never swerved;
In my bosom[43] I treasured the words of His mouth.

13   But He decides,[44] and who can restrain Him?
What He desires, even that He does.[45]

15   Therefore, I am in terror before Him;
[When] I consider, I am afraid of Him.
For God has crushed my spirit,
And Shaddai has terrorized me.

---

him. Read the plural instead of the singular. All this hope, however, is in vain because one cannot find God—a bold utterance, indeed!

[40] Verses 8–9 are an elaboration of the thought expressed in 9, 11. The 9th verse is omitted in the original Greek version and may be a later amplification.

[41] God purposely hides himself from Job, for He knows that justice is on Job's side.

[42] Cf. I Peter 1, 7.

[43] So the Greek text.

[44] So by a slight change of the text.

[45] Verse 14, which is missing in the Greek versions appears to consist of two glosses (a) "for He determines my bound" (*i.e.*, my fate)—a gloss to 13ᵇ and (b) "There are many such things (?) with Him"—perhaps a comment by some sympathizer with Job, to indicate that many more illustrations of sufferings arbitrarily imposed upon man might be adduced.

THE BOOK OF JOB

So that I cannot escape (?), because of the darkness,
And I am enveloped in thick gloom.

Why are times hidden by [46] Shaddai,
So that [even] those who know Him can not see His days?[47]
[The wicked][48] remove landmarks;

24, 1
1–25
The sufferings of the innocent and defenceless at the hands of the ruthless and wicked.

---

[46] Or perhaps to be taken literally in the sense of "from."
[47] This verse has occasioned much difficulty. The thought to be expressed appears to have been intentionally veiled, because of its extreme audacity; and it may be also that the text has been further interfered with in order to tone down its real import that *fate is blind*, that the future is so hidden, that none of God's creatures, not even the most pious and the most learned, can follow the reason for things. It is the same thought that Koheleth expresses when he says (8, 17)

"I realized that no one can penetrate to the core of what happens in earth, that man cannot understand what happens under the sun, despite all efforts to seek a solution . . . and even if a wise man thinks that he knows —yet he cannot find out. Man does not know. (Jastrow, *A Gentle Cynic*, p. 229)

With a view of reducing the boldness of the thought, "not" has been inserted. The Greek text preserves the original reading without "not." If we insert the "not" as the Massoretic text does, the two lines would read

Why are times not hidden by Shaddai,
So that His followers might not see His days?

i.e., it would be better if we did not know what the coming days have in store for us. This appeared to be the more orthodox thought and was, therefore, put in the mouth of Job.

[48] The line is too short by one beat. A word has dropped out and since the subject of the verb is in any case "the wicked" it will not seem too bold to supply this word. The violent oppressors commit crimes without being punished. Note that in this impressive description of the wrongs perpetrated in the world, there is a transition from the deeds of the oppressors (v. 2–4) to the sufferings of the oppressed (v. 5–8) and back again to the oppressors (v. 9), then once more to the oppressed victims (v. 10–12), and back to the oppressors (v. 13–17). Cf. Deut. 19, 14.

THE BOOK OF JOB

      They steal flocks, and pasture them.
3   They drive away the ass of orphans;
      They take the widow's ox for a pledge.
9   [They pluck the orphan from the breast;
      And pledge the infant [49] of the poor.][50]
4   They turn the needy out of the way;
      The poor of the earth hide themselves together.
5   As wild asses in the wilderness they must go forth,
      To seek food as their task.[51]
      In a field that is not theirs [52] they harvest;
      And are forced to garner the vineyard of the wicked one.
      They spend the night without clothing;[53]
      And without a covering in the cold.
      They are wet with the mountain torrents,
      Without a shelter, they cling to the rock.
10   They [54] go about naked without a garment,

---

[49] So read by a slight change in the vocalization of the word preceding "poor."

[50] This 9th verse is misplaced; it evidently belongs here after the third verse. The alternative would be to regard it as a later addition inserted at the wrong place.

[51] A commentator adds, by way of comment to this 5th verse: "The desert must provide the food for their children." The needy driven from the towns seek sustenance for themselves and for their children in the wilderness, like wild asses seeking for prey.

[52] So read according to the Greek text. The description in this verse is of the victims of the rich despoilers, who must garner the fruits in a field which the wicked has stolen, and must work in vineyards that have been seized through violence. An impressive and pathetic picture of the enslavement of the masses through the greed and violence of the possessing classes.

[53] They have been robbed even of their garments. A gloss adds the superfluous "naked" suggested by v. 10. Cf. above 22,6.

[54] The orphans and the children of the poor.

THE BOOK OF JOB

And themselves hungry must carry the sheaves.[55]
They are forced to press the oil between......[56]
They tread the winepresses, and thirst.[57]
The weaklings[58] groan,
And the souls of the wounded cry for help.[59]
They are of those who rebel against light;[60]
They sit not in its paths.[61]
The murderer rises at the break of light;[62]
And at night he is as a thief.
The eye of the adulterer waits for the twilight,[63] 15
And puts a covering on his face.[64]

---

[55] Garnering for the rich owners of the field, while they, the poor, receive nothing.

[56] An obscure word follows. The ordinary translation "between their rows" gives no sense. Various conjectures have been proposed, but none of them is entirely satisfactory.

[57] They are not permitted even to drink the grape juice that they press out.

[58] So Ehrlich's ingenious interpretation of the phrase which occurs, Deuteronomy 2, 34, to describe those not fit for military service and who therefore remain behind with the women and children.

[59] A glossator adds, "But God does not hear the prayer." The last word of that gloss is to be vocalized *tefillah* "prayer." The ordinary translations of this line furnish a good illustration of the absurdities to which one is led by the endeavor to translate an erroneous vocalization. The translation of the American Baptist Publication Society adopts the correct reading.

[60] A splendid line to describe criminals who shun the sunlight in order to carry out their deeds under the cover of darkness.

[61] A variant or comment adds: "They do not know its ways," *i.e.*, of the light.

[62] *i.e.*, at dawn before the city is astir. A comment or variant reads: "He kills the poor and needy."

[63] Again a comment or variant: "Saying, no eye sees me." The original Greek version omits from verse 15–18.

[64] Hardly a mask, but a cloth of some kind so as to conceal his face—a "veil" as Renan (*Job* p. 104) very happily suggests.

THE BOOK OF JOB

They break into houses in the darkness;
They hide themselves by day.[65]
For daybreak[66] is to them [as] dark night;[67]
When it is recognized, [as] the terrors of dark night.
He moves swiftly upon the face of the waters;[68]
He turns aside into the way of the vineyards,[69]

19   In cold [70] as in heat they steal [71]

* * * * * *

---

[65] Read the plural in the first line. A comment reads: "They know not the light."

[66] *i.e.*, they are afraid of the day, and fear it as one does the terrors of the night. The line contains a superfluous "altogether"—a variant to "to them."

[67] Literally, "deep darkness," which is frequently used to express terror aroused by dense gloom.

[68] He takes the refuge on the water when day comes or he hides in the vineyards. At this point and to the end of the chapter, some pious reader or commentator, shocked at Job's audacity in thus describing the various classes of offenders who ply their trade without any interference on the part of a Deity, indifferent to the crimes that are daily committed, inserts pious reflections to counteract Job's extreme cynicism. So at this point, there is an addition, "their portion is cursed in the earth."

[69] So the Greek version which omits "not" and "way."

[70] So read by a slight change of the text.

[71] The rest of the verse is entirely unintelligible. Verse 20 distinctly reflects the point of view of the pious commentator who, in opposition to Job, emphasizes the doom in store for the persistent and cruel offender

> "The womb forgets him;
> Worms feed (?) on him
> He is no longer remembered;
> Iniquity is crushed like a tree."

The language besides is confused, and the beats in the line uneven. The third line may, in fact, be a prose explanation of the first one. Various emendations have been suggested for "womb" and for the verb in the second line, but they are all unsatisfactory.

THE BOOK OF JOB

He lies with the barren who cannot bear;[72] 21
And gives no aid to the widow.
He entices the strong ones by his power;
He rises up, and none is sure of life.
He assures one of safety on which they rely [73] 23
While His eye is on their ways.[74]
If it is not so, who will prove me to be a liar, 25
And nullify my speech?

B [75]

The Reconstructed Third Speech of Bildad [76]

Then Bildad in answer said: 25, 1
Does He rule by terror,[77]

25, 1–6 and
26, 5–14
God's majesty and power.

---

[72] A veiled illusion to sexual indulgences of an immoral character.

[73] This appears to be the meaning of this difficult line. The villain lures his victims under pretense of protecting them.

[74] *i.e.*, on his victims whom he trickily draws into his net. Verse 24 is again an addition on the part of a pious commentator, who furnishes the antidote to Job's poisonous suggestion in regard to the immunity from ultimate punishment of the shrewd and unscrupulous in whose presence no one is safe.

"They are exalted for a while and brought low (gloss or variant "are no more")
And as the tips of the grain they wither. (with a variant or comment: "Like . . . they are cut off")

[75] For the sake of convenience I summarize the rearrangement of chapters 25–31, as set forth above pp. 67–74 and 130–140:

(1) Bildad's third speech, chapter 25, 1–6 and 26, 5–14, with reminiscences of former utterances in the older draft of the book, as for example, 4, 17–19 (Eliphaz) = 25, 4–6.

(2) Job's answer to Bildad's third speech, 26, 1–4; 27, 2–6 and 30, 16–24, concluding with 31, 35–37, but which may originally have been the close of the missing reply to Zophar's speech in the third series. This would give us twenty-two verses, or a little less than the average length of a complete chapter.

THE BOOK OF JOB

He who maintains peace on high?
Is there any limit to His armies?

(3) Zophar's third speech 31, 2-4; 27, 7-23, with 30, 2-8, as an independent fragment, the whole being in line with Zophar's arraignment in chapter 20 of the fate of the evildoers, and of the punishment that will be meted out to them. The beginning of the speech is represented by the section 31, 2-4, which was intentionally torn from its original position. Job's reply is lacking. It is replaced by the two supplementary speeches (chapters 29-31).

(4) A supplementary speech of Job, devoted to setting forth the proper life that he led, and the esteem in which he was held, contrasted with the contempt now heaped upon him because of his sad condition. This speech, which clearly betrays marks of steady amplification as well as of an intentional rearrangement of the sections, is to be subdivided as follows:

(*a*) 29, 1-20.
(*b*) 29, 21-25 as an independent elaboration.
(*c*) 30, 1 and 9-15 and 30, 26-31, forming the close of this supplementary speech.

(5) A second supplementary speech, consisting of 31, 1 and 5-34 (with 30, 25 to be inserted after 31, 15) and 31, 38-40. In this speech Job indulges in elaborate descriptions of all the fine and virtuous things which he did and how he avoided sin and all temptation—descriptions that are none the less fatuous, because they are put in an implied manner. The speech falls into seven sections which need to be arranged in a different order to form a proper sequence. See below p. 304.

These two supplementary speeches have been combined into one under a single heading (29, 1): and in the course of the further editing process, the sections above noted were also inserted into the two speeches, which in turn led to a further rearrangement. The very length of the two speeches (96 verses) precludes the possibility of their being a single composition. Moreover, each speech furnishes internal evidence of being a gradual growth, with a number of independent elaborations. That these supplementary speeches are by different writers from those to whom we owe the speeches of Job in the original book has been made evident in the above discussion pp. 137 *seq.*

(6) Chapter 28, an inserted and entirely independent

THE BOOK OF JOB

And over whom does His authority not extend?[78]
How can man win a suit against God?[79]
And how can woman-born be pure?
Since even the moon is not worthy,[80]   5
And stars are not pure in His eyes.
How much less a man—a mere worm;
And a maggot of a human being!
[26, 1-4 forming part of Job's speech in reply to Bildad, below, p. 289]
The shades below are in terror;[81]   26, 5
The waters and their inhabitants.
Sheol is naked [82] before Him,
And there is no covering to Abaddon.[83]
Over empty space He stretches the North;

---

chapter on the "Search for Wisdom," originally placed at the close of the third series of speeches.

(7) The colophon 31, 40°: "The words of Job are ended" represents the close of the original Book of Job and was transferred from its original position at the close of Job's speech in the third series in reply to Zophar to the end of the second supplementary speech.

[76] Consisting of 25, 1-6 and 26, 5-14. See the discussion above p. 130 *seq.*

[77] So by a very slight change in the text.

[78] So read with Ehrlich by a slight change in the text.

[79] *i.e.*, expect to be acquitted of all guilt. Bildad quotes Job's utterance (9, 2), but gives it a different turn. Verses 4-6 are clearly reminiscent of 4, 17-19 (Eliphaz) and thus betray their dependence upon the speech put into the mouth of Eliphaz.

[80] Literally: "bright," but in the sense of altogether worthy The reference is perhaps to an eclipse of the moon, regarded by the ancients as a punishment of the moon for some offense.

[81] Verses 5-11 and most of v. 14 are omitted in the original Greek version.

[82] *i.e.*, revealed. Nothing is hidden from God. Cf. Prov. 15, 11.

[83] *i.e.*, "Destruction" one of the names of the nether world.

THE BOOK OF JOB

  He hangs the earth over nothing.
  In His thick clouds He binds up the water;
  And the cloud is not rent under their weight.
  He covers the face of the moon;[84]
  And spreads His cloud upon it.
10 He fixes a boundary to the face of the waters;
  To the confluence [85] of light with darkness.
  The pillars of heaven [86] tremble,
  And at His wrath are aghast.
  With His power He stirred up the sea,
  And by His strategy shattered Rahab.[87]
  By His breath He subdued (?) the waters;[88]
  His hand pierced the fleeing serpent.[89]
  These are but the outskirts of His ways,
  And a mere whisper that penetrates to us.[90]

---

 [84] So read—as suggested by Ibn Ezra back in the 12th Century—by a different vocalization of the word translated "throne."

 [85] Literally, the "extreme limit" where light and darkness meet.

 [86] The span of the heavens was popularly supposed to rest on two pillars, one at each end of the vault.

 [87] The sea monster, as the personification of the primæval chaos. See above the note to 9, 13.

 [88] The reading "waters" instead of "heavens" (through the omission of one letter in the Hebrew word) is demanded by the context. The reference is, as in 9, 13, to the myth of creation which, common to Babylonians and Hebrews, represented primæval chaos as a group of monsters that had to be subdued before order could be established. Daiches' explanation of verses 12–13 in the Zeitschrift für Assyriologie XXV, 1–8 misses the point that all four lines refer to the sea.

 [89] i.e., one of the primæval monsters, like Rahab and Leviathan. See the comment to Chap. 40, 25.

 [90] The closing phrase, "The thunder of His might who can grasp," is clearly a misplaced gloss to v. 11—an exclamation

THE BOOK OF JOB

C

THE RECONSTRUCTED SPEECH OF JOB IN REPLY TO BILDAD [91]

Then Job in answer said: 26, 1
How thou hast helped the one without power,   2
Aided the one without strength! [92]   *26, 1-4 and*
Through whom have [these] words been told thee? *27, 2-6.*   4
    Job main-
And whose spirit speaks through thee? [93]   *tains the*
    claim of his
[26, 5-14—part of Bildad's third speech—above, *innocence.*
p. 287.]

---

of some pious reader. The original Greek version omits verses 5–11, of Bildad's speech and all of v. 14, except the closing phrase. Verses 7–13 are again reminiscent of 9, 5–13, there put into the mouth of Job in protest against the exercise of God's power, the existence and unlimited force of which he admits, but here brought forward with the evident intention of proving how presumptuous it is of man to question God's ways. The spirit in which this description of God's supreme control of the universe is to be taken is indicated by the gloss at the end of v. 14, "The thunder of his might, who can grasp?"

[91] This speech, consists of 26, 1–4; 27, 2–6; 30, 16–24, and 31, 35–37. The editorial heading is missing in Jerome's version. See the discussion above p. 134.

[92] The "one without power" and the "one without strength" are not intended to describe Job but God, though, of course, in a sarcastic spirit. In a bitterly ironical tone, Job taunts his opponents with having furnished arguments to defend God, as though *He* were without power and strength. Verse 3 is clearly an endeavor to interpret verse 1, but on the part of a commentator, who wishes to give a less objectionable turn to Job's taunt by applying the terms "without power" and "without strength" to Job.

"How hast thou counselled the one without wisdom,
And hast imparted instruction in abundance!"

[93] A continuation of the sharp sarcasm, to suggest that what Bildad has brought forward is commonplace and trite. For the phrase used, see I Kgs. 22, 24.

THE BOOK OF JOB

27, 2 [94] By God who has taken my right;
And by Shaddai who has vexed my soul;
3 As long as there is breath within me,
And the spirit of God in my nostrils;[95]
5 Far be it from me to justify you;
Till I die I will not relinquish my innocence.[96]
I hold fast to my justification without letting it go;[97]
My mind will never yield its innocence.[98]
[Verses 7-23, part of third speech of Zophar—below p. 294.]

30, 16 My soul is poured out within me;[99]
30, 16–24 and Days of affliction have seized me.
31, 35–37 By night my bones are wrenched from me,[1]

Suffering without end. And my worn-out frame [2] does not permit sleep.
With great force it clutches at my garment,[3]

---

[94] A later editor has inserted the heading, "And Job again took up his speech as follows," which he found at the beginning of Chap. 29 and repeated here.

[95] A quotation from Genesis 2, 7, which is thus assumed in its present form. A pious commentator in order to give a different turn to Job's bold insistence upon this innocence, inserts (v. 4) —perhaps based on Psalm 34, 14,

"My lips shall not speak unrighteousness,
Nor my tongue utter deceit."

[96] *i.e.*, the claim of my innocence.
[97] So read, following Ehrlich.
[98] Again, the claim of my innocence.
[99] The line is missing in the original Greek version.
[1] *i.e.* the pain is so excruciating at night that it seems to him as though his bones were being wrenched out of their sockets.
[2] So Ehrlich's interpretation, by a comparison with the Arabic equivalent which designates bone from which the flesh has been removed. Job says that he is a mere skeleton without flesh, so that his bones ache when he lies on them.
[3] Verse 18 describes by way of contrast, his sufferings by day when he is clothed, and the pain seizes him now at the

THE BOOK OF JOB

And grasps me at the hem of [4] my undergarment.
Into the mire He has cast me,
So that I am utterly undone.[5]
I cry unto Thee, but Thou dost not answer;   20
I stop, and Thou starest at me.[6]
Thou art turned cruel to me;
By the force of Thy hand Thou torturest [7] me.
Thou liftest me up with the wind,[8]
And the storm [9] tosses me about.
I know that Thou wilt deliver me to death,
To the gathering place [10] of all the living.
But it [11] is not forthcoming [12] upon request;[13]   24

---

upper garment, now at the lower garment. The dress consists of a lower garment, hanging from the loins, and an upper garment, covering the upper part of his body. He has pains everywhere throughout his body.

[4] So read by a slight change in the text.

[5] Literally: "Dust and ashes," an idiomatic expression to convey the idea of being completely undone. It occurs again 42, 6, probably quoted from our passage.

[6] Without, however, helping me. It is all the same whether I cry or whether I suffer in silence.

[7] So the Greek text.

[8] An explanatory gloss is added, "Thou causest me to ride," *i.e.*, on the wind. Both the line and the gloss are missing in the original Greek version.

[9] So read by a slight change in the text. The metaphor in this verse is that of a ship at the mercy of the wind, tossed about in an angry sea.

[10] Literally: "gathering house."

[11] *i.e.*, death.

[12] Literally: "it does not stretch forth the hand."

[13] So to be rendered, instead of the meaningless "ruinous heap," retained in the translation of the American Jewish Publication Society.

THE BOOK OF JOB

Nor does release [14] come in one's distress.[15]

[Verse 25, belonging to Job's second supplementary speech is to be placed after 31, 15, below, p. 306.

Verses 26-31—the conclusion of Job's first supplementary speech—below, p. 303.]

31, 35-37 [16] [O that there were some one to hear me![17]
Here is my brief[18]—let Shaddai refute me.[19]
Aye, I will lift it on my shoulder;

---

[14] So read by a slight change in the text. Job complains that although he knows that God will not grant him a release from his pains and that death is in store for him, yet death does not come though one longs for it. A pathetic outcry of one who feels himself doomed, and who yet is not permitted to die.

[15] The following verse (v. 25) belongs to Job's second supplementary speech. It may have been added on the margin of a codex and inserted by a later copyist into a wrong place. I place it after the section 31, 15. Below p. 306.

[16] Conclusion either of Job's speech in reply to Bildad, or of the missing speech of Job in reply to Zophar. See above, p. 67 seq., and the summary, p. 285.

[17] The line is omitted in the original Greek.

[18] Literally, "my cross," the word used being *Taw*, the name of the last letter of the Hebrew alphabet, corresponding to our T and having originally the form of a cross. The cross is the mark or signature attached to a document, and is here used for the document itself, authenticated by the signature.

[19] Literally: "answer me," but in the legal sense of presenting a counter argument. What follows (in prose form) "and the indictment (literally: "book") which my adversary has written," is an amplifying comment to "Here is my brief," to suggest Job's anxiety to refute any charges that might be brought against him. The adversary is, of course, God. The line is superfluous and interrupts the context. As a comment, however, added by way of explanation to "my brief" it is intelligible. The famous quotation "Oh that mine adversary had written a book" (so the Authorized Version) thus turns out to be both a mistranslation and misconception of our passage.

THE BOOK OF JOB

I will wear it as my crown.
With steady gait I will confront him;
[And] as a prince approach him.] [20]

D

THE RECONSTRUCTED THIRD SPEECH OF ZOPHAR[21]

What [22] is the portion of God above,	31, 2
And the heritage of Shaddai on high?	31, 2–4; 27, 7–23 and 30, 2–8
Is it not calamity for the evildoer,	
And disaster to those who do wrong?	*Again the doom of the wicked.*
Does not He see my ways,	

---

[20] Verses 38–40ᵇ form part of Job's second supplementary speech, below p. 305.

[21] See the discussion above p. 133. The speech, consisting of 31, 2–4; 27, 7–23 and 30, 2–8, forms a parallel to Zophar's second speech (Chapter 20), further elaborating the description of the punishment in store for the wicked, even though for a time he flourishes. The fragment appears to be an attempt on the part of a writer to try his hand at a refutation of Job's charge that the wicked flourish in this world quite as frequently as they are punished, if not more so; it has been assigned to Job by an orthodox commentator with deliberate intent, so as to convey the impression of Job's conversion to the conventional point of view.

The three verses (31, 2–4), inserted into the second supplementary speech of Job (see above p. 286), are clearly out of place where they stand and interrupt the context. The thought is entirely along the lines of 27, 7–23 and 30, 2–8 and forms an appropriate beginning to a speech, setting forth again in variant form, the awful fate in store for the wicked. I have, therefore, no hesitation in placing the verses here, where they form a proper link with the section 27, 7–23, which begins rather abruptly. They were torn from their place with deliberate intent, in order to represent Job as giving expression to the orthodox view regarding the justice of God in dealing out punishment to the wicked in this world.

[22] The conjunction "And" was added by the editor, who transferred the verses to Chap. 31.

THE BOOK OF JOB

And count all my steps?[23]

[27, 2-6 part of Job's speech in reply to Bildad's third speech, above p. 290.]

27, 7 May [the fate of] my enemy be as that of the wicked,
And my adversary [have the fate] of the evildoer.[24]
For what is the hope of the impious,[25]
When God threatens(?)[26] his life?
Will God hear his cry,
When trouble comes upon him?
10 Can he count upon [27] Shaddai?
Approach [28] God at all times?
[I will teach you concerning God's power,
And not conceal what Shaddai brings about.
Behold all of you have seen it;
Why then this foolishness that you display?][29]
This is the portion of the wicked from God,
And the heritage of the oppressors from Shaddai.[30]

---

[23] Giving a different turn to Job's complaint, 13, 27.

[24] A general curse, levelled by Zophar at Job, who is the wicked and the evildoer.

[25] A gloss adds, "that there should be any profit."

[26] So demanded by the context.

[27] The verb indicates a cordial relation to God, as that of a favorite child to his father.

[28] So read by a slight change in the text.

[29] Verses 11-12, it will be observed, represent an address in the plural, whereas one expects the singular on the supposition that Zophar is speaking to Job. Either the change was intentionally made after the fragment had been inserted into a supposed speech of Job's, or the verses represent a later addition to adapt the speech to Job, as though he were addressing the three friends.

[30] Parallel to 20, 29 (Zophar) and no doubt taken over from the former speech.

THE BOOK OF JOB

If his children be multiplied, it is for the sword;
And his offspring shall not have bread enough.[31]
Those that remain [32] shall be buried by pestilence; 15
And there shall be no widows to mourn.[33]
Though he heap up silver as dust,
And provide garments as clay;
He may provide, but the righteous will put on,
And the innocent shall divide the silver.
He builds his house as a spider's web,[34]
As a [vineyard] booth for the keeper.[35]
He lies down rich, but it [36] will not continue;
He opens his eyes, and it is gone.
Terrors overtake him by day;[37]   20
The tempest removes him by night.
The east wind carries him off and away;
And sweeps him out of his place.
Its arrows shoot without sparing;[38]

---

[31] A direct answer to Job's assertion 21, 7-11, showing clearly that 27, 13-23 *cannot* be placed in the mouth of Job.

[32] *i.e.*, those that are left over from the sword and famine.

[33] *i.e.*, the remaining sons and their wives will also die of the plague.

[34] So the Greek text. What the wicked builds will be as fragile as a spider's web; their riches will not be permanent. This is directly contrary to Job's assertion (21, 13 *seq.*), but in accord with what Bildad (8, 13-15) says.

[35] So the Greek and the Syriac versions. The reference is to the booth or hut erected temporarily in the vineyards during the vintage season to house the one who guards the vineyard against theft.

[36] *i.e.*, his wealth.

[37] So read by a slight change in the text, instead of "waters."

[38] *i.e.*, the arrows of misfortune are not spared in hunting him down. Cf. Jer. 50, 14.

And he is pierced [39] by its force.[40]
One shall clap one's hands over him,[41]
And in his own place [42] one shall hiss at him.

[For chapter 28, an independent composition on the "Search for Wisdom" see below p. 310; for chapter 29-30,1 part of Job's first supplementary speech, below p. 298.]

[30, 2-8 an independent fragment, containing and elaborating the same description of the awful fate in store for the wicked.][43]

30, 2   Of what profit is the strength of their hands to them,[44]
When old age lays its hold upon them?
Gaunt with want and famine,
They take to the desert for refuge.[45]
Plucking the salt-root with wormwood,
5   And with the roots of the broom as their food.
Driven forth from the community,[46]

---

[39] So Ehrlich's reading.
[40] Literally: "hand," but designating the force of the evil fortune or punishment.
[41] In joy at his discomfiture. Cf. 30, 8.
[42] Better than "out of his place."
[43] Barton, Journal of Biblical Literature, vol. 30, p. 74, proposes to take verses 2-8 of Chap. 30 as part of Bildad's speech, beginning with Chap. 25, but Barton's whole theory of the reconstruction of this speech involves too many transpositions without sufficient motive. Besides, it is Zophar (Chap. 20) and not Bildad who dwells so emphatically upon the fate of the wicked.
[44] So read instead of "to me." Verses 2-3 and 4ᵃ are missing in the original Greek version.
[45] There is an obscure word in 3ᵃ, but the general sense is clear. A gloss, descriptive of the desert (?) as the place of "storm and the hurricane" is added.
[46] So by a slight change of the text.

THE BOOK OF JOB

One shouts after them as after a thief.[47]
Forced to dwell in the clefts of the valleys,—
In caves and in rocks.
Among the thorny growths they groan;
Huddled together under nettles.
Worthless and nameless,　　　　　　　　　　8
They are scourged out of the land.[48]

The words of Job are ended.[49]　　　31, 40ᵃ

[47] *i.e.*, they are driven off with derisive shouts, as a thief is hounded out of the settlement.

[48] Clearly a parallel to 27, 23 and betraying the independent character of this fragment.

[49] The colophon to the original Book of Job see above p.67. Job's reply to Zophar's third speech is lacking. It was perhaps suppressed because too objectionable from the orthodox point of view; and at all events replaced by the two supplementary speeches of Job, embodied in chapters 29-31, in which, however, later editors in their rearrangement inserted portions of Zophar's third speech (30, 2-8 and 31, 2-4) and of Job's speech in reply to Bildad's third speech (30, 16-24) and the conclusion (31, 35-37).

IV

TWO SUPPLEMENTARY SPEECHES OF JOB

(Chapters 29–31)

A

THE FIRST SUPPLEMENTARY SPEECH OF JOB [50]—
RECONSTRUCTED

29, 1   And Job again took up his speech [51] as follows:
1–25   Oh that I were as in the months of old,
The happy past.   As in the days when God watched o'er me;[52]
When His lamp hung [53] over my head;
When by His light I could venture into darkness.[54]

---

[50] Consisting of 29, 1–20 with 21–25 as an independent elaboration of the same thought as in 7–11; 30, 1 and 9–15, and 26–31 as the close. In my translation I divide the speech into three sections as follows:

(a) 29, 1–20, (b) 29, 21–25, as an independent supplement, followed by (c) 30, 1 and 9–15, and 30, 26–31 as the conclusion.

[51] The unusual heading in place of the conventional "in answer said" betrays the independence of this speech from the body of the book. The term *mashal* here used is a very general one for "discourse" or speech; but which in time acquired the sense of a speech with some didactic purpose. Hence it becomes the designation for the "Book of Mashals," *i.e.*, Proverbs; it is also used as parable, which is essentially an utterance of a didactic character. The same heading was appended by some editor to 27, 1. See above, p. 290, note 94.

[52] See the parallels in Dante and Chaucer, quoted by Strahan, *Job*, p. 242.

[53] So by a slight change of the text.

[54] This is the meaning of the Hebrew phrase, as Ehrlich *Randglossen*, 6, p. 293, points out.

THE BOOK OF JOB

As I was in the days of my bloom,
When God was close [55] to my tent.
[When Shaddai was with me   5
And my children about me.][56]
When my guests [57] washed in cream,
And a messenger to me[58] poured streams of oil,[59]
When I went forth to the gate, [60]
And took my seat in the broad place;[61]
Youths saw me and withdrew,[62]
And the aged remained standing.[63]
Princes refrained from speaking,[64]
And laid their hand on their mouth.[65]
The voice of the nobles was hushed,
And their tongue cleaved to their palate.[66]   10

---

[55] More literally: "in close converse."

[56] Verse 5—somewhat banal and prosaic—is probably a later insertion to explain the force of the preceding one. Ehrlich's explanation is farfetched, besides involving an unnecessary correction in the first part of the verse.

[57] Not "my steps" but "those who come or wander to me," *i.e.*, the wayfarers who sought Job's hospitality, as Ehrlich has most happily suggested.

[58] So by a slight change of the text, instead of the meaningless "rock."

[59] Meaning that streams of oil were poured out for him. Cream instead of water to wash one's feet, and oil in abundance are symbols of the overflowing plenty which prevailed in Job's household. Verse 6 is missing in the Syriac version.

[60] A gloss adds "unto the city." The gate is the place where the tribunal, composed of the leading citizens, sat.

[61] *i.e.*, the plaza at the gate of an Oriental town.

[62] Out of respect.

[63] A gloss adds "rose," to the verb "stood."

[64] Out of respect for Job.

[65] The sign of silence.

[66] *i.e.*, they kept back anything that they had to say.

THE BOOK OF JOB

The ear that heard envied me,[67]
And the eye that saw emulated me.
For I delivered the poor that cried out,
And the orphan and the one without help.
The blessing of the forsaken was poured on me;
And I cheered the mind of the widow.
Righteousness I put on and it clothed me;
And my judgment[68] was [my] mantle and diadem.[69]

15 Eyes was I to the blind,
And feet to the lame.
A father, I to the needy;
And I searched out the cause of the unknown.
And I broke the jaws of the wicked,
And plucked the prey from his teeth.
And I thought to die in my nest,
To lengthen my days as the phœnix.[70]
My root exposed to water,

---

[67] Literally, "looked upon me as fortunate."
[68] *i.e.*, the just decisions rendered by him.
[69] Symbols of royalty.
[70] An interesting metaphor to express two hopes—a long life, always regarded as a sign of Divine favor, and to die peacefully in one's home. The phœnix, according to the widespread belief in antiquity, was supposed to live for 500 years and when his time was come, he consumed himself by setting fire to his nest. The correct translation "Phœnix" instead of "sand" is found in the translation of the American Jewish Publication Society as also on the margin of the RV. It probably underlies the Greek translation (though misunderstood by later redactors) and has ancient Rabbinical authority (see Marcus Jastrow, *Talmudic Dictionary* I, p. 433 sub Ḥōl). One cannot help wondering whether if "phœnix" had been suggested by some modern commentator, it would have been adopted by translators who retain untenable translations, (merely because they are traditional) in hundreds of passages that are far more unreasonable than "sand" instead of "phœnix."

THE BOOK OF JOB

And dew falling all night on my branch.
My glory freshened,[71]   20
And the bow in my hand renewed.[72]

Unto me men listened and waited,[73]
And kept silent for my counsel.
After I had spoken, they spake not again;
And my speech dropped upon them.
They waited for me as for rain;
And they opened their mouth as for latter rain.[74]
When I smiled upon them, they gained confidence,[75]
And at sight of me could hardly contain themselves.[76]   25
I choose their way [77] as chief:
And I sat as a king with [his] troops.[78]

---

[71] *i.e.*, with ever renewed strength.

[72] There is a strange mixture of metaphors in these two verses (19 and 20) to express practically the same idea as in v. 18—that Job hoped to end his days as he had lived, with his vigor unimpaired like a tree whose roots are constantly fed by water and which does not dry up, and like one whose strength is maintained by constantly being supplied with fresh weapons.

[73] 29, 21–25, is an independent fragment, expressing the same lament over the contrast between *then* and *now* as 29, 1–11. I place it here, so as to make it evident that it is merely another attempt to describe what is already set forth fully in 29, 7–11.

[74] Cf. Prov. 16, 15.

[75] So by a slight change of the text.

[76] Such the meaning of the line, demanded by the context.

[77] *i.e.*, guided them. The line has a superfluous word added by way of comment.

[78] *i.e.*, he was looked up to as the army looks to the king, who is also the general. A comment, "As one who comforts

THE BOOK OF JOB

30, 1
1. 9–15 and 26–31
The unhappy present.

But now those younger than I mock;
Whom I would have disdained to set with my flock.[79]
[30, 2–8—part of the reconstructed third speech of Zophar see above, p. 296]

9   Their song[80] have I become,
And a by-word among them.

10 They abhor me [and] stand aloof;
And refrain not from spitting in my face.
For they have severed[81] my cords and afflicted me;[82]
And cast off the bridle before me.
The rabble rises up at my right;[83]
They have cast up against me their...... [84]

---

mourners," is added, to suggest a different interpretation for "sitting as chief," as though referring to his sitting among those who looked to him not only for guidance, but also for comfort. The entire verse is lacking in the original Greek version.

[79] *i.e.*, as shepherds of the flock. The line has been amplified to read "Whose fathers I would have refused to set with the dogs of my flock." In its present form, the line has five beats—clearly much too long.

[80] *i.e.*, their jest. Because of the manifest incongruity of verses 2–8 with v. 1, the editor, who felt the lack of sequence, repeated at the beginning of the 9th verse, the word "now" with which chapter 30 begins.

[81] Read as plural.

[82] So read by a slight change.

[83] So read by a slight change of the text.

[84] The text as it stands "the ways of their destruction" gives no satisfactory sense. I suspect "ways" to be a gloss to "my path" in v. 13; and the remaining word to designate "siegeworks" or the like. A commentator added by way of explanation:
"Headlong they send me"—more literally, "they upset my feet."

THE BOOK OF JOB

They block (?) my path,
They scale [85] my bulwark (?).[86]
As through a wide breach they come;
As a storm they roll themselves upon me.[87]
My honor is chased as the wind,   15
And my welfare passes away as a cloud.

[30, 16–24—part of Job's speech in reply to Bildad's third speech, above p. 290. For verse 25, to be transferred to Job's second supplementary speech, see below p. 306.]

For I hoped for good, but evil has come,   30, 26[88]
I waited for light, but darkness set in.
My bowels are stirred, without rest;
Days of affliction have overtaken me.
In mourning I go about without sunshine;[89]
I have joined the assembly of those crying for help.[90]

An associate to jackals have I become;
[And] a companion to ostriches.[91]

---

[85] So read with Ehrlich.

[86] The text reads "my being" or "my calamity," but the context demands a suitable parallelism to "path." I therefore suggest a term like "bulwark." The last phrase, "with none restraining them," (so to be read following Ehrlich, instead of "no helper to them" which is nonsensical), is an explanatory gloss.

[87] A commentator adds "terror is turned upon me." The line is missing in one of the older Greek versions.

[88] 30, 26–31 close of the reconstructed supplementary speech of Job.

[89] *i.e.*, I move about in darkness—solitary.

[90] *i.e.*, I have joined, as it were; the guild of the helpless. So Ehrlich's explanation.

[91] Jackals and ostriches are frequently used in Biblical poetry as symbols of desolation and mourning.

THE BOOK OF JOB

30   My skin has become black upon me,
And my bones are burned with heat.[92]
My harp is turned to mourning,
And my pipe become a lament.[93]

B

A SECOND SUPPLEMENTARY SPEECH OF JOB[94]—
RECONSTRUCTED

31, 1   A covenant I made with my eyes;
Never to have a thought [95] of a virgin.
[Verses 2-4 forming the beginning of Zophar's third speech above, p. 293; Verses 5-8 below, p. 309.]

31, 1; 9-12; 38-40; 13-15; 30, 25; 31, 16-34; 31, 5-8 Job sets forth his virtues and his avoidance of all sin and temptation.

[92] He is consumed by fever, so that his skin is parched, and the marrow of his bones dried out.

[93] Harp and pipe are usually instruments of joy.

[94] Consisting of 31, 1 and 9-34; 38-40, together with 30, 25 which has slipped into a wrong place (see below, p. 306). The speech consists of seven sections that have been pieced together. They all deal with the same thought—Job's virtuous life. The speech betrays its composite character by its abrupt transition from virtues of private life to those bearing on public duties, and back again to the former. We obtain a more orderly sequence by a rearrangement as follows: 31, 1; 9-12; 38-40; 13-15; 30, 25; 31, 16-34 and lastly 31, 5-8 which forms a forcible climax. I adopt this rearrangement with all the less hesitation because I am convinced that chapter 31 is not of one piece or by a single author; and if this be admitted, a rearrangement of the seven sections into which the speech falls secures a logical instead of a confusing sequence. In the case of a composite production a confusion of sections could easily take place through the editor, who pieced chapters 25 to 31 together in the interest of Jewish orthodoxy, as above p. 130 *seq.* set forth. Verses 35-37 of this chapter must be detached from their present position; they form the close of the original Book of Job in its enlarged form. See above at the conclusion of the reconstructed speech of Job in reply to Bildad's third speech.

[95] So by a slight change of the text. See Matthew 5, 28. Verses 1-4 are missing in the original Greek version.

If my mind[96] should ever be enticed unto a wo- 9
man,
Or I should lie in wait at my neighbor's door;[97]
Might my wife grind for another, [98]   10
And others bend over her.
For that [99] were incest and a grievous offense;[1]
Aye, a fire consuming unto Abaddon.[2]
If my land had cried out against me,   38–40
And its furrows wept together;
If I had sapped its strength without paying for it,
And caused the tillers thereof to be disappointed;[3]
Let thistles grow instead of wheat,
And cockle instead of barley.
If I had ever rejected [4] my servant's claim,   13
Or that of my maid in their suit against me,
What could I do, if God sought revenge?[5]

---

[96] *i.e.*, I vowed that if my mind, etc.
[97] *i.e.*, with a view of visiting his neighbor's wife.
[98] An allusion to sexual intercourse, as the parallelism shows. This line is missing in one of the older Greek versions.
[99] *i.e.*, the mere thought of seducing a woman.
[1] Read as in v. 28 of this chapter. The text has a superfluous "it."
[2] One of the names of the nether world as 26, 6. An utterly destructive fire is meant. A commentator adds a superfluous line:
"Rooting out all my produce,"
which is clearly a misplaced comment to v. 8ᵇ. See also below, p. 309.
[3] By not giving them their full pay. So Ehrlich's interpretation, which is also that adopted by the translators of the American Jewish Publication Society.
[4] *i.e.*, by his superior station had secured a rejection of a just claim on the part of those dependent upon him—an easy matter at all times.
[5] So the reading according to the Greek text.

THE BOOK OF JOB

          What could I answer, if He held me to account?
15   [Has He not formed him in the womb as He made me?
          And did He not fashion her in the same womb?][6]
30, 25 [7] [If I had not wept for the unfortunate,
          And if my soul had not grieved for the needy;]
31, 16 If I had ever refused the request of the poor,
          And turned away from the longing[8] of the widow;
17   And had eaten my morsel alone,
          And the orphan had not shared it with me;[9]
19   If I had ever seen a homeless [10] without a garment,
          And the poor without a covering;
20   If his loins [11] had not blessed me,
          And he had not warmed himself with the fleece of my sheep;
          If I had ever lifted my hand against an orphan,

---

[6] The banal and pietistic reflection is almost offensive. One suspects that the verse may be a later insertion.

[7] Here I would place 30, 25. See above, p. 303.

[8] Literally: "eyes," in the sense of what one longingly looks at and hopes to obtain.

[9] Verse 18, which is missing in the original Greek version appears to be an insertion on the part of an excessively pietistic commentator, who thought it necessary to assign as a reason for Job's kindness to orphans that God had been *his* guardian.

    "For He reared me from my youth as a father,
    And from my mother's womb guided me."

The two lines do not refer as is assumed in the ordinary translations to the orphan but to Job. The subject of the two verbs is God, and the reading of the second verb ("guide") must be slightly changed so as to embody the suffix of the first person.

[10] *i.e.*, a tramp.

[11] Namely, the loins of the poor, in gratitude for having been covered by the benevolent Job.

THE BOOK OF JOB

Because I saw my support in the gate;[12]
Let my shoulder fall from its socket,   22
And my arm be broken at the elbow.[13]
If I had made gold my hope,[14]   24
And to pure gold said, "My trust";
If I had rejoiced at the abundance of my wealth, 25
And that my hand had gotten much;
If I had looked for the appearance of the new moon,[15]

---

[12] The gate is the place of the tribunal. The thought is the same as above, 13–14, against taking advantage of one's influence before the tribunal.

[13] Verse 23—only partially preserved in the Greek version—is clearly a prose addition in the style of the excessively pietistic commentator:

"For a terror to me is the hand of God, which I could not endure."

Read by a slight change "hand," instead of "calamity."

[14] The line is missing in the original Greek version.

[15] This is without much question the meaning of the line. The usual translation which takes the word "light" (*i.e.*, ôr) to refer to the sun is erroneous, since the verb which follows and which refers to the rejoicing at the appearance of the new moon, clearly shows that in both lines the moon is meant. As a survival of primitive moon-worship Arabs continue to this day to greet the new moon with salutes and shouts of rejoicing. (See Doughty, *Arabia Deserta* I, p. 166 and 319). Similarly, Orthodox Jews still have special prayers at the time of new moon. Job is here represented as saying that he was careful not to yield to the temptation to pay obeisance to the moon, instead of confining his worship to the Supreme Author of the Universe. One cannot help suspecting that verses 26–28 may be due to a later commentator, who as an extremist in maintaining Judaism pure from heathenish associations, regarded the custom of saluting the new moon and of ceremonies at the time of the full moon as a species of idolatry, and who tried his hand at enlarging on this long recital of all the sins and wrongs from which Job kept himself free.

THE BOOK OF JOB

And for the coming of the bright moon;[16]
And had secretly been enticed,[17]
To kiss my hand to it;
This also might have been a grievous offense;
For I should thereby have denied God on high.
29 If I had rejoiced at the destruction of my hater,
Or exulted when evil befell him,[18]
31 If any of my household [19] could ever say,[20]
That any of them [21] did not have enough.[22]
No stranger ever lodged outside;
My doors were e'er open to the traveller,
If silently [23] I had covered my transgressions,
Hiding my iniquity in my bosom;

---

[16] Meaning the full moon.
[17] This line is missing in the original Greek version.
[18] Verse 30 reading (in prose form):

"I did not permit my mouth (literally: "palate") to sin by asking for his life from God."

is again to be taken as an insertion by the same commentator who finds it necessary to emphasize the description of all that Job did not do, and to comment upon it in more or less banal fashion. Instead of "by a curse" read with Ehrlich, by a different vocalization, "from God." This simple and happy emendation which at once makes the point clear is a good illustration of Ehrlich's skill in restoring a corrupt and obscure passage, by virtue of his keen penetration into the genius of the Hebrew language, and his complete grasp of the vocabulary and of grammatical niceties.

[19] Literally, the "men of my tent," meaning, however, as the word used for "men" indicates, the menials.
[20] Omit "not," as the Greek version does.
[21] Literally, "his flesh."
[22] *i.e.*, every one got more than enough.
[23] So read with Ehrlich, by a slight change of the text, instead of the meaningless "like a man."

THE BOOK OF JOB

Because I greatly feared the multitude,[24]
And the contempt of the folk [25] affrighted me; [26]
[Verses 35-37 at the close of Job's speech in reply to Bildad's third speech. See above p. 292.]
If I had ever followed falseness,   5
And my foot had hastened to deceit;[27]
If my step had turned out of the [right] path,
And my mind had followed after my eyes;[28]
Let me sow and another eat;
And let my produce be rooted out.[29]

---

[24] *i.e.*, for fear of public opinion.

[25] Literally, "families"—here used as a synonym for populace.

[26] The last part of this verse "So that I kept quiet and did not go out of doors" is a gloss—and a rather superfluous one—to amplify the fear of facing those who might suspect him of wrongdoing.

[27] Verse 6 reading:

> "Let Him weigh me in a just balance,
> That God may know my integrity."

is again an inserted exclamation of the pietistic commentator, who, not content with the patronizing tone throughout the chapter, saw fit to increase it still further by insertions that overstep all reasonable bounds of self-appreciation.

[28] *i.e.*, followed after lust, with an allusion to Numbers 15, 39. "Follow not after your minds and eyes." A superfluous line follows:

> "If any blemish clung to my palms"

which is either a comment to 7ᵃ or is half of a distich of which the other half is lost.

[29] To this the superfluous line in v. 12 (above)

> "rooting out all my produce"

is a misplaced comment.

V

THE SEARCH FOR WISDOM [30]
(Chapter 28)

28, 1
1-11
Man's search for precious metals and stones.

There [31] is a mine for silver,
And a place for gold to be refined.
Iron is taken out of the dust,
And copper molten out of the rock.[32]
Man sets a bound to darkness,[33]
Penetrating [34] to thick gloom and dense shadows.
He breaks a shaft through a strange people;[35]
Forgotten of men they grope about;[36]

---

[30] Chap. 28 is an entirely independent production, with striking analogies to the glorification of wisdom in Proverbs, Chap. 8-9. It was inserted into the Book of Job by some later editor as appropriate, though having no connection with the problem with which the book deals. See further above, p. 135 *seq.*

[31] In order to connect the chapter with what precedes, an editor has added the particle "for."

[32] Literally, "stone," here used generically for any hard substance—mineral or otherwise.

[33] To explain this somewhat obscure phrase a commentator has added "To the uttermost bound he searches." This is omitted in the original Greek version.

[34] So read with Ehrlich, by a slight change of the text instead of "stone."

[35] So read by a different vocalization of the consonantal text. The mining operation which the author has in mind and with which he is so familiar refers either to the Sinaitic Peninsula or—and more probably—to the Lebanon region. In either case, the miners could be spoken of as a foreign people. The line is missing in the original Greek version.

[36] The verb describes those who grope their way in darkness or totter like a drunkard. A commentator, however, refers

THE BOOK OF JOB

[In a land from which produce [37] grows, 5 [38]
But which underneath[39] is stirred up by fire;[40]
A place whose stones are sapphire,
And where dust is gold.]
A path unknown to the bird of prey,
And which the eye of the falcon has not seen;[41]
Which proud beasts have not trodden,
Beyond which the lion has not passed.
He attacks[42] a flinty rock;
He overturns mountains by the roots.[43]
He breaks light shafts [44] in the rocks; 10
And his eyes see precious things.
He explores [45] the sources[46] of the streams;

---

the verb to miners and adds, by way of explanation, "hanging of foot," as though let down by a rope into the shaft.

[37] Literally, "bread" in the general sense of food.

[38] Verses 5–9ª are missing in the original Greek version. Verses 5–6 clearly interrupt the context. The many verses in this chapter that are missing in the original Greek version (4ª; 5–9ª; 14–19; 21ᵇ; 22ª; 27) confirm the view here taken of the growth of the chapter by subsequent insertions, which may represent snatches of other poems in celebration of wisdom.

[39] *i.e.*, still deeper down.

[40] Referring to the hard interior with its misshapen masses of rocks, suggesting a tremendous upheaval as by the eruption of a volcano, in contrast to the softness and smoothness of the cultivated soil on the surface.

[41] The miners pass into regions inaccessible even to strong birds, accustomed to penetrate into the clefts of rocks that cannot be scaled by man.

[42] Literally: "puts forth his hand."

[43] *i.e.*, blasting, which was known to the ancients. See Pliny, *Hist. Nat.* XXXIII, 21.

[44] So read, following Ehrlich.

[45] So the Greek text.

[46] So the Greek text.

THE BOOK OF JOB

*12-22
Wisdom
hidden from
man.*

And what was hidden is brought to light.
But Wisdom [47] where is she to be found?
And where is the place of understanding?
Man knows not the way to her;[48]
Nor is she to be found in the land of the living.
The Deep [49] says; "she is not in me";
And the sea says, "not with me." [50]

15 [51]

[She cannot be gotten for gold, [52]
Nor can her purchase price be weighed out in silver.
She cannot be valued with gold of Ophir,[53]
Nor with the precious onyx and sapphire.
Gold and glass cannot equal her;
Nor are vessels of gold an exchange for her.
Corals and crystals are naught beside her;[54]
For the value of wisdom is above pearls.
The Topaz of Cush[55] is not equal to her;
She cannot be valued with purest fine gold.]

---

[47] Here personified, as in Proverbs Chap. 8.
[48] So the Greek text, instead of "price." By a change in a single letter of the Hebrew text, we obtain the correct reading.
[49] Tehôm—the personification of the deep as in Genesis 1, 2.
[50] *i.e.*, neither the deep nor the sea possess Wisdom. The verse is missing in the original Greek version.
[51] Verses 15-19 are missing in the original Greek version, and represent a later insertion based on Prov. 3, 14-15 and 8, 10-17.
[52] A strange word stands in the Hebrew text—perhaps the name of a special kind of gold. Siegfried refers to I Kgs. 6, 20, where the term is used in connection with gold.
[53] Ophir (in southern Arabia?) was famous as the source of the finest gold. See above 22, 24 and I Kings, 9, 28.
[54] Literally: "not worth mentioning."
[55] *i.e.*, Ethiopia.

THE BOOK OF JOB

Wisdom,—whence cometh she? 20
And where is the place of understanding?
She is hid from the eyes of the living,
And concealed from the bird of heaven,[56]
Abaddon[57] and death say:
"Our ears have heard of her."[58]
God knows the way to her;   23–28
And He knows her place.   *Wisdom is with God.*
For He encompasses the ends of the world;
He sees all under heaven.
When He gave a weight[59] for the wind, 25
And measured out the waters;
When He assigned a law for the rain,
And a path for the thunderbolt;[60]
Then He saw her and proclaimed her,
Established her, aye singled her out;[61]
[And said in regard to man:
"Behold, the fear of Yahweh[62] is wisdom;
And departing from evil is understanding."][63]

---

[56] The line is missing in the original Greek version.

[57] Literally: "Destruction" here as 26, 6, and 31, 12, a name for the nether world. The line is missing in the original Greek version which combines verse 21ᵃ and 22ᵇ into one distich.

[58] But we have never seen her.

[59] *i.e.*, force and power.

[60] Verses 25–26 are based on Prov. 8, 22–31.

[61] Verse 27 is missing in the original Greek version.

[62] So the original reading as in Prov. 1, 7, changed subsequently to *Adonai* "Lord," though many MSS. retain Yahweh.

[63] As shown by the introductory line, verse 28 is an addition by some pious commentator, who quotes Prov. 1, 7 (a saying similar to 9, 10), as an appropriate close to the chapter.

VI

FIRST APPENDIX TO THE BOOK OF JOB

The Four Speeches of Elihu With Three Inserted Poems

(Chapters 32–37)

A

Introductions to the First Speech

32, 1 [64] (a) And these three men [65] ceased answering Job
1–5 because he was justified in their eyes.[66]

Five editorial comments.

[64] The first five verses (in prose) consist of a series of five editorial comments, each of independent origin and rather awkwardly combined, resulting in redundancy and in some confusion that is still further aggravated by later glosses. The first comment was added originally to the close of the book which terminated—as above, p. 71 set forth—in its first draft with chapter 21 or in the enlarged one with 31, 35–37, as the close of Job's reply to Bildad or possibly to the last reply to Zophar.

[65] The phrase "these three men"—instead of "three-friends" (2, 11) shows that the editorial comment is by a different hand than the one to whom we owe the prose introduction to the original book. The reading of the Greek text "his three friends ceased" is clearly a later correction to conform to the usage in 2, 11.

[66] The reading of the Greek text and the Syriac version and also of some Hebrew manuscripts "in their eyes," instead of "in his eyes," (as the received text has it), represents the original wording, which in this form would constitute an intelligible comment on the part of a reader or commentator who sympathized with the point of view set forth by the compiler of the speeches of Job and of the three friends in their earliest form. The comment thus incidentally furnishes a proof that the original purpose of the Book of Job was to show the untenability of

THE BOOK OF JOB

(b) And the anger of Elihu, the son of Barachel, the Buzite [67] of the family of Ram [68] was kindled, [69] because he (*i.e.*, Job) regarded himself justified as against God. [70]

(c) And against his three friends [71] was his anger kindled, because they could not find an answer. [72]

---

the conventional view that only the wicked suffer in this world, and that the good enjoy the blessings of God as long as they live. The second comment (v. 2) protesting against the assumption that Job was justified, betrays on the other hand the spirit of the orthodox opponents to the original book, and emanates, therefore, from an editor who regarded Elihu as the triumphant champion of the rule of Divine justice in this world. Another editor found it necessary to state (v. 3) that Elihu was also angry at the three friends because they found no answer. The fourth comment (v. 4) is the remark of a pedantic commentator who, regarding the book in its final form as a unit, naïvely assumes that Elihu was present during the Symposium between Job and his friends, and thinks it necessary to explain why Elihu hitherto had not been introduced to the reader. Finally the fifth comment (v. 5) may represent the *original* introduction, added with a view of connecting the appendix with the original book.

[67] Buz is mentioned in Jer. 25, 23 with Dedan and Tema in northern Arabia. The Prophet Ezekiel (1,3) was likewise a Buzite.

[68] Occuring Gen. 22 21. The Greek text adds "of the land of Uz."

[69] A pedantic glossator adds: "against Job his anger was kindled."

[70] The word "as against God" (or "rather than God") may be a gloss subsequently added.

[71] The phrase "his three friends" as against "these three men" in v. 1, shows that the comment in v. 3 is from a different source.

[72] A glossator has added "so that they might show Job to be in the wrong," which translation is preferable to the one found in the AV and its successors: "and yet had condemned Job."

THE BOOK OF JOB

(d) But Elihu held back [73] while they were speaking,[74] because they were older than he.

5 (e) And Elihu saw that there was no answer in the mouth of these three men.[75]

B

THE FIRST SPEECH OF ELIHU

32, 6 [Then Elihu, the son of Barachel, the Buzite, in answer said:[76]]

6–22 *Another series of introductions.*

(a) Young am I, in years,
And you are aged;[77]
Therefore I held back and feared,

---

[73] Or "waited." The text has an insertion "Job" after the verb, probably a gloss to "himself" in v. 2, and which has crept in at a wrong place.

[74] So read by a different vocalization of the consonantal text.

[75] A glossator in order to connect this independent (and probably original) introduction to the speeches of Elihu with the previous comments added: "And his anger was kindled" the superfluity of which is self-evident. The verse is missing in the original Greek version.

[76] Verse 6ᵃ is an editorial addition to make the introductory phrase correspond to the conventional one used in the case of the speeches of Job and his three friends. Chapter 32, 6–22, is entirely taken up with the preliminaries to Elihu's speech. It consists of (1) the editorial connecting link (v. 6ᵃ), (2) two independent introductions running parallel to one another (a) 6ᵇ–10 = (b) 11–17, likewise with explanatory comments, and (c) an ironical addition (18–22), made by a commentator who did not think much of Elihu's argument and sought to make him appear ridiculous by representing him as bursting with an irresistible desire to relieve his mind, and as determined to express his views at all hazards. A fourth introduction in imitation of the third is found 33, 2–7 and a fifth one has slipped in at the close of chapter 33, 31–33. See below p. 323.

[77] The line lacks a word to make up three beats. Perhaps "very" has dropped out.

THE BOOK OF JOB

To declare my opinion to you.
I thought, let the aged [78] speak,
And those of many years teach wisdom.
However, it is the spirit in man,
And the breath of Shaddai that gives understanding.
Grey beards are not [always] wise;
Nor do the old [always] have discernment.[79]
Therefore, I say; "listen to me; 10
Let me also declare my opinion."

(b) [I waited,[80] forsooth, for your words; 11–17 [81]

---

[78] Literally, "days," meaning those of many days.
[79] Cf. the note to 12, 12.
[80] To this word "I waited" there is added a comment (v. 16) "I waited," *i.e.*, "because they did not speak, for they stood there without answering further." According to this commentator, the words "I waited" mean that Elihu waited for the three men to answer. The verse is missing in the original Greek version.
[81] Verses 11–17 represent another and entirely independent draft of an introduction to Elihu's speech, and form a parallel to verses 6–10.

We have a similar combination of several drafts in the orations of Ezekiel. In chapter 1, verses 15–21 form a variant description of the prophet's vision verses 1–14, while in chapter 8 we have a third description and in chapter 10 a fourth, the latter running closely parallel to 1, 15–21. Again in the message revealed to Ezekiel in the vision, we can detect several drafts that have been combined. Thus in chapter 2, verses 6–7 are clearly parallel to 3–5, just as 8–10 are paralleled by 3, 1–3. There are thus four independent introductions to which we may add two more (a) 3, 4–9 and (b) 3, 10–11. It is only by thus assuming a series of independent drafts, combined by a conscientious editor who wished to preserve *all* the material that had come down to him, that we can get order out of the frightful confusion in the present combination of this material in the Book of Ezekiel. Such imperfect methods of editing are natural at a

THE BOOK OF JOB

    To your arguments I listened.
    While you carefully selected words,[82]
    I reflected about you.
    And [83] there was none that convinced Job;
    None that could answer his points.[84]
    Beware lest you say, "*we* have wisdom;[85]
    Let God refute him—not man."

14   Since words he has not measured with me,[86]
    I shall not answer like your speeches.[87]

17   Let me now present my argument;[88]
    Let me declare my opinion.[89]]

---

time when literary composition in the proper sense was regarded as secondary as against the zeal of editors to preserve all records—however fragmentary or imperfect—that lay before them.

[82] The line, as well as the whole of verse 12, is missing in the original Greek version.

[83] A glossator adds "behold."

[84] Literally, "his words." To this we again have a comment in v. 15 (missing in the original Greek version),

> "They were [so] startled that they could not find any answer,
> Words failed them."

[85] Elihu warns the friends against seeking to excuse their failure by putting the task of answering on God, saying "Let God do it. We give it up."

[86] Or, by following in part the Greek version and changing the person of the verb, we may obtain "I will not set forth such words as these." So Gray in the American Journal of Semitic Languages, Vol. 36, p. 102.

[87] So by a slight change. Verses 15–16, (missing in the original Greek version) are glosses to v. 12 and to v. 11, respectively, as indicated above notes 80 and 84.

[88] More literally "doctrine." So read instead of "my portion," by a transposition of the consonants of the word in the text, as suggested by Ehrlich.

[89] Verse 17 is clearly a parallel to v. 10, to mark the close of the first introductory draft.

THE BOOK OF JOB

(c) [For I am full of words;[90]
The spirit within me constrains me.
Indeed, my inside is as wine without outlet,
That even in new wine-skins is ready to burst,[91]
Let me speak that I may find relief;   20
Let me open my lips to give answer.
Without regard to any man's feelings,
Without evasion, because of any one;
For I know not how to evade,
E'en though my Maker might forgive me.[92]]
Now listen, Job to my speech,[93]   33,

---

[90] Verses 18–22 must be looked upon as an ironical amplification of the introduction to Elihu's speech, added by some one who sympathized with the spirit of the original Book of Job that ended in a *non sequitur*, and who aimed to hold up Elihu to ridicule, as one who talks merely to relieve his mind. What he says would, according to this commentator, be mere escaping gas, "words full of sound and fury, signifying nothing."

[91] Matthew 9, 17.

[92] This is clearly the sense of the concluding line, not that God would "soon take me away," as usually rendered.

[93] Verses 2–7 represent a second insertion on the part of the ironical commentator who added, 32, 18–22, with a view of further emphasizing the empty boasts of Elihu and his "big" talk which issues in banalities.

> [Behold, I open my mouth;
> My tongue utters what is in my bosom.
> My words [reflect] the frankness of my mind;
> And what my lips speak is sincerity itself.
> The spirit of God has made me,
> And the breath of Shaddai has given me life,
> If thou canst, then refute me,
> Array yourself and stand before me.
> I am like you in relation to God;
> Out of clay, I too, have been formed.
> Let terror of me not startle thee;
> And my authority (?) not weigh upon thee.]

The irony is delicious, especially when one considers that in the two introductions in chapter 32, Elihu is represented as young

THE BOOK OF JOB

<small>8

8-11
*Job's claim
to innocence.*

10

12-22
*God sends
warnings to
man through
visions and
tribulations.*</small>

And hearken to all my words,[94]
For thou hast said in my hearing;[95]
And I heard the sound of the words:
"I am pure, without transgression,
Guiltless (?), without iniquity in me;[96]
But He devises occasions [97] against me,
As His enemy He counts me.
He puts my feet in the stocks;
He keeps watch over all my steps."[98]
Now to this I answer, thou art not right;
[In supposing] God too severe towards man.
Why dost thou contend [99] against Him,
Because He answers not all thy [1] words?
For God *does* answer[2] once,
And even twice without one's regarding it;[3]

---

and modest. At the end of v. 2 we must read by a slight change "in my bosom" (so Ehrlich) instead of "in my palate." In v. 3 the word "knowledge" is a gloss to "my words." In v. 5 the last word "stand forth" is a variant or comment to "array thyself before me." In v. 6, instead of "as thy mouth," we must read by a slight change of the text "like thee." Verse 4 harks back to 32, 8. See above, p. 316, note 76.

[94] The Greek text omits the word "all," found in the Hebrew, while in the original Greek version the entire line is missing.

[95] The line is omitted in the original Greek version.

[96] Alluding to Job's utterances as *e.g.*, 9, 21; 10, 7; 16, 17; 23, 10–12. The Hebrew text has a superfluous "I" and a corrupted synonym to "pure," which must have emphasized Job's innocence.

[97] *i. e.* He frames up charges against me.

[98] As one closely watches a prisoner,—a direct quotation from 13, 27.

[99] Note again the legal phraseology as in Job's speeches.

[1] So read by a slight change.

[2] *i.e.*, responds to the summons.

[3] The line is missing in the Greek version.

THE BOOK OF JOB

In a dream (and) in a night vision;[4] 15
In slumbering upon one's couch,
He opens the ears of men,
And startles them with sufferings.[5]
To lead man away from his deeds,[6] 17
And to remove [7] pride from man.[8]
He is chastened by pain on his couch, 19
And by the enduring torture of his bones;[9]
So that his life has distaste for food, 20
And his soul, for the daintiest bit.[10]
His flesh is consumed beyond recognition;[11]
And his bones corroded [12] to unsightliness.
And his soul is brought near to the pit,
And his life to the slain.[13]
Yet, if there be an intercessor,[14] 23–26
Intercession and Relief.

---

[4] A gloss (omitted in the original Greek version, as also 16°), with an allusion to Gen. 2, 21 adds "when deep sleep falls on man." God speaks to man in this way without his knowing it.

[5] *i.e.*, nightmares.

[6] So by a slight change in the text, supported by the Greek translation.

[7] So by a slight change in one letter of the text.

[8] Verse 18 is a misplaced comment to v. 28. See below.

[9] So by a slight change in the text. The line is missing in the original Greek version.

[10] This line is likewise omitted in the original Greek version.

[11] More literally, "from being seen."

[12] More literally, "scraped bare." I follow the rendering of the American Jewish Publication Society.

[13] So read by a different vocalization of the consonants.

[14] A commentator adds "angel" to suggest the kind of intercessor meant. The Targum renders by the Greek *paraklētos* "comforter," used in the theological sense of "Holy Spirit." Then follows a comment "one in a thousand" (like 9, 13), which

THE BOOK OF JOB

  To testify to a man's righteousness;
Then He graciously says: "release him,-[3]
For I have found a ransom [16] [for his soul."]

25 His body [17] becomes softer than a child's;
He returns to the days of his youth.
He prays unto God, who is gracious to him;[18]
And who restores to a man his right.[19]

27-30
Confession and Redemption.
 He[20] steps before men and says:

is either out of place, or is added to suggest that intercession rarely takes place. If this be correct, the addition must have been made by a skeptical reader.

[15] A commentator adds: "from going down into the pit" (suggested by v. 28ª) which, however, makes the line too long. One of the Greek versions has a further addition.

> "He renewed his body like mortar on a wall,
> And filled the marrow of his bones."

[16] Namely the good deeds formerly done by the sinner, in accordance with the testimony borne by the intercessor. The point of view is pithily expressed in the maxim, "Righteousness saves from death" (Prov. 10, 2 and 11, 4). The line is too short by one beat. Perhaps a word like the one suggested in the translation has dropped out. The Greek version shows that something has happened to the text at this point. See Beer, *Text des Buches Hiob*, p. 212.

[17] Literally: "his flesh." Similarly in the Babylonian tale of the suffering king (above, p. 37) we read in the description of his restoration to health

> "He restored my form to complete strength"

(Jastrow, *Journal of Biblical Literature*, Vol. 25, p. 179.) All the ravages of disease and suffering had disappeared.

[18] A superfluous line reading:

> "And looks with joy upon him,"

is to be regarded as a comment or variant to "who is gracious to him."

[19] *i.e.*, the place due to the righteous man.
[20] *i.e.*, the man restored to his position through Divine grace.

"I sinned and perverted the right,[21]
But He redeemed me from passing to the pit,[22]
And my life to enjoy the light."
[Behold all this God does,
Twice and thrice with a man;[23]
To keep his soul from the pit,
To enjoy light in the land of the living.][24] 30

---

[21] A pedantic commentator adds, "but He did not do the same to me," *i.e.*, God did not punish me as I deserved. The ordinary translation of this addition: "And it profited me not" is entirely astray.

[22] To this 28th verse, a commentator to make still clearer what was meant, added v. 18, (which got into the text at the wrong place)

"He kept his soul from the pit
And his life from passing into oblivion (?)."

The last word of the couplet is obscure (see 36, 12), but the context demands a parallel term to the nether world.

[23] *i.e.*, God gives man two and even three chances to prolong his days by a return to a virtuous life.

[24] I follow Ehrlich's emendation of the text. The two verses (29–30) are omitted in the original Greek version; they hark back to v. 14, and probably represent a later addition. The closing three verses of the chapter (31–33) are clearly again a variant form of the introduction, chapter 33, 2–7. They evidently belong at the beginning and not at the end of a discourse. The editor who came across them may have put them on the margin, whence they were inserted by a copyist as a supplement. The three verses (with the exception of the first line) are missing in the original Greek version—a further indication of their supplementary character. They read as follows:

"Give heed, Job, hearken to me;
Keep silent, while I speak.
If thou hast anything to say, answer me;
Speak, for I desire thy justification
If not, hearken thou to me,
And be silent, while I teach thee wisdom."

THE BOOK OF JOB

C

SECOND SPEECH OF ELIHU [25]

34, 1 [Then Elihu in answer said:][26]
1–4
Introduction. Hear my words, you wise men.
Listen to me, you that have knowledge.[27]
[For the ear is there to test words,
As the palate to taste food.][28]
[Let us choose the right for ourselves;
Let us ascertain among us what is good.][29]
5 Now Job says; "I am innocent,

---

[25] Chapter 34. Into this speech an entirely independent fragment, beginning with a special introduction (v. 16), has been dovetailed with the result of creating a painful confusion in the sequence of the thought. This fragment, consisting of verses 16–20; 23–27 and 30, deals with a theme entirely *foreign* to Elihu's second speech. Elihu makes the point that Job places himself on a plane with the wicked in accusing God of injustice. Instead, Job ought to humbly submit and throw himself on the mercy of God. The inserted fragment, on the other hand, treats of God's indifference to the rank of sinners and illustrates this thought by detailing how He deals with kings and nobles who have abused their position. The manner of dovetailing is quite in keeping with the method of composition which we find in the Pentateuchal Codes and in the Historical Books of the Old Testament. See *A Gentle Cynic*, p. 109 *seq*.

[26] Clearly an editorial addition, (like 32, 6ᵃ) since Job does not answer Elihu, and the second speech is not even addressed to Job. It is an independent composition by some one who tried his hand at the conundrum propounded by Job. A later editor put the speech into the mouth of Elihu.

[27] The form of address, "Hear"...... "Listen" is clearly based upon the usage of the prophets, for example, Isaiah 1, 1, just as the late poem inserted at the close of Deuteronomy (chapter 32) follows this usage.

[28] Quoted from 12, 11, and missing in the original Greek version.

[29] This fourth verse is missing in the original Greek version.

THE BOOK OF JOB

But God has taken away my right.[30] 5–12
Despite my being right, I suffer;[31] *God is supreme*
Without transgression, my wound[32] is mortal." *and just.*
Was there ever a man like Job,
Drinking in scorn like water?[33]
He has joined the company of evildoers, 8
To walk with the wicked.[34]
Far be it from God to be wicked; 10b
From Shaddai to [commit] iniquity.[35]
For the work of man He requites;
According to a man's way, it happens to him.
[Surely, God does not act wickedly,
And Shaddai does not pervert judgment.][36]

---

[30] Literally, "judgment," meaning Job's just cause—quoted from 27, 2.

[31] So read by a slight change of the text.

[32] Literally, "My arrow," *i.e.*, the arrow within me. Cf. Job 6, 4 where Job speaks of the arrows of God that are in him. The line is missing in the original Greek version.

[33] Taken from 15, 16 (Eliphaz). The verse is missing in the original Greek version.

[34] Literally, "men of wickedness." The following verse (v. 9) is superfluous and shows by the lack of the parallelism to be a prose comment on the part of some one who thought it necessary to repeat the substance of verses 5–6. The verse reads:

"When he says that man profits naught by seeking favor with God."

The word translated "profit" is indicative of later usage.

At the beginning of the tenth verse there is an insertion,

"Therefore, hearken unto me, you men of understanding,"

which is probably a misplaced comment, or a variant to v. 2ª.

[35] The line is too short. A verb as suggested in the translation needs to be inserted.

[36] Practically a repetition of v. 10 and perhaps a variant verse.

THE BOOK OF JOB

<small>13-15. 21 and 28-29
God's merciful control.</small>

To whom has He given charge o'er the earth?
And to whom has He assigned any part of the world?[37]
Should He resolve to withdraw His spirit,
And to take back His breath;[38]

15   All flesh would forthwith perish,
And man would again become dust.[39]
[16-20—the inserted poem on "The Punishment of Unworthy Rulers" below, p. 335.]

21   For His eyes are upon the ways of man,
And He sees all his steps.[40]
[23-27, part of the inserted poem, below, p. 335.]

28   He brings [41] before Him the cry of the humble,
And He hears the cry of the afflicted.

29   But if He is silent, who can condemn [Him]?
If He hides His face, who can challenge Him?[42]

---

[37] God rules the world by Himself and in His own way.

[38] *i.e.*, "the breath of life" which God breathed into man, according to Genesis 2, 7.

[39] An allusion to Genesis 3, 19. At this point the fragment (16-20; 23-27; 30 see above, p.80), dealing with God's indifference to the high rank of rulers and how He overthrows them when they merit it, is introduced. For the translation, see below p. 335

[40] Verse 22, prosaic in form, adds by way of comment, "There is no darkness nor dense shadow in which the evildoers (same expression as in v. 8) can hide themselves." Verses 23-27 form part of the insertion.

[41] The form of the verb has been changed by the editor who dovetailed the two compositions into one another.

[42] The original Greek version omits verses 28-33. A glossator, realizing the confusing transition in the second part of the chapter from people in general to the individual and back again to the group adds, "for a people and for an individual alike," to indicate the two-fold application of the utterances.

THE BOOK OF JOB

To God one should say: "I bear it,[43]	31
I will not [again] be an offense [to Thee].[44]	31–33 *Repentance, not Defiance is demanded of man.*
Since I cannot see, O teach me;	
If I have done wrong, let me not do it again.[45]	
For Thou choosest—not I;	
And what Thou knowest, speak."[46]	
Men of understanding will agree with me,[47]	34–37 *Condemnation of Job.*
And every wise man who hears me;	
That Job speaks without knowledge,	35
And that his words are devoid of wisdom.	
Job should be tried continuously,[48]	36ᵃ

The gloss may have originally been intended more specifically for v. 21ᵃ "For His eyes are on the ways of man." Verse 30 closes the inserted poem.

[43] Or perhaps the verb is to be taken in the sense of, "I have been overbearing."

[44] The line is too short by two beats. Some such words as suggested in the translation need to be supplied.

[45] At the beginning of v. 33 are two glosses (a) "Shall one requite one according to thy idea"—apparently a rhetorical exclamation on the part of some pious commentator, who took v. 31 in the sense of a defiance of God, translating as the Jewish tradition would have it, "I have borne it, though I offend not."

(b) "For Thou hast rejected"—a comment to "For Thou choosest"—to explain that God's choice *i.e.*, His "decision" has been the rejection of Job's claim.

[46] *i.e.*, instruct me out of the abundance of Thy knowledge.

[47] Literally: "say unto me."

[48] This the sense demanded by the context. The first word of the verse is a corruption of the name Job and belongs after "answers" in the gloss that follows upon this line.

A glossator adds "because of the answers [of Job] after the manner of iniquitous men." The Greek version tries to soften the severe condemnation of Job by rendering "Be admonished, O Job."

THE BOOK OF JOB

37 Because to his sin he adds blasphemy.[49]
Among us he claps, [his palms];[50]
And he multiplies his words against God.

D

FRAGMENT OR DRAFT OF A THIRD SPEECH OF ELIHU[51]

35, 1
1-16
Righteousness and sin affect man—not God

[And Elihu in answer said:][52]
Dost thou think this to be just,[53]
That thou sayest, "My case[54] against God's?"
Arguing:[55] "What is it to Thee?
What profit hast Thou[56] from my sin?"[57]

---

[49] This the force of the word (literally) "transgression" in this connection.

[50] *i.e.*, shows his contempt for us. The line is too short by one beat. The addition "his palms" (like 27, 23) is suggested by Budde, *Hiob*, p. 222.

[51] The fragment consists of sixteen verses only; and of these four entire verses (8–9; 15–16) and parts of three others (7b, 10a, 12a.) are missing in the original Greek version, leaving only nine and a half—clearly a mere draft of some speech. It deals with Job's assertion of his innocence and attempts to find an answer by suggesting that God should not be held to be responsible for suffering that comes through the deeds of men,—a strange argument indeed, that entirely begs the question.

[52] Again an editorial link, like 32, 6 and at the beginning of chapter 34.

[53] Literally, "judgment."

[54] Literally, "my right" in the sense of claim or case. Job says: "I'll stake my case against anything that God may bring forward in answer." Cf. 9, 21.

[55] Literally: "When thou sayest," *i.e.*, in further argument.

[56] Text says, "have I" but this is clearly an error, or an intentional change to avoid a too drastic charge against God.

[57] The reference is to 7, 20 where Job exclaims, "Have I sinned, what have I done to thee?" The Greek version omits the verse.

THE BOOK OF JOB

I will answer thee,
And thy friends with thee:[58]
Look unto the heavens and see;
And behold the high skies above thee![59]
If thou hast sinned, what dost thou to Him?
And be thy transgressions ever so many, what is it to Him?
If thou be righteous, what givest thou to Him?
Or what does He receive from thee?[60]
Thy wickedness affects a man like thee;[61]
Thy righteousness, a son of man.
By reason of great oppression they [62] cry out;
They appeal against the arm of the mighty.[63]

---

[58] Who could not find a satisfactory answer.

[59] Clearly based on 11, 8 (Zophar) and 22, 12 (Eliphaz).

[60] The righteousness of man is of no benefit to God, any more than the wickedness of man is of harm to Him. The original Greek version omits 7^b as well as 8–10^a. Cf. 22, 2 (Eliphaz).

[61] Men suffer through their wickedness and benefit through their virtues—an interesting thought that one's conduct affects one's fellows but not God.

[62] *i.e.*, people in general.

[63] *i.e.*, when things get too bad through the oppression of the wicked, people rebel and seek help against the oppressors, but they ought not regard God as the cause of their misfortune, which is due to men. The abrupt transition in v. 9 suggests the possibility of some omission. Duhm (*Job*, p. 169) places v. 16 at this point, which would make the subject in v. 10 Job, *i.e.*, "But Job does not say where is God," etc. The objection to the introduction of v. 16 after v. 9 is that it spoils the point of the argument, to wit, that God is not to be held responsible for evils which come through man. To be sure, it *may* be that v. 9 was added so as to lead to this argument, in which case verses 10–11 would mean that people ought to appeal to God; but this assumption is somewhat arbitrary.

THE BOOK OF JOB

10 But one does not say "Where is God, my maker?"
Who assigns lights[64] for the night,
11 Who teaches us through beasts of the earth,
And through the birds of heaven gives wisdom.[65]
13 Surely, it is idle [to say] that God does not hear,
And that Shaddai pays no regard.[66]
15 [That His anger punishes for nothing,
And that He takes not strict note of transgression.[67]
But Job opens his mouth with vanity;
He multiplies words without knowledge.][68]

---

[64] So Ehrlich proposes to read by a change in the text instead of "songs," which gives no sense in this connection. The point which Elihu makes is that when people suffer through the violent deeds of men, they should not blame God, who has nothing to do with the matter. God's deeds are to be seen in nature and in His care of the beasts and the birds. If God pays no attention to appeals, it is not because He does not hear them, but for some good reason, and, correspondingly, when He punishes it is not without cause, nor because He is not concerned with the transgressions of man. The argument smacks of sophistry, but is interesting just because of its subtlety.

[65] Cf. 12, 7. A pious reader adds the reflection: (v. 12) "If they seek for help and there is no answer, it is because of the haughtinesss of the evildoers." The first half of the verse is not found in the original Greek version. Read "if" at the beginning of the verse, by a slight change, instead of "these."

[66] Verse 14 (in prose form) appears to be again the addition of a pious commentator to suggest that one must under all circumstances maintain one's trust in God. "Even though thou shouldst say that thou canst not perceive Him, the case is before Him, and thou shouldst wait for Him," *i.e.*, for God's decision.

[67] So read by the addition of a letter. *i.e.*, one must not talk as Job does and say that God does not concern himself with the transgressions of men. He does, although He is not to be blamed if men commit violence and bring sufferings on others.

[68] Based on 34, 37^b. The two verses 15–16 are missing in the original Greek version and impress one as a later amplification of v. 13.

THE BOOK OF JOB

E

A Fourth Speech of Elihu [69]

[And Elihu continued as follows:][70]   36, 1
Suffer me a little, and I will tell thee;[71]
For there are things still to be said for God.   1–4
I must prolong my discourse,   *Introduction.*
Though I will justify my doing so.[72]
For, assuredly,[73] my words are not false;

---

[69] 36, 1–23. 26 and 37, 23–24.
[70] Again the usual editorial link. The address in this chapter is directed to Job. This speech—the fourth if we count the fragment or draft, chapter 35—furnishes no new argument but attempts again to drive home the truth that God is just, has no need to recall any decision and that when affliction comes, it is in order to recall men to Divine obedience. Those who profit by the lesson will live; those who do not will perish. This is set forth verses 1–23 with v. 26 as perhaps a later insertion and 37, 23–24, as the forcible close of the speech. Into this speech a nature poem, 36, 24–37, 13 (except v. 26 of Chap. 36) with 37, 21–22 forming the close, has been inserted, descriptive of God's majesty in a storm. It is a beautiful composition for the preservation of which we should be grateful, but we must also recognize that the poem is an independent production and stands in no connection with the Book of Job, as little as does chapter 28 or the poem on the punishment of unworthy rulers, dovetailed into chapter 34. It has affinities with the group of nature poems which we have in chapters 38 to 41. See below, p. 337. Chapter 37, 14–20 is again an independent fragment, forming another transition to the nature poems.
[71] *i.e.,* on God's behalf in answer to Job's charge against Divine justice. This introduction clearly betrays the supplementary character of the speech and that it is by another author.
[72] The common translation of both lines of this verse is wide of the mark.
[73] This is the force here of the particle generally rendered "indeed."

THE BOOK OF JOB

<small>5
5-7
God's firmness and justice.</small>

It is undefiled truth[74] [that comes] to thee.
Surely, God is firm and does not recall;[75]
He is firm, and strong of mind.
He permits not the wicked to flourish;[76]
And He judges the cause of the afflicted.
He withdraws not His eyes[77] from the righteous;
But seats them on a throne to be exalted.[78]

<small>8-15
Suffering as a warning and a discipline.</small>

And if He binds them [79] in fetters,
[And] they are encompassed with cords of affliction;
It is to recall to them their deeds,
And their transgressions, when they become haughty.[80]

<small>10</small>

Then He opens their ear to dicipline,
And tells [them] to return from iniquity.
If they hearken and obey,
They will round out their days in joy.[81]
But if they hearken not, they pass to oblivion,[82]
And die without knowledge.

---

[74] More literally: "some one of perfect knowledge"—meaning himself.

[75] God is not obliged to recall any decision once made.

[76] The line is too short by one beat. Some word like "in joy" or perhaps "forever" has dropped out. The original Greek version omits verses 6–9, as well as 11–13, 16, 20, 25ᵃ, 26 and 29–33.

[77] The Greek text says "His judgment."

[78] There are two glosses to this verse: (a) "with kings" and (b) "forever."

[79] So by a slight change of the text.

[80] This is the kernel of the fourth speech that sufferings are sent to those who err as a warning to return to a virtuous life. It is the same thought as in the first speech (33, 16 *seq.*).

[81] A gloss or a variant adds "and their years in pleasures."

[82] The same word as is used 33, 18 to express "the nether world."

THE BOOK OF JOB

But the impious assume [Divine] anger;[33]
[And] cry not for help when He binds them.
Their soul perishes in youth,
And their life in the age of vigor.[84]
[Though] He oppresses[85] the afflicted with suffering,   15
Yet He opens their ear through tribulation.[86]
He even leads thee from the mouth of distress,[87]   16
And covers thy table with fat.   16–21 *God's grace in testing man.*

   *   *   *   *   *   *
   *   *   *   *   *   *

..........lest it entice thee by................ 18

---

[83] An interesting thought that those who are utterly depraved assume, as Job does in chapter 21, that God is an arbitrary Being, morose and hostile by nature.

[84] The word used as a parallelism to "youth" is a curious one, *kedeshim* or "Hierophants"—the designation of the male devotees in the Canaanitic cult, who were evidently chosen when they were young, as were their female counter-parts, the *kedeshoth* or "sacred prostitutes."

[85] So by an inversion of two letters instead of "delivers," which is clearly out of place here.

[86] Again the same thought that God sends affliction to those capable of repentance, as a means of revealing to them their guilt.

[87] A gloss adds "[into a] broad expanse where there is no narrowness." Verse 17 and the first part of v. 18 are unintelligible. The Greek version reads as v. 17,

"He does not withhold judgment from the righteous"

which is only half of the distich to be expected and appears to be a substitute for the unintelligible verse in the original which is ordinarily rendered:

"Thou art full of the judgment of the wicked;
Judgment and justice take hold on them."

It is better to confess ignorance than to leave such translations stand. The two lines are not in accord, and besides are totally

THE BOOK OF JOB

And let not a great ransom mislead thee.[88]

    *   *   *   *   *   *
    *   *   *   *   *   *
    *   *   *   *   *   *
    *   *   *   *   *   *

21   Beware of turning to iniquity,

22–23 and 26; and 37,23–24   That thou choosest this in preference to affliction.[89]

God is supreme.   Behold God is exalted in His strength;
Who is a teacher like Him?

23   Who dares to call Him to account?
And who can say, "Thou hast done wrong?"

26   [Behold God is old beyond knowledge;
The number of His years is beyond reckoning.][90]

[Verses 24–25 and 27 to Chap. 37, 13 and 37, 21–22, an inserted poem on "God's Majesty in the storm," for which see below, p. 337, while 37, 14–20 is an independent fragment on "The Wonders of Creation," likewise dovetailed into this fourth speech of Elihu. See below, p. 341.]

---

out of connection with what precedes and what follows. Similarly 18ᵃ, "For, lest wrath lead thee away," bears no relation to 18ᵇ and appears to be a variant reading to 16ᵃ with the word *af* taken erroneously as "wrath." Something has happened to the text at this point, and it is a hopeless endeavor to try to straighten it out.

[88] *i.e.*, do not try to escape Divine wrath by offering a bribe. Verses 19 and 20 are again utterly obscure. They, as well as 17 and 18ᵃ, have proven to be the despair of commentators and it is not possible to make even a reasonable guess at their meaning. In the original Greek version v. 19ᵇ and 20 are missing.

[89] *i. e.*, it is better to suffer and thus be warned of perhaps some unintentional misstep, than to deliberately plunge into wrong in the hope of escaping punishment.

[90] The verse is missing in the original Greek version, and

THE BOOK OF JOB

He is exalted in power and justice; 37, 23-24 [91]
The one abounding in righteousness does not
 afflict.
Therefore, men fear Him;
Albeit the wise cannot fathom it. [92]

F

THE PUNISHMENT OF UNWORTHY RULERS [93]
(INSERTED POEM)

If there be understanding, hear this; [94] 34, 16
Give ear to my words.
Is it conceivable that He who governs is a hater
 of justice? [95]

---

may well be a later insertion (reminiscent in part of 5, 9) that has gotten into the midst of the "storm" poem, instead of being placed directly after v. 23.

[91] These two verses of chapter 37 form the appropriate close of the fourth and last speech of Elihu.

At the beginning of v. 23 "Shaddai—we cannot find Him," is an explanatory comment either to 19ᵇ or to 24ᵇ, which has crept into the text at a wrong place. See below, p. 342, note 39.

[92] Literally; "See," *i.e.*, as we say "see through it." Even the wisest cannot understand the hidden ways of God—a thought similar to the one uttered by Koheleth as his final word (Eccl. 8, 17).

"Even though a wise man thinks that he knows—yet he cannot find out."

[93] An inserted poem—chapter 34, 16-20; 24-27; 30. See above, p. 326. As a further proof for the independent character of this little section, one may instance that some of the Greek versions have a separate heading before v. 16, "Elihu in answer said."

[94] The address in this introduction is in the singular, whereas Elihu's speech proper is directed to the wise man in general (v. 2).

[95] Literally: "judgment."

THE BOOK OF JOB

Wilt thou condemn One who is supremely just?[96]
Who says to a king, "Thou worthless one";
"Thou wicked one" to nobles?[97]
Who pays no regard to princes,
And favors not rich against poor?[98]
20 For all in a moment die,
In the middle of the night are shaken off.[99]
24 The mighty He shakes indiscriminately,[1]

---

[96] *i.e.*, God—the subject also of the verbs in the following lines.

[97] This line is missing in the original Greek version.

[98] A pious commentator adds the banal remark, "the work of His hands."

[99] *i.e.*, deposed. Two glosses are added (a) "They pass away" as the explanation of the second verb, which is somewhat obscure, (b) "the mighty ones(read the plural!) are taken away without a [visible] hand"—a further explanation of what is meant by v. 20. As a variant to the "mighty ones" by which rulers and princes are meant, some commentator has suggested that the verse refers to the "people"; and this word for "people" has crept into the text at a wrong place. Verses 21–22 belong to the main speech, while v. 23 (in prose) is a comment to v. 20 about the suddenness of the change in the fortunes of rulers.

"For He does not fix a time for going to God for judgment"

God calls rulers away without notice. Instead of "again," read by a slight change the word for "time"—adopted also by the translators of the Amer. Jewish Publ. Society. The original Greek version omits 23ᵃ.

[1] More literally: "without search" but here, clearly, in the sense of "indiscriminately." The Greek version because of the word "without search" adds, from 5, 9,

"He does great things beyond searching,"

just as we have seen this same sentiment added at 9, 10, and for a third time 37, 5. Such a quotation deliberately introduced—for the Greek translator must have found it in the text before him—shows the liberties taken with the text by editors, who felt free to add anything which seemed appropriate.

THE BOOK OF JOB

And sets others in their stead.[2]
In this way He takes note of their works;   25
He overturns [them] at night, and they are crushed.
Because from Him they turned away,   27
And paid no regard to His ways.[3]

G

GOD'S MAJESTY IN THE STORM[4]
(A SECOND INSERTED POEM)

Remember to glorify His work,   36, 24
Whereof men have sung;
Which all can see;[5]   25
Which man has looked on since distant days.[6]
How He draws up the drops of water,   27
Which are distilled as rain through His vapor;   27–28 *Rain.*
Which the clouds pour down,[7]
And drop upon the multitude.

---

[2] To this utter condemnation, verse 26 (in prose) is added by way of comment. It consists of two parts (*a*) "in place of the wicked," to explain "in their stead," (*b*) "He exults over them (same verb as in 34, 37. See above, p. 328) in open sight," *i.e.*, he humiliates the unworthy rulers in the sight of all..

[3] Verse 30 which is missing in the original Greek version (as also 28, 29 and 31–33) is again a comment (in poetic form) to the deposition of rulers as expressed in verses 24–25,

>"Against the rule of an impious man,
>Against the ensnarers of the people."

[4] The inserted poem in Elihu's fourth speech (see above, p. 331), consisting of 36, 24–25 and 27 to 37, 13; and 37, 21–22.

[5] The line is missing in the original Greek version.

[6] Literally: "from afar," meaning, however, from far off days. For verse 26, see above, p. 334.

[7] The line is missing in the original Greek version.

<small>29–37, 4
Thunder and
lightning.</small>

Who[8] can grasp the spreading of clouds,
Aye, the thunderings of His pavillion?[9]
30   Behold, He spreads His light[10] over it,[11]
Until it covers the tops of the mountains (?).[12]
32   He covers with light[13]......................

---

[8] The particle at the beginning of this line should be transposed to the following one. The entire verse is missing in the original Greek version as are also verses 30–33.

[9] Literally, "His tent"—meaning the heavens.

[10] *i.e.*, the lightning. Duhm and others read by a slight change "cloud," but this is unnecessary.

[11] *i.e.*, over the cloud. The reference is to the lightning flashing across the cloud.

[12] The text reads "roots of the sea," but this gives no sense. The emendation suggested by Duhm is radical and somewhat arbitrary, but it is the best that has been offered for what is clearly a currupt text. Verse 31 is a reflection added by a later editor,

"For through them He judges peoples;
He gives food in abundance."

to suggest that the clouds and the rain with the accompanying lightning are both destructive and beneficial forces.

[13] The balance of this line is unintelligible, as is also v. 33 which appears to consist of a series of glosses (perhaps to 37, 7–8) that have been combined into an absolutely untranslatable line. It is preferable to confess being baffled (as Siegfried, Ehrlich and others do), rather than to attempt a translation which is either nonsensical or fanciful. In reading the current translations of this verse, it is difficult to decide in which of the two categories they belong. 33[b] consists of four words (a) "cattle (b) even (c) over (d) that which comes up"—a perfectly hopeless jumble. The RV in its despair adds the word "storm," after "over," which the translators of the Jewish Publication Society adopt, but without indicating that it is *not* in the Hebrew text. As for 33[a] why mislead the public to suppose that the Hebrew words are to be rendered as "The noise thereof telleth concerning it"? What possible sense is there in such a line or in the following one rendered:

"The cattle also concerning the storm that cometh up?"

THE BOOK OF JOB

And commands it where it should strike.[14]
At this my heart indeed trembles,   37, 1
And is moved out of its place.
Hark in trembling to His voice,
And to the sound that issues from His mouth.
Across the heavens He sends it,
And His light [15] unto the ends of the earth.
He thunders with His voice majestic,
And nothing restrains them[16] when His voice is heard.[17]
[Marvellous things [God][18] does,   5ᵇ
Great deeds beyond knowledge,][19]
For to the snow He says, "Fall to earth";   6–8
And the rain is the outpouring of His strength.[20]   Snow and rain.
He seals up the activity of mankind,[21]
That every one may know His work.
The beasts go into coverts,
And remain in their dens.

---

[14] *i.e.*, the lightning.

[15] *i.e.*, again the lightning. A gloss (4ᵃ) adds "Behind it (*i.e.*, behind the lightning), a voice roars."

[16] *i.e.*, thunder and lightning. Verse 5ᵃ "God thunders with His voice" is a comment or variant to 4ᵃ.

[17] Cf. Psalm 29, 3–9 for a similar description of God's voice—the thunder.

[18] Perhaps to be supplied. The line lacks one beat.

[19] A quotation—slightly altered—from Eliphaz's speech, 5, 9, who also specifies the downpour of rain as one of the manifestations of God's greatness.

[20] A gloss explains *geshem* ("rain") as equivalent to *mātār* "downpour."

[21] A man is forced to stop work and to seek refuge during the rain storm. The line is missing in the original Greek version.

THE BOOK OF JOB

9–10 *Cold and ice.*
    From the South [22] comes the storm,
    And the cold from the North.[23]

10
    For by the breath of God ice is formed,[24]

11–12 and 21–22 *The passing of the storm.*
    And the expanse of water congealed.
    Even as the sunshine drives away the cloud,[25]
    And its light scatters the mass of clouds.

12
    He causes it [26] to move about in its circuit;[27]
    By His direction over the face of the universe.[28]

---

[22] Literally, "chamber" for "chambers of the South" (Job 9, 9), *i.e.*, the constellations of the South, and used poetically for the South.

[23] A poetic term for the North is used in the text, the specific meaning of which escapes us. It may refer to the Polar Star.

[24] An impressive picture of a gifted poet, who pictures the ice as formed by God's cold breath upon the waters, just as His warm breath gives life. Cf 38, 29–30. The original Greek version omits the line.

[25] So read the line by a change in the first word—following Ehrlich. The verse is missing in the original Greek version as are also verses 12–13.

[26] *i.e.*, the light—meaning the sun.

[27] A gloss v. 12^b (in prose form) adds "for all their work as He commands them," *i.e.*, clouds and sun play their part in nature according to God's orders to them.

[28] A gloss adds "towards the earth" in explanation of the phrase "over the face of the universe." Verse 13 (in prose form) is the reflection of a pious commentator and should be translated as follows:

"Whether as a scourge for the earth or for grace, He lets it (*i.e.*, the sun) run its course," *i.e.*, for better or worse.

I follow Ehrlich in making two slight changes in the text, called for in order to yield an intelligible meaning. The original Greek version omits verses 11–13. Verses 14–20 form the third inserted poem. See below, p. 341.

THE BOOK OF JOB

And now [29] there is brightness in the skies;   21–22 [30]
A wind blows and it brightens up.
From the North a golden [31] splendor comes;
To God, the awe-inspiring, be the glory!

H
THE WONDERS OF CREATION [32]
(A THIRD INSERTED POEM)

Give heed to this, O Job;   37, 14
Stand still and consider God's wonders!
Dost thou know how God brings these things   15
    about? [33]
How light breaks through His clouds?
Dost thou know of the spreading of clouds? [34]
The marvels of the Perfect in knowledge?
That thy clothes become warm,
    When the earth is hushed in the south wind? [35]

---

[29] There is a meaningless gloss, "They see not the light," which is evidently misplaced. It may belong to 37, 11, "its light scatters the mass of the clouds," to suggest that the light comes mysteriously.

[30] Forming the close of the poem and describing the passing of the storm.

[31] Or "brilliant."

[32] The little section 37, 14–20 inserted into the fourth speech of Elihu, is clearly supplemental as shown by the separate heading. It draws the lesson from the "storm" poem, and forms the transition to the magnificent series of nature poems, embodied in chapters 38–41; and may well have been suggested by these poems with which it has the question form in common.

[33] So read instead of "on them."

[34] By a change in a single letter, we obtain the same phrase as 36, 29 in the "storm" poem, to which it harks back.

[35] *i.e.*, lies breathless in the hot south wind. Verse 18 takes up a new thought which would be in better place after 38, 3, but

THE BOOK OF JOB

[Canst thou spread out with Him the expanse,[36]
Firm as a molten mirror?]
19   Teach us [37] what to think of it;[38]
Because of the darkness, we find not our way.[39]

---

since this necessitates the change from "with Him" to "like me" for which there is no warrant in any of the versions, it seems preferable to let the verse stand where it has been placed, and regard it as a later addition by some one who wished still further to emphasize the marvels of creation before which men should be speechless.

[36] The "expanse" (Genesis, 1, 6) or firmament was pictured by the ancients as a solid polished substance; hence the metaphor comparing it to a molten mirror. The verse is missing in the original Greek version and is clearly out of the context.

[37] Some Hebrew manuscripts read "me."

[38] Literally "to say"—not, however, "to Him" as is usually rendered but "concerning it." The reference is not to God, but to the marvellous phenomena which renders one speechless.

[39] The verb used conveys the idea of arranging one's words or thoughts in a proper manner. The gloss in v.23, "*i.e.*, Shaddai—we cannot find Him," may have been intended to explain our passage, or possibly 24^b. (See p. 335, note 91). At all events, the thought is that man must content himself in the presence of the marvels of creation to worship in silence. To further emphasize that silence alone is becoming to man, some pious reader added v. 20, which, however, strikes one as an anti-climax

"Should one declare to Him, 'I wish to speak?'
Does a man order his own destruction?"

Literally: "that he be swallowed up." The commentator has in mind Job's audacity in declaring that he will insist upon speaking to God (*e.g.*, 7, 11; 10, 1; 13, 3,etc). and insinuates that such speech is equivalent to ordering one's destruction.

VII
SECOND APPENDIX TO THE BOOK OF JOB

A Collection of Eight Nature Poems[40]
(Chapters 38-41)

A

The Pæan of Creation[41]

[Then Yahweh answered Job:][42] 38, 1
[Who is this that darkens counsel,
By words without knowledge?
Gird up thy loins like a warrior;[43]
That I may ask thee to tell me:][44]

---

[40] See above pp. 82-86.
[41] Consisting of 38, 1-18.
[42] The usual editorial link. One of the Greek versions adds "After Elihu had ceased speaking," to connect the chapter still closer with what precedes. A gloss to the line adds "from (or out of) the storm," inserted by a commentator who, regarding the Book of Job in its present form as a literary unit and as an actual narrative, took the poetical references in the closing verses of the inserted poem on the majesty of the storm and the miracle of the clearing sky after the storm (37, 21-22) literally. Thereupon, in order to connect the appearance of Yahweh with what preceded, he added the words "out of the storm" (not "whirlwind" as usually rendered). They are clearly out of place. The repetition of the editorial link at 40, 6 is taken from our text.
[43] *i.e.*, get ready for a contest. For work or battle, the lower garment is tucked up around the loins so as not to interfere with the freedom of movement.
[44] Verses 2-3 represent the introduction added by the editor who collected the nature poems and connected them with

THE BOOK OF JOB

4–11
Earth and sea.

Where wast thou when I laid the earth's foundations?
Declare, if thou hast the knowledge!
5 Who determined its measures, that thou shouldst know?[45]
Or who stretched the measuring line o'er it?
Whereupon are its sockets fastened?
Or the corner-stone thereof who laid it?[46]
When the morning stars sang together,[47]
And all the Sons of God shouted for joy?[48]
9 When I made the cloud its garment,[49]
And thick darkness its swaddling band.[50]

---

the Book of Job as speeches in the mouth of God. According to Ehrlich and others, verse 37, 18 should be inserted here so as to begin the description of God's work of creation with the heavens. But see note 35, above, page 341.

[45] *i.e.*, Who has ever measured the earth and told thee? See verse 18.

[46] *i.e.*, dost thou know anything about it? Wert thou present?

[47] *i.e.*, dost thou know anything of the time when the morning stars, etc.

[48] See the note to 1, 6 and the references to this famous verse in Shakespeare, Milton and Tennyson, given by Strahan, *Job*, p. 317.

[49] *i.e.*, again where wast thou when, etc.

[50] *i.e.*, of the earth. In view of this application of the line to the earth rather than to the sea, to describe the enveloping of the earth through clouds and darkness, verse 9 is to be placed before v. 8. Note that in some of the poems, God is introduced as speaking (*e.g.* 38, 9–10; 39, 6), whereas in others, (*e.g.*, 38, 41; 39, 17) God is spoken of in the third person. Such a variation of itself points to the independent origin of the separate poems into which chapters 38–41 may be divided. For most of them we need not even assume that they represent an address by God to man, but merely have the question form because of its stronger rhetorical force.

THE BOOK OF JOB

Who [51] barred the sea with doors,   8
When from the depth[52] it broke forth?
And I established[53] for it my decree,   10
And to the doors set a bolt?[54]
And said: Thus far come, but no further.
And here shall thy proud waves break?[55]
Hast thou ever commanded the morning,   12–15 *Creation of day and light.*
And assigned to the daybreak its place?
To take hold of the ends of the earth,
And to shake the wicked out of it?[56]
So that it is reversed as a clay seal,[57]   14
And is dyed [58] as a garment.[59]
Hast thou come to the springs of the sea?   16
And walked in the recesses of the deep?   16–18 *—The deep.*
Have the gates of death been opened to thee?

---

[51] So read by a slight change of the text.
[52] Literally "womb." An explanatory gloss adds: "came forth."
[53] So read by a slight change in the text, supported by the Greek version.
[54] So by a slight change.
[55] So the Greek text.
[56] The wicked are dispersed with the morning dawn. Similarly, in Babylonian hymns to the sun-god we read that Shamash drives away crime and reveals guilt (Jastrow, *Aspects of Religious Belief and Practice in Babylonia and Assyria*, p. 111 and *Religion Babyloniens und Assyriens*, I., p. 432 *et seq*.)
[57] I follow Ehrlich's interpretation, (improving upon a suggestion made by Ewald, *Book of Job* p. 301 note) that the reference is to the inscription on a clay seal which is written backward and on being impressed on a soft object is reversed and comes out in perfect form. So the sun changes the chaos of night into order.
[58] So by a slight change in the text.
[59] Verse 15 is a reflection, added by a pious commentator.
"Their light is withheld from the wicked;
And the haughty arm is broken."

THE BOOK OF JOB

And hast thou seen the gates of dense darkness?[60]
Hast thou surveyed the earth in its breadth?
Declare, if thou knowest its measure.[61]

B

The Phenomena of the Heavens[62]

19–24
The mystery of snow and hail.

[Which is the way to the dwelling of light,
And darkness—where is its place?
20   That thou mayest track it to its bounds,
And discern the paths to its house.][63]
22   Hast thou come to the storehouses of snow,
And seen the chambers [64] of the hail?
Which I have reserved against time of trouble,
Against the day of battle and war?
By what way passes the wind?[65]

---

[60] A synonym here for the realm of the dead, situated in the deep or in the hollow of the earth.
[61] So by a slight change of the text.
[62] Consisting of 38, 19–38.
[63] Verses 19–20 probably represent the beginning of the second poem, though it is also possible that they are an insertion, suggested by v. 24. At all events their extreme beauty justifies their inclusion in the text, despite a certain doubt of their genuineness. Verse 21, to be taken ironically, reads:

"Thou knowest, for thou wast born at the time,
And the number of thy days is great."

This is clearly an insertion that reveals the rather bad taste of some zealous and pious commentator, who is more concerned in pedantic fashion with rebuking Job, than impressed with the beauty and majesty of this paean.
[64] The Hebrew text repeats "storehouses" though one would expect a synonym.
[65] Read "wind" for "light" in the text—a suggestion originally made by Ewald, and adopted by many commentators, including Ehrlich

THE BOOK OF JOB

Or is the east wind scattered o'er the earth?
Who has cleft a channel for the waterflood,   25
And a way for the thunderbolt?[66]
[To cause it to rain[67] on a land uninhabited;
On the wilderness where are no men.
To saturate what is waste and desolate,
And to cause verdure to spring forth.][68]
[Has the rain a father?
Or who has begotten the dew-drops?
From whose womb comes the ice,
And who has engendered the hoarfrost of heaven?
So that water is congealed as a crystal,   30
And the face of the deep is frozen.][69]
Canst thou bind the chains of the Pleiades,
Or loosen the bands of Orion?[70]
Canst thou lead out the Dippers at their season, [71]

25–28 Storm and rain.
29–30 Cold and ice.
31–33 The constellations.

---

[66] A reminiscence or an actual quotation from 28, 26ᵇ in the inserted "Search for Wisdom."
[67] The miracle of rain that fertilizes even the stoniest soil was particularly impressive to the ancients and is, therefore, dwelt upon so frequently in the Book of Job.
[68] Verses 26 and 27 are omitted in the original Greek version, and may well be later insertions.
[69] These three beautiful verses (28–30) appear again to be an insertion—perhaps taken from the same poem of which we encountered another fragment above verses 19–20. It would be quite in keeping with the ancient Oriental mode of composition to thus dovetail two poems into each other that have an affiliation. Compare the description of the source of cold and ice in the "storm" poem 37, 9–10, above, p. 340.
[70] An impressive metaphor to describe the combination of stars into a constellation, as though they were bound by invisible chains and bands.
[71] Probably the greater and the lesser Bear, though Schiaparelli, *Astronomy in the Old Testament*, p. 82, argues for

THE BOOK OF JOB

<small>34–38
Clouds and
storm.</small>

Or guide the Lion and his young?[72]
Knowest thou the ordinances of the heavens?[73]
Or on earth canst trace its constellations?[74]
Canst thou lift thy voice to the clouds,
To answer thee,[75] with abundance of water?

35   Canst thou send flashes of lightning, to go forth;
And to say to thee, "Lo we are here?"[76]

37   Who can empty[77] the clouds [on high?][78]
Or can pour out the water-skins of heaven,
When the ground runs thick into mire,
And the clods cleave fast together?

---

an identification with Lucifer and Hesperus, which is most unlikely. The verse is missing in the original Greek version.

[72] According to Schiaparelli *l. c.*, p. 57 Aldebaran and Hyades. The verse is omitted in the original Greek version.

[73] Cf. Jer. 31, 35–36.

[74] *i.e.*, from thy position on earth canst thou make a map covering the *entire* starry heaven? The word translated constellation is, literally, "its writing," which is also used in Babylonian ("writing of heaven") for the mapping out of the starry firmament.

[75] So read by a slight change of the text.

[76] Verse 36 which contains two obscure words:

"Who has placed wisdom in the . . .
Or has given understanding to the mind (?)

appears again to be the reflection of some pious commentator, with a view of giving expression to his amazement at the Divine power manifested in the universe.

[77] So the meaning of the verb, as in Arabic.

[78] Text has "by wisdom," which spoils the beauty of the line, and may have been separated by accident from v. 36. Some word, however, is needed to complete the three beats of the line. The parallelism suggests "on high."

THE BOOK OF JOB

C

ANIMAL LIFE[79]

Dost thou hunt the prey for the lion,	38, 39
To still the hunger of young lions?	39–40 *Lions.*
As they crouch in their dens,	40
And lie in wait in the covert?	
Who provides his food for the raven,[80]	41
When his young ones cry unto God?[81]	*Raven.*
Dost know when rock goats bring forth?[82]	39, 1
Or dost mark when hinds are in travail?[83]	1–4 *Goats and hinds.*
When they throw off[84] their young,	
And separate themselves from their burdens?	3
Their young grow up[85] in the open,	
Go forth and return not again.	

---

[79] The third of the nature poems (38, 39–39, 30) consists of the description of the ways of the animal world in further illustration of the wonders of God. Ten animals or eleven if we count both ostrich and stork (13–18) are singled out. The poem is again a composite production, as is shown by the lack of any arrangement or sequence in the animals enumerated—wild animals and birds being promiscuously combined.

[80] Instead of "raven" some commentators read by a change in vocalization "at evening" and thus eliminate the raven altogether, because hardly in place between the lion and other wild animals.

[81] A commentator adds "roaming about without food."

[82] The entire line, which has a superfluous word "time" (making the line too long) is missing in the original Greek version.

[83] Verse 2 appears to be a variant or a comment to verse 1. It reads:
> "Dost thou count the months which they round out?
> Dost thou know the time of their bringing forth?"

[84] A commentator adds "crouching" to explain the rare verb used. The word makes the line too long.

[85] Comment, "wax strong."

THE BOOK OF JOB

<small>5
Wild-asses. 5-8</small>

Who sends the wild ass to roam free?
Or has loosened the bonds of the unbridled?
For whom I have made the wilderness his house,
And the desert [86] his dwelling place.
He scorns the tumult of the city;
Nor hears the shoutings of the driver.[87]
He roams the mountains for pasture,
And seeks out whatever is green.[88]

<small>9-12
Wild-ox.</small>

Will the wild ox [89] be content to serve thee?
Or will he abide by thy crib?[90]

<small>10</small>

Canst thou with a cord bind him,[91]
To harrow thy furrows [92] after thee?
Canst trust him, [93] because of his strength?
And leave thy labor to him?

<small>12</small>

Wilt thou to him confide thy seed?[94]

---

[86] Literally "salt" land—as a picture of desolation.

[87] Those who have travelled in the East and have heard the constant shouts of the drivers to their horses will appreciate this description.

[88] The 8th verse is omitted in the original Greek version.

[89] The *re'em* now definitely identified through the frequent references to the *rimu* in Cuneiform Inscriptions and through illustrations of this animal on Assyrian monuments.

[90] There is a gap in the *original* Greek version from 39, 9 to 40, 8ª, so that we cannot be certain how much of the description of the horse (19-25) has been amplified or whether the single verse (v. 26) devoted to the hawk may not be a later insertion.

[91] So read, instead of repeating "wild ox," which the Greek version properly omits.

[92] So the Greek version, instead of the Hebrew "valleys," though in the preceding line we have "furrow" which represents the variant and better reading.

[93] *i.e.*, utilize him.

[94] The line as it stands is too long. By omitting the super-

THE BOOK OF JOB

And to heap up thy threshing floor?[95]
[Verses 13-18 below, p. 352.]

Dost thou give strength to the horse?   19
Dost thou clothe his neck with a mane?[96]   19-25
Dost thou bring smoke from his nostrils,[97]   *The horse.*
With the loud blast of his snorting?   20
He paws in the valley with joy;
He goes out in might to the encounter.
He laughs at fear without tremor;
And turns not back from the sword.[98]
The quiver rattles against him,
The glittering spear and the javelin.
He stamps the ground with storm and rage,   24
And cannot be held back at the trumpet's sound.[99]

---

fluous "to bring in" before "thy seed" (*i.e.*, thy produce)—it is reduced to three beats.

[95] The wild ox, if let loose in the fields will uproot and destroy the crops. Verses 13-18 are clearly an independent fragment, taken from some poem that like ours was devoted to a description of the ways and habits of animals, but as a *direct* nature poem, not in the form of a question to suggest man's inability to control the wild brood of creation. The translation, will be found below (p. 352), as a supplement to our composition. The insertion appears to have been suggested by verses 26-30—the description of the hawk and vulture, which would lead to inserting the description of the ways of the ostrich.

[96] The mane as the symbol of strength.

[97] So read with Ehrlich, by a slight change of the text. The traditional translation of this line, describing the horse as "leaping like a locust" is unpoetical as well as absurd.

[98] The line is missing in the Greek versions.

[99] Verse 25ᵃ—superfluous line—is an explanatory comment: "When the trumpet sounds, he says 'Aha!'" to emphasize that the approaching battle acts as a spur.

THE BOOK OF JOB

25ᵇ He smells the battle from afar,
    The captain's thunder and the roar.[1]

The hawk. 26 Does the hawk migrate[2] through thy wisdom,[3]
    Spreading his wings to the South?

The vulture. 27-30 Does the vulture mount at thy order,
    To make his nest on high?
    He settles on rock and abides there,
    Upon the crag of the rock as a stronghold.[4]
    Whence he spies out the prey;
    His eyes seeing it from afar.

30 With his young[5] he sucks up[6] the blood;[7]
    And where the carcasses are, he is to be found.

D

The ostrich. INDEPENDENT FRAGMENT[8] ON THE OSTRICH

13-18 The wing of the ostrich[9] fails;[10]
    A cruel[11] mother is the stork.[12]

---

[1] Strahan, *Job*, p. 329, appropriately quotes Layard's fine description of the horse of the Arab (*Discoveries in the Ruins of Nineveh and Babylon*, pp. 326-331). The horse in the ancient East is used in battle or for hunting, never as a beast of burden for which the ass is employed. Poetic descriptions of the horse are a standing feature in the poetry of ancient Arabia. Indeed, the section in Job is quite in the style of Arabic poetry.

[2] So by a slight change of the text, furnishing a reading that replaces the guess "soar" for a stem not otherwise found in Hebrew.

[3] *i.e.*, dost thou tell the hawk when to migrate on the approach of winter?

[4] Quoted from Jeremiah, 49, 16.

[5] So by a slight change.

[6] Read the singular, since the vulture must be the subject in both parts of the verse.

[7] Quoted as a proverbial saying Matthew 24, 28 and Luke 17, 37.

THE BOOK OF JOB

For she leaves her eggs in the ground,
To hatch in the dust;
Forgetting that foot may crush them,   15
And that the beast of the field may trample them.
She hardens her young to do without her;
To no purpose her labor [and without profit (?)].¹³
For God has deprived her of wisdom,   17
And not given her a share in understanding.¹⁴

[40, 1-14, forming the first epilogue, and a part of the second, see below, p. 361 *seq*.]

---

⁸ 39, 13–18 omitted in all the older Greek versions. See Beer, *Text des Buches Hiob*, p. 243.

⁹ The Targum renders as "wild cock." "Peacock" in the older English versions is a pure guess.

¹⁰ So read, following Hoffman, whose emendation of the meaningless word in the text is accepted by Budde, Ehrlich and others. The ostrich fails to protect her brood.

¹¹ So read instead of meaningless "pinions" by a change of the text, demanded by the context.

¹² A misplaced gloss or a comment by one who did not understand the obscure because corrupt verse, adds "and feathers." To the writer of this fragment, the ostrich and stork are closely related birds—at least sufficiently so as to warrant the poetical license in using the one for the other. What the fragment says applies, however, only to the ostrich.

¹³ *i.e.*, she has no joy of motherhood in return for her effort in laying her eggs. The close of the line reads "without fear," but this gives no sense. The word is a gloss that has slipped into a wrong place and entailed the dropping out of the correct reading which must be supplied from the context. Some word is needed to make up the three beats.

¹⁴ Verse 18, as it stands, gives no sense that could conceivably fit into the context. What possible connection is there even between the two parts of the verse, which are usually rendered:

> "When the time comes she raises her wings on high,
> And she laughs at the horse and his rider."

Nor have the various attempts at emendation of the text been

THE BOOK OF JOB

FOUR POEMS DESCRIPTIVE OF THE EXTRAORDINARY STRENGTH AND HUGENESS OF ANIMALS THAT CANNOT BE TAMED BY MAN

E

THE HIPPOPOTAMUS [15]

40, 15   Behold, the great beast [16] as compared to thee;
Eating grass as an ox.
See his strength in his loins,
And his force in the muscles of his body.
His tail [17] is stiff like a cedar;
Closely knit are the sinews of his thighs.
18   His bones pipes of brass;

---

successful. I venture to see in the final words "scorning the horse and his rider" a gloss or comment to v. 19^b, while the balance of the verse appears to have been intended as a comment either to v. 26 (hawk) or to v. 14, to further indicate the indifference of the stork to her brood, by describing how at the time when they need her, she leaves them. In the endeavor to connect the two glosses, the text has, however, been corrupted beyond the point of certain restoration.

[15] 40, 15–24. An independent poem to which 40, 6–7, with 42, 3^a and 4, originally served as an introduction (see below note 65), but in the course of the editorial process, the introduction was combined with the epilogue to the series of four poems on the huge beasts.

[16] Text uses the plural *Behemōth* "beasts" as frequently in poetic Hebrew for "great beast." Similarly in Psalms 137, 1, "rivers" for "great river," *i.e.*, the Euphrates. There is added a gloss, "which I have made" (missing in the Greek version). It represents a later insertion to bring the independent fragment into connection with the theme of God's power in creating such animals.

[17] The "tail" may be euphemistic for the sexual member, to which the "thighs" in the parallel line point.

THE BOOK OF JOB

His gristles like bars of iron.[18]
The mountains [19] bring him food;   20
And he scorns the beasts of the field.[20]
Under lotus he lies;
In the covert of reed and fen.
[Lotus trees form his shade;
And willows of the brook encompass him.][21]
Though the river [22] overflows he trembles not;
Confident as when Jordan oversteps its bank.
Who can overcome him with his eyes?[23]
Pierce his nose with hooks?[24]

---

[18] V. 19 reading;
"He is the first (*i. e.* the mightiest) of God's ways,
A creature of gigantic build,"
is an addition on the part of some commentator. The text of the second line is corrupt. I follow Ehrlich's suggestions for two textual changes in order to get a satisfactory parallel.

[19] Or "rivers" which reading one can obtain by a slight change.

[20] The text has a superfluous word at the close of v. 20.

[21] Perhaps a variant verse.

[22] *i.e.*, the Nile as the river *par excellence*, in contrast to the petty Jordan. The vast overflow of the great Nile is as insignificant to him as the small Jordan overstepping its banks.

[23] So the text, which Ehrlich explains as a reference to an attempt to hypnotize the hippopotamus by one's stare, which is possible in the case of lions and tigers, though—one feels inclined to add—a rather risky procedure.

[24] The abrupt ending suggests that something has been omitted at this point. Duhm, (*Hiob*, p.197) is of the opinion that 41, 1-4 represent the conclusion of the description of the hippopotamus and that, since these verses apply also to the crocodile, they have been transferred to the poem on the crocodile 40, 25-32 (=41, 1-8). Such a supposition is, however, unnecessary. The original Greek version omits verse 24 as well as 23[b].

THE BOOK OF JOB

F

THE CROCODILE[25]

40, 25   Canst thou draw the crocodile [26] with a fish hook?
And with a cord press down his tongue?
Canst thou put a ring [27] through his nose?
And with a hook pierce his jaw?
Will he indulge in supplications to thee,
Or softly speak unto thee?
Will he cut a covenant with thee,
To take him as a servant forever?
Wilt make a toy of him as a bird,
And bind him for thy maidens?
30   Will the guilds barter for him?
Divide him among the merchants?[28]
Canst fill his skin with barbed irons,

---

[25] 40, 25–41, 4 (or 41, 1–12). Note that the AV and RV follow the Greek translation in beginning the 41st chapter at this point. There are no less than three poems on the crocodile that have been put together, (a) 40, 25–41, 4 (or 41, 1–12) (b) 41, 5–13, (or 41, 13–21), (c) 41, 14–26 (or 41, 22–34).

[26] "Leviathan"—the name of this mythical monster of primitive myth is here used as in Psalms 104, 26, for any great beast of the waters—figuratively, therefore, for the crocodile though not limited to this monster. The same beast is referred to by Ezekiel 29, 3 under the title of the "great dragon" and there used as a metaphor for Egypt. It is interesting to note that Herodotus (II §70) states that the crocodile *is* caught by a hook. The passage in Ezekiel (29, 4) likewise assumes this method of capturing him.

[27] So the Greek text.

[28] Text "Canaanites"—used as a general term for merchants, as also Prov. 31, 24; Is 23, 8, etc., because of the fame acquired by Canaanites as the merchants *par excellence*.

THE BOOK OF JOB

And his head with fishhooks?
Try to lay hand upon him;
Think of the battle—thou'lt not do it again.
One's hope would forsooth be dispelled;   41, 1
At mere sight of him, one would be cast down.
Inconceivable [29] that any should stir him;
For who could stand up against him?[30]
Who could attack him [31] and come out whole?
There is none such [32] under heaven.
[None can deny [33] his structure;
His strength without comparison].[34]

---

[29] By a transposition of two letters of the text we obtain the reading "I do not recall," *i.e.*, I cannot conceive,—here used as the strongest kind of a statement, *viz.*, it is inconceivable. Similarly in v. 4.

[30] So the Greek text and several Hebrew manuscripts instead of "before me"—a reading which represents an intentional change *ad magnam gloriam dei* to give to verses 2–4 an entirely different interpretation from the one intended by the author of the description of the crocodile, which is continued in these verses.

[31] So instead of "me" the Greek text which is undoubtedly correct. The change to "me" is again intentional. (See above p. 111).

[32] Read *lô hû* "there is none" instead of *lî hû* "to me there is" which is a further change to make the phrase read:

"To me is everything under heaven"

but which is clearly out of place at this point. For the phrase "there is not" as in our passage, cf. Jer. 5, 12.

[33] Literally, "I cannot pass over in silence," *i.e.*, one cannot ignore. The entire fourth verse is missing in the original Greek version, and may well be a later addition.

[34] So by a change of the text, demanded by the context. The common translation of this verse is wide of the mark.

THE BOOK OF JOB

G

A FURTHER DESCRIPTION OF THE CROCODILE [35]

41, 5   Who can do justice [36] to his covering?[37]
His double armor [38] who can describe?[39]
Who can open the doors of his mouth?[40]
About his teeth lies terror;
His back [41] is a cluster of shields;
A mass that is closely sealed.
Touching one the other;
That no air can come between them.
[Joined one to another;
So close as not to be sundered].[42]

10   His sneezings flash light;
His eyes are like eyelids of morning.

---

[35] An independent composition comprising 41, 5–13 or 41, 13–21, according to the enumeration in the AV and RV.

[36] Literally: "reveal," not, however, as usually taken in the sense of "uncover," but as "setting forth."

[37] Literally: "garment."

[38] So read by a transposition of the letters of the text and the insertion of *yod*, giving us *siryōnō*, "his armor," which forms the proper parallelism to "garment," *i.e.*, the skin of the crocodiles. "Double bridle" in our English translations is meaningless; nor is "double jaws" much of an improvement.

[39] Text "enter," but the context demands a verb like "describe."

[40] So read—following the Syriac version—instead of "his face" by the omission of the second letter of the word in the text. The "doors of the mouth" (cf. Micha 7, 5 and Psalm 141, 3) are, of course, the jaws. Ehrlich, who accepts this reading proposed by Budde, takes the phrase, somewhat figuratively to mean to get an insight into the nature of the beast.

[41] The Greek text has "breasts."

[42] This verse as well as 8ᵃ is omitted in the original Greek version. It impresses one as a variant to the preceding verse.

THE BOOK OF JOB

Out of his mouth go torches;
Sparks of fire leap forth.
Out of his nostrils goes smoke,[43]
As a seething and boiling [44] pot.
His breath kindles coals;
And flames go forth from his mouth.

H

A Third Description of the Crocodile[45]

Strength abides in his neck;[46]   41,

. . . .

Closely knit are the flakes of his flesh,   15
Firm and [also] immovable.[47]
At his hindparts the waves are in terror;[48]   17
The billows of the sea [49] retreat.[50]
Sword does not avail against him,

---

[43] As in the description of the horse above 39, 20.
[44] So by a slight change in the text instead of "rushes," which gives no sense.
[45] Likewise an independent composition, 41, 14–26 (or 41, 22–34) and duplicating in part the two other poems.
[46] The second half of this verse is hopelessly corrupt. The ordinary translation

"dismay (or 'terror') dances before him"

is devoid of meaning and forms no parallelism.
[47] A repetition, therefore, of verses 7–9 in the second poem The line is omitted in the original Greek version. Verse 16 represents a double comment (a) "His heart, (*i.e.*, here 'his body'), is firm as a stone." (b) "firm as the nether millstone."
[48] So Ehrlich's reading and interpretation.
[49] So by an emendation of the word translated "terror" or "despair." The phrase occurs in Psalm 93, 4.
[50] So by a change in one letter of the word.

THE BOOK OF JOB

    And the spear [51]..........................
    Iron he esteems as straw;
    Copper as rotten wood.
20 The arrow pierces him not;[52]
    The stones of the sling become stubble.[53]
    A club is counted as stubble;[54]
    He laughs at the rattling of javelin.
    His underparts are sharp potsherds,
    Tracing a threshing sledge[55] upon the mire.
    He makes the deep boil as a pot;
    He stirs up the sea like a salve pot.[56]
    Behind him a shining path,
    Making the deep appear hoary.
25 Upon earth there is not his like;
    A creature made without fear.
    Powerful, whatever is mighty fears him;[57]
    The king over all the proud beasts.

---

[51] The balance of this second part of the verse—omitted in the original Greek version—is unintelligible, because of the hopelessly corrupt text.

[52] The same verb in the same sense as 20, 24.

[53] The line is omitted in the original Greek version.

[54] The line is missing in the original Greek version.

[55] The threshing sledges in the Orient are still made, as in antiquity, of wood smooth on one side, but provided with sharp-pointed nails on the other, that leave their deep traces in the ground. To these ruts, the poet compares the impress of the stiff prickly hide of the crocodile as it lies in the mire.

[56] *i.e.*, the medicine pestle in which steaming mixtures are prepared. Cf. 41, 12.

[57] So by slight changes in the text.

VIII

THE FOUR EPILOGUES TO THE BOOK OF JOB[58]

A

AN EPILOGUE ADDED TO THE FIRST SPEECH OF YAHWEH

(40, 1-5)

[Then Yahweh answered Job as follows:][59]   40, 1
Is the contest with Shaddai to continue?[60]
Then let the accuser [61] of God give answer.
And Job in answer to Yahweh said:
"I am entirely unworthy to answer Thee;[62]

---

[58] The first two epilogues in poetic form (a) 40, 1–5 and (b) 40, 6–14 with 42, 1–6, emanate from orthodox circles that found it necessary to represent Job as repenting of his audacity. They are in direct contradiction to the original close of the Symposium (42, 7ᵇ–9) which represents even God as approving of Job. See further above, p. 61.

[59] Again an editorial link in conventional form; and entirely meaningless here, since Job has not been speaking. It is quite certain that verses 1–2 were not in the *original* Greek version. See Beer, Text des Buches *Hiob*, p. 246.

[60] The verb in the text is entirely unintelligible. What possible meaning can there be in the customary translation of this line:
"Shall he that reproveth contend with the Almighty?"
Some such verb as is suggested in my tentative translation is demanded by the context. The two lines (of which the first is lacking in the later Greek versions) probably represent an editorial addition to lead up to Job's confession of his inability to reply to God—all in the interest of the conventional orthodoxy.

[61] Literally, "the one who argues" in the legal sense of presenting the charge.

[62] The Greek version varies considerably.

THE BOOK OF JOB

My hand I lay upon my mouth.
5   Once I have spoken, but never again;[63]
    Twice, but now no more."[64]

B
An Epilogue Added to the Second Speech of Yahweh
(40, 6-14 with 42, 1-6.)[65]

40, 6   [Then Yahweh answered Job:][66]
8   Wilt thou disavow my decision?[67]

---

[63] So read instead of "I will not answer," which is clearly an error, and not in the Greek version.

[64] One is reminded of Hamlet's last words; "The rest is silence."

[65] The second epilogue—likewise in poetic form—was originally attached to the poems on the hippopotamus and the crocodile. Its proper place is, therefore, at the beginning of chapter 42 but it has been combined with a part of the original introduction to the four poems, namely 40, 6–7. These two verses must be taken in connection with 42, 3 and 4. This reconstructed introduction, clearly based on 38, 1–3, therefore, reads as follows:

> Then Yahweh answered Job:
>> Gird up thy loins like a warrior,
>> That I may ask thee to tell me.
>> Who is this that darkens counsel,
>> [By words] without knowledge?
>> [Hear now and I will speak;
>> I will ask thee to tell me.]

To remove the confusion we must, therefore, detach from the epilogue 40, 6–7.

In the epilogue proper (40, 8–14) verses 9–10 appear to be due to later expansion, and verse 12 is a paraphrase of verse 13. Verse 14 impresses one as a later addition, so that the epilogue in an earlier form consisted of three verses only, 8, 11, 13 in which God calls upon Job to humble himself. These four verses would then correspond to 40, 2 of the first epilogue.

[66] Copied from 38, 1, including the words "out of the storm," though these are omitted in at least some Hebrew manuscripts. See note 42 above, p 343. The editorial link is entirely omitted in the Sinaitic codex of the Greek version.

[67] Literally: "judgment" in the sense of judicial decision.

THE BOOK OF JOB

Condemn me so as to justify thyself?
[Hast thou an arm like God?
Canst thunder with a voice like Him?
Deck thyself with majesty and excellency? 10
Clothe thyself with glory and beauty?][68]
Repress the fury of thy wrath; 11
And lower every kind of haughtiness.[69]
Hide them [70] in the dust together; 13
Bind their faces in a hidden spot.
[Then, indeed, I will praise thee,[71]
For thy right hand will bring thy salvation.]
Then Job answered Yahweh:[72] 42, 1
I know [73] that Thou canst do everything; 2
And nothing [74] is too difficult for Thee.[75]

---

[68] To be taken as a continuation of the query.

[69] Verse 12 (briefer in the Greek text) is a paraphrase of the preceding verse by a commentator who, however, takes "haughty" for the "wicked," whereas Job's haughtiness is meant:
"And humble every haughty one;
And tread down the wicked in their place."
i.e., crush the wicked completely.
The first of these two lines is lacking in the Syriac version.

[70] Thy wrath and thy haughtiness.

[71] So to be rendered, "not confess unto thee." This verse of the epilogue is under suspicion of being a later addition.

[72] One important Greek codex omits the line. See Beer, *Text des Buches Hiob*, p. 255. Job's confession clearly forms part of the second epilogue, to correspond to the confession (40, 3–5), in the first epilogue. Verses 42, 1, 2, 3ᵇ, 5–6, constituting this confession, therefore, belong immediately after 40, 14.

[73] There appears to have been a variant reading "Thou knowest"—meaning God—but the versions favor "I know."

[74] So the Greek text.

[75] The first part of verse 3.
"Who is this that darkens counsel without knowledge" (not found in the Codex Sinaiticus of the Greek version) is taken

THE BOOK OF JOB

3ᵇ What I did not understand, I uttered;
Things far beyond me of which I had no knowledge.[76]
5 From hearsay I had heard of Thee;
But now my eye has seen Thee.
Therefore, I recall and repent,
[In utter worthlessness.][77]

C

THE PROSE EPILOGUE TO THE SYMPOSIUM[78]
(42, 7ᵇ–9)

42, 7ᵇ And Yahweh said unto Eliphaz the Temanite:
"My wrath is kindled against thee,[79] and against thy

---

over from 38, 2 except that "by words" has been omitted, though probably by accident. It is clearly out of place and belongs. as indicated, to the introduction which in the editing process was combined with the epilogue. See above, note 65.

[76] Verse 4,
"Hear now and I will speak,
I will ask thee to tell me,"
is similarly a variant to 38, 3 and 40, 7ᵇ and taken over from there. The verse is entirely out of place and meaningless where it stands. It belongs like 42, 3ᵃ to the introduction to the four poems on the huge beasts. That verses 3ᵃ and 4 should thus have been actually inserted into the text and made part of a speech of Job shows the lack of any critical spirit on the part of those to whom we owe the present text of Job. And yet until modern criticism set in, such insertions were accepted as part of a sacred book, which by such editorial methods becomes a hopelessly confused one.

[77] Literally: "in dust and ashes," but which as Ehrlich has shown is an idiomatic expression for "utter worthlessness." The same phrase occurs 30, 19 and since the line is too short as it stands, it may be that the phrase represents an addition taken over from 30, 19. See above p. 291.

two friends; for you have not spoken what is proper [80] as my servant Job has. Therefore, take now seven bullocks and seven rams, and go [81] and offer them up as a burnt offering [82] on your behalf; and my servant Job shall intercede for you [83] that I do not do something abominable [84] to you. And Eliphaz the Temanite and Bildad the Shuhite and Zophar the Naamathite went and did as Yahweh had spoken to them. And Yahweh accepted Job.

---

[78] In prose like the prologue (chapters 1–2). For the original place of this epilogue see above, p. 60 *seq*. The additional words

"And it was after Yahweh had spoken these words unto Job"

represent the editorial link to connect the original close of the book with the two "orthodox" epilogues. But these two epilogues form such a contrast to the original close, that even the editorial link cannot bring about a smooth transition. For surely, God cannot approve of Job and be angry at his friends, *after* Job has confessed his guilt, and which confession obviously acquits his friends.

[79] An imitation of 32, 3–4.

[80] Or "right." The word in the text points to a complete approval of what Job said. Only one who had the boldness of the writer of the original Book of Job, ending with Job's complete vindication, could venture to go so far as to suggest that God himself recognized the justice of Job's reproaches against the cruelty and injustice of Divine government. The unorthodox writer could, of course—if he were so inclined—take refuge behind the plea that the misfortunes of Job were merely a test, though he would involve himself in the contradiction that according to the philosophical poem Job did not endure the test since he defied God. Such logical subtleties, however, would not disturb an ancient writer.

[81] An unnecessary comment adds, "to my servant Job."

[82] According to the Priestly Code (Lev. 4, 28), it would have been a she-goat as a "sin offering."

[83] Text adds (taken over from v. 9) "for him I accept"—literally, "lift up his countenance," *i.e.*, in the sense of favoring

THE BOOK OF JOB

D

THE ORIGINAL CLOSE OF THE FOLKTALE[85]

(42, 10–17)

42, 10 And Yahweh turned the fortune of Job,[86] [and Yahweh restored everything to Job in double amount.][87] And all his relations[88] and his former acquaintances [heard all the things that befell him, and][89] came to

---

one or acting out of regard for one, and which is clearly added so as to connect the original close of the folktale with the epilogue to the Symposium.

[84] The word used comes close to the term in the Priestly Code to describe an "abomination," like a carcass that must not be eaten. It is here used in a more general sense to denote an awful punishment. "Unseemly" as found in the translation of the American Jewish Publication Society is too mild, though an improvement on "folly" as the AV renders. The text again adds tautologically:

"For you have not spoken what is right to me (or "of me") as my servant Job has"—repeated from v. 7.

[85] 42, 10–17 (in prose) now attached to the special epilogue to the Symposium. The abrupt beginning points to an omission of some details that either were not in keeping with the epilogue attached to the Symposium or that were regarded as superfluous. The folktale must have had further links connecting chapters 1 and 2, with the happy ending, as a reward for Job's piety and silent endurance. See above, p. 61 *seq.*

[86] Literally: "restored the captivity (like Ps. 14, 7) in the sense of removing one's distress and trouble. A glossator adds, "because of his interceding for his friend"—which is as commonplace as it is unnecessary. The Hebrew text has "his friend" in accord with v. 7 in which Eliphaz alone is addressed. The versions, however, have the plural, which is accepted in our English translations, though without any mention of the original reading.

[87] Probably a later amplifying addition in view of the statement in v. 12.

[88] Literally, "All his brothers and all his sisters"—an expression to indicate all his relations.

[89] So the Greek version.

THE BOOK OF JOB

feast with him in his house, [to sympathize with him; and to comfort him for all the evil which Yahweh had brought upon him.][90] And each one gave him a *kesita* and each a golden ring.[91]

And Yahweh blessed the latter end of Job more than his beginning; and he had fourteen thousand sheep and six thousand camels and a thousand yoke of cattle and a thousand she-asses. And he had double 13 the number of seven sons [92] and three daughters.[93]

---

[90] Added by the one who attached the epilogue to the Symposium and who aimed to weld the two epilogues into a consistent whole. An orthodox writer would not have used phrases which might reveal the original character of the book as justifying Job.

[91] This is a genuine folktale touch. The *kesita* is a coin (Gen. 33, 19, Jos, 24, 32) and it, as well as the golden ring, probably represents a congratulatory gift that it was customary to bestow on some one who had recovered from an illness or who had escaped some danger. The word for ring *nezem* (Gen. 24, 22) is a ring placed by women on the nose to hold up the veil, but perhaps it is here used in a more general sense. In no case is a ring placed through the nose meant. That custom is not found among the Semites. The Greek version renders *kesita* which it no longer understood as "lamb." These gifts have, of course, no significance in the form of the story adapted to the Symposium.

[92] A strange form to express "double seven" is used and as Ehrlich points out with intent to avoid a confusion with the expression "sevenfold." The Targum confirms the interpretation by using the common term fourteen. It will be observed that only the number of the sons are doubled, but not that of the daughters. Sons from the Oriental point of view are an asset; daughters a liability.

[93] As an amplification of the folktale of Job, the names of the three daughters of Job are added (v. 14):

"And the name of the one was Jemima and the name of the second Kezia and the name of the third Keren-happuch."

The names appear to be plant names and of foreign origin,

THE BOOK OF JOB

15 And there were no women in all the land so fair as the daughters of Job. And their father gave them an inheritance with their brothers.[94] And Job lived after this a hundred and forty years [95] [and saw his children and his grandchildren,—four generations. And Job died, old and full of days.][96]

---

perhaps transliterations from the Arabic. Kezia is the plant Cassia while Keren-happuch, literally "horn of eye paint," might designate the "Stibium box," used by women. In Arabic Jemima is the "dove," but it is more likely that it here designates some plant. It is likely that in some version of the folktale the names of the sons were also mentioned, as well as the name of Job's wife.

[94] Again a bit of folk-lore, that is, however, devoid of significance in the present form of the story. The post-exilic Priestly Code (Num. 27, 1-11) permits such an inheritance only in case there are no sons.

[95] The Greek version has 170.

[96] Verse 16[b] and the whole of verse 17 are omitted in the original Greek version. They are clearly later additions—suggested by Gen. 35, 29—just as the names of the three daughters are fanciful amplifications of the folktale. Such additions are common at the end of ancient books. The Greek version of Theodotion has four additional notes or statements pointing to the continued expansion of the folktale, in the style of the Jewish "Midrash." They are:

(a) "It is written that Job will again arise with those whom the Lord will resurrect."

(b) "According to the 'Syriac' book (i.e., probably an Aramaic version) he (i.e., Job) dwelt in the land of Uz on the borders of Idumæa and Arabia and his name was formerly Jobab (cf. Gen. 36, 33). He took to wife an Arabic woman and had a son whose name was Ennon. He himself was the son of Zare (i.e., Zerah, Gen. 36, 33), one of the sons of Esau and Bozrah (a misreading of Gen. 36, 33, which says 'from Bozrah' in connection with Zerah), so that he was the fifth from Abram."

(c) A third addition, giving the list of the Edomite kings on the basis of Gen. 36, 31-39, though only four are mentioned here, as against eight in Genesis:

"And these are the kings who ruled in Edom, over which he himself ruled:

THE BOOK OF JOB

First, Bela the son of Beor, whose city was Dinhabah (cf. Gen. 36, 32).
After Bela, Jobab, who was called Job (cf. Gen. 36, 33),
After this one, Husham of the land of the Temanites (Gen. 36, 34).
After this one, Hadad, son of Barad (Bedad, Gen. 36, 35), who slew Midian in the field of Moab and the name of his city was Gethaim" (=Awith or Gawith, cf. Gen. 36, 35).

(d) "The friends who came to him were:
Eliphaz of the sons of Esau (cf. Gen. 36, 10), king of the Temanites,
Bildad the tyrant of the Shuhites,
Zophar, the king of the Mineans."

The "Syriac book" mentioned as the source of the second statement appears to have been an Aramaic version with Midrashic additions. The same statement is found in the work of a certain Aristeas on "The Jews," which shows us that the source in question must have been in existence in the second century A. D. during which Aristeas lived. We cannot be sure that the additions in the Greek version are earlier than the translation made by Theodotion, whose date is somewhere toward the end of the second century A. D. Both Aristeas and Theodotion may, therefore, have used the same source, or Theodotion may be dependent upon Aristeas. At all events since the source is distinctively Jewish, we have in these additions to the Greek version the proof that the story of Job, as well as the book, was subject to constant elaboration for at least two centuries after the completion of the original Book of Job. See further on the additions to the Greek version Dillman, *Hiob*, (4th edition) pp. 360-361, and Cheyne, *Job and Solomon*, p. 96 note 1, and for a different view, the article on "Aristeas" in the Jewish Encyclopædia.